Revolutionary War Soldiers

of

Western
North Carolina

Vol. #3

Compiled by:
Emmett R. White, Sr.

Southern Historical Press, Inc.
Greenville, South Carolina
2011

Please Direct All Correspondence and Book Orders to:

Southern Historical Press, Inc.
PO Box 1267
375 West Broad Street
Greenville, S.C. 29602

ISBN # 0-89308-806-4

Printed in the United States of America

FOREWARD AND APPRECIATION

Vol. III of the Revolutionary Soldiers of Western North Carolina represents the final volume of this series. Hopefully, the material presented will be of assistance to the many thousands of persons who are seeking to learn more about their Revolutionary ancestry and history. They will also see the manner in which these brave men moved westward and helped forge our great new nation.

I would like to extend my deepest thanks and appreciation to Ms. Nancy Young of Murrells Inlet, South Carolina, who dutifully and unselfishly typed, collated, indexed, and prepared the data for this work.

Emmett R. White, Sr.
Rutherford College, NC 28671-0010

THIS VOLUME IS DEDICATED IN LOVING MEMORY OF

OUR SON MATTHEW

Contents

Adams, Philip

Summary of Early Life:

Philip Adams was one the earlier settlers of what is now Catawba County, North Carolina, then Rowan County. He obtained land via crown grants on Elk Shoals Creek, and later, on Lyles Creek (near the head of Clarks Creek). He and his wife Catherine and family, were neighbors of George Pope and George Wilfong.

Summary of Partisan Activity:

In the summer of 1776, the Cherokee Indians (allied with the British) began a massive raid on the western North Carolina frontier. Militiamen, under the command of Colonel Christopher Beekman and Lieutenant Colonel Charles McDowell were called out in defense. Philip Adams, along with Captain Mathias Barringer, was conducting a foray into Indian country in the vicinity of Upper Creek in what is now Burke County, North Carolina. Both Adams and Barringer were killed by the Indians in ambush. At that time they were near a small branch that flowed into Upper Creek.

Summary of Later Events:

Catherine Adams was named executor of Philip Adams' estate when probate was begun in 1777. Probate continued for a number of years, into 1793. There were children, as indicated by a petition to Rowan County for support of his orphans. (These are in loose records borrowed in Raleigh and not recorded by authors. They may well contain additional families' names, etc.) Lincoln County, North Carolina land records give a "Conrad Adams" as heir to Philip Adams property, from Lincoln County, Virginia.

Land Holdings and Transactions:

1. NC Crown Grant (Governor William Tryon) Patent Bk

18, #16, 6 April 1765. 640 acres in Mecklenburgh County on both sides of Elk Creek, including a shoal and adjacent to land of Bastian (Sebastian) Cline. This is now Catawba County, North Carolina.

Note: This is an excellent example of a Crown Grant being issued well within "Granville's" district. During 1765, the Granville line had not been extended beyond the Catawba and thus the border was indeterminate. Obtaining a Crown Grant was quicker and easier and established definite ownership. Dozens of Crown Grants were issued in a similar fashion during this time period.

2. NC Crown Grant (Governor William Tyron) Patent Book 18, #552 "Mecklenburgh County", 30 October 1765, 350 acres both sides of Elk Creek, including the forks (near John Haun and George Pope), now Catawba County, North Carolina.

3. NC Crown Grant (Governor William Tryon) Patent Book 23, #6461 (with Henry Pope), 28 April 1768, 268 acres in "Mecklenburgh" County on branches of Lyle's Creek, adjacent to George Pope (now Catawba County).

The Lyles Creek property was later transferred to George Wilfong "for said deceased orphans". See Burke land records

References:

Huggins, Edith W. "Burke County Records" Vol. I. pp 30, 70, 116, 128. Vol. II, pp 161, 42. Vol. III, p 43. SHP 1987.

Linn, Jo White. "Wills and Estate Records of Rowan County, North Carolina". Salisbury, NC 1980, p 99.

Hofmann, Margaret M. Colony of North Carolina 1765-1775. Abstracts of Land Patents; Vol. 2. Weldon, NC 1984. Nos. 16, 552, 3185, 5062, 6461.

Burke County, North Carolina "Minutes of the Court of Pleas and Quarter Sessions (1791-1795)". Abstract by Daniel Swink. 1986 Lawndale, NC. pp 3, 15.

Pruitt, Dr. R. B. "Abstracts of Deeds Lincoln County, North Carolina 1786-1793". (1988) p 59.

Adams, William

Summary of Early Life:

William Adams was living on Mulberry Fork of Johns River during the Revolutionary period.

Summary of Partisan Activity:

William Adams was a Captain of Mounted Militia in Charles McDowell's Burke Regiment. Lt. William Sumter was one of his superior officers.

Summary of Later Life:

Burke County records show a will probate of William Adams in September 1785. Elizabeth Adams is listed as executor, along with sons James, William and Robert Adams.

Land Holdings and Transactions:

1. 100 acres, Burke Co. NC, on Mulberry Fork of Johns River. The land lay adjacent to that of John Brevard, William White and to Col. Osborne's Old Survey. Ent. 5 Jun 1778 # 160 Grant # 26 Book 28, p. 26. cc. James Taylor White, Thomas Wakefield.

References:
Burke Co. NC Land Records Burke Co. Library. Morganton, NC.
U.S. National Archives, RW Pension records of William Osborne (W 4303).
Huggins, Edith W. Misc. Burke Co. NC Records in 4 vols. Vol.II p.161.

Alexander, Elias

Major Elias Alexander, a field officer and Kings Mountain veteran, appears to have lived a short time in Burke County. He is more closely identified, however, with Rutherford County, where he lived most of his life. For further information see Clarence Griffin's book, <u>The History of Old Tyron and Rutherford Counties</u>.

Alexander was sheriff of Burke County at one time. He also entered and owned land in Burke, but disposed of his holdings, perhaps indicative of his move to Rutherford County. He is listed on the 1790 Census of Rutherford County. There was another Elias Alexander in Burke County as listed in the 1790 Census, perhaps accounting for some of the confusion.

References:
Burke County Land Grant Data in Burke County Library Huggins, Edith W. Burke County Records Vols. I-IV.
Griffin, Clarence W. <u>The History of Tryon and Rutherford Counties</u>. (Spartanburg SC – Reprint 1982 from original 1937 ed.) p 170.
1790 AIS Census Burke County and Rutherford County NC. Burke listing is "Elisa Alexander".

Alexander, Noble

Summary of Early Life:

Noble Alexander was the son of William and Elizabeth Alexander and a brother of Revolutionary soldier, Samuel Alexander (see Vol. I). The Alexanders lived on Upper Creek in Burke County during the American Revolution.

Summary of Partisan Activity:

Noble Alexander was an officer in Charles McDowell's Burke Regiment of militia. In the 1780-81 period, he served as an ensign under Major George Pope. Alexander was among those troops who opposed Cornwallis' crossing of the Catawba River in early February 1781. After the death of General William L. Davidson and the defeat of the Americans at Torrence's Tavern, Alexander assisted in re-grouping the scattered militiaman.

Summary of Later Life:

Noble Alexander died December 5, 1826. His brother Samuel Alexander was executor.

Land Holdings and Transactions:

470 acres John Fox's Co. 1796-1800

Census Locations:

1800 Burke County, North Carolina
1810 Burke County, North Carolina
1820 Burke County, North Carolina

References:
AIS Census Indices 1790-1820.
US National Archives Pension Data. Richard Matlock.
NC Revolutionary Accounts Vol. IX, Book 14, Part VII. (from Weynette P; Haun previously cited.)
Moore, Robert P. Articles in Burke County NC Heritage Vol. I. 1981 ed., pp.

66-67.
Burke County Land Grant Data. Burke County Library, Morganton, NC.

Baker, Beal

Summary of Early Life:

Beal Baker was born in Baltimore County, Maryland on February 9, 1756. He was a brother of Elias Baker who was also a Revolutionary war soldier. By the beginning of the Revolutionary War, the family was living in Rowan County, North Carolina, Captain Richard Graham's District. Other Bakers living in the area included Absolam, Jehu, Joshua, Charles, and Elias Baker. In 1786 Beal Baker, Elias Baker and Margaret Baker acted as executors to the estate of one Charles Baker, deceased. (Lincoln County, NC Bk 16, p.158) Father?

Summary of Partisan Activity:

Beal Baker served a total of two tours of duty, each lasting about three months. He first entered as a substitute for his younger brother, who had been drafted. In March 1779, he was mustered in at Charlotte and placed in a company of militia commanded by Captain William Armstrong. Armstrong's company became part of a North Carolina Regiment headed by the Marquis de Malmedy, a French officer. Under Malmedy, they marched to the Savannah River and then to a place called Pond Ponds. Later they were engaged in the battle of Stono Ferry on June 20, 1779. Baker was not in the actual battle, being at that time with the supply wagons.

It appears that members of the Baker family moved from Rowan County to Burke County North Carolina ca 1780. His second and final tour of duty was as a volunteer militiaman in a company commanded by Captain John Hasselbarger of Burke County. They were part of McDowell's Burke regiment. The brigade was commanded by Brigadier General Griffith Rutherford. In the fall and winter of 1781, they marched to Wilmington in order to free that city from the British (the British had already left). Baker's company was stationed at Clayton's Place, eighteen miles above Wilmington, on the northeast Cape Fear River. At completion of his tour, he was discharged by Colonel Francis Defore, a French officer.

7

Summary of Later Life:

Beal Baker was married in 1782 to Sarah Brown (b. Feb. 15, 1759). The marriage took place in Burke County. The magistrate was James Alexander. Elias and Sarah Baker were also present (brother and sister-in-law).

The Bakers lived in that part of Burke County that later became part of Lincoln County and finally Catawba County, North Carolina.

After living in Lincoln County a few years, they moved to Franklin County, Georgia, and lived there forty or fifty years. In later life, they moved to Hall County, Georgia where Beal Baker applied for federal pension on November 5, 1832. He was awarded an annual pension of twenty dollars per anum. The Revolutionary soldier Beal Baker died in Hall County, Georgia on August 31, 1842, age 86 years. His widow applied for pension in 1849 and received an award also of twenty dollars per annum.

A John Baker is listed as a son. An Elias Baker is also listed on 1830 Census of Hall County (reference of the soldier as Gwinnett County, Georgia).

Land Holdings and Transactions:

1. It appears that the Baker family lived on a branch of Clark's Creek (now Catawba County, NC) known as Anthony's Mill Creek.

Census Locations:

1830 Hall County, Georgia

References:
US National Archives Pension statements #W5212.
AIS 1830 Georgia Census Index.
Pruitt, A. B. Abstracts of Deeds of Lincoln County North Carolina 1786-1793.
     (1988 ed.) #652

Baker, Charles (*See Vol. I, p 12 for another Charles Baker, any relationship unknown*)

Summary of Early Life:

Charles Baker was born in Baltimore County, Maryland on December 22, 1760. He was living in Burke County with his father and family at the beginning of the American Revolution. Lawrence Evans was a neighbor.

Summary of Partisan Activity:

Charles Baker first entered military service in the summer of 1780 as a volunteer militiaman. He served out a tour of duty of three months and was stationed on the western Catawba frontier, guarding against possible incursions by the Cherokee Indians. He served in Captain James Davidson's company of Colonel Charles McDowell's Burke regiment. He served mainly at Wofford's Fort on the North Catawba River.

His last tour of duty was again for three months. He served in a militia company commanded by Captain Samuel Killian of McDowell's Burke Regiment. He mentions other officers, Joseph McDowell (Q. M.), Joseph McDowell (P.G.). His duties once again were on the Catawba frontier.

Summary of Later Life:

Shortly after the Revolution in 1783, Charles Baker was married to Catherine Evans (b. Aug. 15, 1767), the daughter of Lawrence Evans and a sister of Henry Evans. In 1786, Charles and Catherine Baker moved to Lincoln County, Tennessee, and remained there until 1795. In 1795 they moved to Madison County, Kentucky.

Charles Baker applied for Revolutionary War Pension in Madison County, Kentucky, on April 4, 1842, and was awarded a pension of twenty dollars per annum. The Revolutionary soldier Charles Baker died in Madison County on October 27, 1843.

After his death, Catherine Baker had considerable difficulty in receiving her pension, based on her husband's service. This was due to lack in documentation of her marriage. She finally won approval for pension in 1852, shortly before her death on November 5, 1852 in Fayette County, Kentucky.

Surviving children of Charles and Catherine Baker were:

David E. Baker
John Baker
Rachel m. James Fleming
Margaret m. Asa Shepherd
Charles

An earlier statement by Catherine Baker elicited that she had twelve children, of which she raised eleven.

Census Locations:

1800 Madison County, Kentucky (from 8/12/1800 tax list)
1810 Madison County, Kentucky
1820 Madison County, Kentucky
1830 Madison County, Kentucky

References:
U.S. National Archives. Revolutionary War Pension Statements #W9337.
Clift, G. G. "Second Census of Kentucky". 1800, GPC 1976, p 11.
AIS Indices 1810 Kentucky Census (1974 ed.), Bountiful, Utah.
Index to the 1820 Census of Kentucky, (1975 ed.), Volkel, Lowell ;Thomson, Ill.
Kentucky 1830 Census Index . (1974 ed.) Smith, Dora W. ;Thomson, Ill.

Baker, Elias

Summary of Early Life:

Elias Baker was born on January 22, 1760 in Baltimore County, Maryland. At the beginning of the American Revolution, Baker was a resident of Rowan County, North Carolina, in Captain Richard Graham's District. He was a brother of Beal Baker, also a Revolutionary War soldier.

Summary of Partisan Activity:

Elias Baker first entered military service in the year 1777 as a volunteer militiaman in Captain John Graham's Company, Rowan County Regiment. The company Lieutenant was Francis Ross. He served a three-month tour of duty on the Catawba Frontier, guarding against the incursions of the hostile Cherokee Indians.

His next tour of duty was in 1778-1779. He served in South Carolina in Colonel Malmedy's Regiment, in a company commanded by Captain Joseph White and Leiutenant Benjamin Knox. The oreverall commander was General Benjamin Lincoln. On June 20, 1779, Baker fought in the battle of Stono Ferry, South Carolina. He was discharged by General Rutherford and returned home.

It appears that Baker moved from Rowan County to Burke County ca 1780-81 (now Catawba County NC).

During the fall and winter of 1781, he participated in the Wilmington Expedition, headed up by Brigadier General Griffith Rutherford. He served in a company commanded by Captain John Hasselbarger and Lieutenant George Sigmon of Colonel Charles McDowell's Burke Regiment.

In his pension statements he mentions fellow soldiers Beal Baker (brother), Samuel Killian, William Frizelle, Benjamin Baker, John Lowery, and Thomas Lowery.

Note: Rowan County records indicate the Bakers failed to sign the oath of allegiance. One of them, Jehu Baker, was a known Loyalist. No indication as to whether they may have signed it later.

Summary of Later Life:

Elias Baker, on June 15, 1780 was married to Sarah Holbrook, daughter of John Holbrook of Mecklenburg and Rowan County. This, more than likely, was about the time they moved to Burke County (later which was part of Lincoln and then Catawba County NC). After the war, he remained in Lincoln County until after 1790 (he appears on the 1790 census). They moved first to Elbert County, Georgia, then to Franklin County, Georgia where he remained for about twenty years. He moved to Madison County, Illinois for a while and finally to Gwinnett County, Georgia, where he applied for federal pension on October 25, 1832. He was awarded a pension in the amount of thirty dollars per anum. Still later Elias Baker moved to Chattooga County, Georgia, where he died on November 18, 1843 at the age of 83. His widow, Sarah Baker, applied for and received a pension based on her late husband's service. It was approved in 1849, and at that time, she was described as being old and infirm and unable to appear at court in person.

Census Locations:

1790 Lincoln County, North Carolina 2nd Company.
1830 Gwinnett County, Georgia

References:
US National Archives Pension Statements #W5773.
Linn, Jo White. Abstractsof the Minutes of the Court of Pleas and Quarter
    Sessions. p 43.
 Rowan County NC. 1775-1789, Vol III. Salisbury 1982).
AIS Reprint of 1790 Census.
AIS Georgia 1830 Census Index (Bountiful, UT; 1976 ed.).

Baldwin, Isaac

Summary of Early Life:

Isaac Baldwin was a member of the well-known Loyalist family of Lower Creek, in Burke County during the American Revolution, but now a part of Caldwell County, North Carolina. Four other members of the family were written up in Volume II of this work. One, John Baldwin, in a pension declaration stated that he had lived in Burke County, North Carolina "since his infancy".

Summary of Partisan Activity:

The partisan activity of Isaac Baldwin is described in detail by Draper (Kings Mountain and Its Heroes). This data is also included in "The Loyalists at Kings Mountain", by Professor Bobby Moss of South Carolina.

Draper states that Isaac Baldwin was a leader of a Tory band who had stolen and plundered. He also had whipped several victims severely. Baldwin was at Kings Mountain, probably in the regiment commanded by his neighbor, Colonel Veazy Husbands. Husbands was killed in the battle, and Baldwin was captured (October 7, 1780). At Bickerstaff's, while awaiting execution, he managed to escape (aided by a younger brother). Returning to his father's home in Burke County, Baldwin was killed by a patriot, who had earlier spotted him (he was killed by a rifle butt to the head).

Land Holdings and Transactions:

1. Burke County, North Carolina entry data for Jacob Baldwin. 300 acres on Lower Creek adjacent to William Sumpter, Daniel Jackson, and Isaac Baldwin. Ent 10 August 1778.
2. Burke County, North Carolina entry data of Henry Williams. 500 acres Lower Creek including two improvements, one of Isaac Baldwin (10 August 1778), and one of John Hayes – on John Hayes Creek (ent 29

13

December 1778).
3. David Jaxon (Jackson). 100 acres North Fork on John Hayes Creek joining "Isaac Baldwin's". Ent 29 Dec 1778.

References:
Draper, Lyman C. <u>Kings Mountain and Its Heroes.</u> Originally published 1881 Genealogical Publishing Company, Reprint, Baltimore, 1997. pp 341-342.
Moss, Bobby G. "The Loyalists at Kings Mountain." Scotia Hibernia Press Blacksburg, Sc 1998. p 4.
Huggins, Edith W. Miscellaneous Burke County Records. Vol I, pp 56, 125,127.

Ballew, William

Summary of Early Life:

William Ballew was born in Bedford County, Virginia ca 1752. William Ballew was one of the several members of the family that came from Central Virginia, and settling in Pre-Revolutionary Rowan County (later Burke, Caldwell, and McDowell Counties). From land grant records, he lived on the north side of the Catawba River, near present Baton (Caldwell County) and Rutherford College (Burke County). The Flemings and Connellys lived nearby.

Summary of Partisan Activity:

The North Carolina Revolutionary Army Accounts verify the service of William Ballew as a militiaman (Morgan District). The Morgan district militia was commanded by Benjamin General Charles McDowell of Burke County. Colonel Joseph McDowell of Quaker Meadows commanded the Burke County Regiment of militia.

Summary of Later Life:

William Ballew in ca 1773 married Elizabeth Connelly (born 1756). They were the parents of the following offspring:

Abraham b. 1774	Joshua b. 1782	Elizabeth b. 1791
John b. 1776	Mary b. 1784	Cyrus b. 1793
William b. 1776	Barnabas b. 1786	Jane b. 1795
David b. 1778	Joseph b. 1788	Thomas b. 1797
Hiram b. 1780	Peter b. 1790	Harvey b. 1797

This corresponds with the 1790 Census, which lists nine males and one female, other than husband and wife.

William Ballew served as a civil servant throughout the late 1790's and extending into the early 1800's. He served as a juror many times. William Ballew was still living in the 1830's as indicated by census and estate records.

Land Holdings and Transactions:

1. 212 acres Burke County, NC on north side Catawba River. The land lay adjacent to that of Abraham Fleming, William Connally and to his own land. cc. William Ballew; William Connally. Ent 25 Apr 1804 #4992, Grant 3391, iss 12 Dec 1805, Bk. 119, p. 255.
2. 25 acres Burke County, NC on north side of Catawba River. The land lay adjacent to that of his own land "opposite his improvements" (on south side Catawba?). Ent 5 Dec 1778 #827, Granted 11 Oct 1783 #702, Bk. 50, p 260.
3. 73 ½ acres Burke County, NC on North side of Catawba River adjacent to Abraham Fleming and "including his own improvements for complement". Ent 30 Dec 1778 #1345, Granted 28 Oct 1782 #352, Bk. 44, p 133.

Census Locations:

1790 Burke County, North Carolina 2nd Company
1800 Burke County, North Carolina
1810 Burke County, North Carolina
1820 Burke County, North Carolina
1830 Burke County, North Carolina

References:
Miscellaneous Ballew Family Data Vertical Files, Burke County Library, Morganton, NC.
Ballew Family Journal (Ballew Family of America, Atlanta, GA 31145), April 1998 issue.
Hamlin, James S. Annandale, Va, 22003 Brochure on Ballew Family, Burke Co Library 1998.
AIS Census Indices 1790-1830.
Land Grant Data Burke County Library Morganton, NC.
NC DAR Roster of Soldiers from NC in the American Revolution 1967 Reprint (GPC) of 1932 ed, p 351.
NC Revolutionary Army Accounts Vol VI, Book 24, p 4 from Weynette Haun Revolutionary Army Accounts Publications, Durham NC (27704) multiple, mainly in 1990's.

Barringer, Matthias

Summary of Early Life:

According to data in the Heritage of Catawba County, Vol. I, Matthias Barringer was born in Germany in 1730 (DAR records say ca 1747), the son of Wilhelm and Paulina Barringer. He had an older brother, John Paul, who came to America in the early 1740's. Matthias was to follow him and was to bring along their parents. Both Wilhelm and Paulina died, however, while making the voyage (1748). Paul had settled in what is now Cabarrus County on South Buffalo Creek. Mathias lived in the same area for a while, but then acquired land in what is today Catawba County, North Carolina. He received a Crown Grant for 640 acres of land on Clarks Creek in 1764, which included "his improvements". Matthias was married to Margaret Bushart Barringer. Matthias Barringer became an officer in the Colonial militia with the rank of Captain.

Summary of Partisan Activity:

Early in the Revolutionary Period, Matthias Barringer became a member of the Rowan County, North Carolina Committee of Safety (1774-1775). He functioned actively as a committee member. He received a commission as an officer in the Rowan Militia – first as an ensign and later a Captain.

In March of 1776, Barringer participated in the Cross Creek Expedition of General Rutherford. This was part of the Moore's Creek Bridge Campaign. The Rowan Militia did not take part in the battle, but did conduct "mop-up" activities later.

In the summer of 1776, the Cherokee Indians conducted a massive raid on the western frontier (now Burke and McDowell Counties). Members of the Rowan Militia responded immediately to counter the raid. Captain Barringer, along with several of his neighbors, went on a foray against the Indians in the Upper Creek area of Rowan (later Burke) County. Captain Barringer and a neighbor militiaman, Philip Adams, were killed, as were several others. One man, Philip Frye, survived.

Summary of Later Events:

Following the death of Mathias Barringer, his estate transactions were begun in Rowan County Court in May 1777. George Pope and Conrad Tippong were appointed administrators. As Burke County had been formed in the same year, Tippong entered 640 acres for Matthias Barringer, Jr. including his mother's improvements. It mentions a Granville Patent, but was actually the 640 acres Crown Grant issued earlier in 1764. The children of Matthias and Margaret Barringer were:

Matthias Barringer, Jr. (1767-1844) m. Catherine Haas
Catherine m. John Setzer

The log home of Matthias Barringer survived until 1952, when it was accidentally destroyed by fire. His property was the site of a muster ground – used frequently during and after the Revolutionary War.

Land Holdings and Transactions:

1. Rowan County, North Carolina Crown Patent (Arthur Dobbs, Governor) 21 April 1764. 640 acres in Mecklenburg County on Clark's Creek, adjacent to Jacob Egnar, "including his own improvements". #7230, p. 71. *Due to the indeterminate position of Granville's line west of the Catawba, Crown Grants were frequently issued for tracts well within Granville's District – and labeled "Mecklenburg County" instead of Rowan.*

References:
Hofmann, Margaret. Colony of North Carolina 1735-1764, Abstracts of Land Patents. Vol. I, Weldon NC, 1982 #7230 p. 513.
Huggins, Edith W. Burke County Records Vol. I, p. 110.
The Heritage of Catawba County Vol. I. Winston Salem NC, 1986, pp 47-48.
Linn, Jo White. The Minutes of the Court of Pleas and Quarter Sessions of Rowan County NC 1775-1776. Salisbury 1982, pp 17,55.
Revolutionary Army Accounts; Journal "A" 1775-1776 as given in Haun, Weynette Parks. Durham NC 1988 ed. p 53.

Wheeler, John Hill; <u>Historical Sketches of North Carolina</u> (originally printed
        Philadelphia 1851) Reprint Regional Publishing Company Baltimore.
        1964. pp 36-337 (Rowan County Committee of Safety Minutes).
Clark, Murtie June. <u>Colonial Soldiers of the South</u> (GPC, Baltimore1983) p
        646.
<u>A History of Catawba County.</u> Ed. by C. J. Preslar, Jr. Salisbury 1954.
<u>DAR Patriot Index.</u> (Nat. Soc.DAR) Washington DC 1966, p 39.
Whitener, R. Vance. Data on Barringer Family, (copy) vertical files Burke
        County Library Morganton, NC (1916).

Blackwell, John

Summary of Early Life:

John Blackwell, the son of John Blackwell, Sr. was born in Culpeper County, Virginia in 1755. At the beginning of the American Revolution, he was living in Burke County, NC (or Rutherford?).

Summary of Partisan Activity:

John Blackwell first entered military service as a volunteer militiaman, serving on the Western Catawba Frontier for a period of fifteen months in a company commanded by Captain John Connally. Their duties consisted of guarding against the incursions of the hostile Cherokee Indians and in erecting frontier forts for protection.

Blackwell's next tour of duty was as a volunteer militiaman in Colonel Charles McDowell's Burke Regiment, serving in a company commanded by Captain Thomas Kennedy. Other officers included Major Joseph White and Major Joseph McDowell. He participated in the South Carolina actions of Colonel McDowell in July and August 1780. He mentions, in his pension statements, skirmishes at Ned Hampton's place and at Paris's place on Tyger River. After hearing of the news of the American disaster at Camden, McDowell retreated back into North Carolina. Blackwell tells of their defeat by the British near Gilberttown (probably the action at Bedford's Hill or Allen's Mountain). Blackwell, a short while later, joined a company of militiamen commanded by Captain Alexander Erwin of Burke County. Colonel Benjamin Cleveland commanded the regiment. Under them, Blackwell took part in the battle of King's Mountain on October 7, 1780. He describes the numerous dead and many prisoners being taken.

Blackwell's last tour of duty was as a volunteer militiaman in Captain McFarland's Company of McDowell's Regiment. He took part in Rutherford's Wilmington Expedition of late fall and

winter of 1781, commanded overall by Brigadier General Griffith
Rutherford of Rowan County. He served about four months on
this tour.

Summary of Later Life:

John Blackwell was married to Mary Anthony, daughter of
Paul Anthony. Blackwell remained in Burke County until 1784,
moving to Abbeville County, South Carolina, Ninety-Six district.
He left Abbeville County about 1797 or 1798 and moved to
Franklin County, Georgia. In 1818, he moved to Hickman County,
Tennessee.

John Blackwell applied for Revolutionary War pension in
Hickman County, Tennessee on July 4, 1836. He was awarded an
annual pension of $26.66. John Blackwell died February 12, 1839.

Census Locations:

1790 Abbeville County, South Carolina, Ninety-Six District
1820 Hickman County, Tennessee
1830 Hickman County, Tennessee

References:
US National Archives; Pension Statements; # S2083.
Preston, Peter and Sally. Mathews, Virginia 23109, material in Vertical files,
        Burke County Library, Morganton, NC.
1790 SC Census; Genealogical Publishing Company, Baltimore, 1972 ed.
Sistler, Byron. 1830 Census – West Tennessee, 1971 ed.
AIS 1820 Tennessee Census 1974 ed.

Blalock, John

Summary of Early Life:

John Blalock was born in Brunswick County, Virginia on September 4, 1762. He continued to live in Brunswick County for the duration of the American Revolution.

Summary of Partisan Activity:

John Blalock first entered Revolutionary War military service in Brunswick County, Virginia in January 1778. He was placed in a company commanded by Captain Turner Bynum of Colonel Dowlman's regiment. He served in the Suffolk area. Blalock volunteered again for Captain Bynum's Company of Dowlman's regiment in July 1778. They served in the Portsmouth area. He mentions a skirmish near Dismal Swamp. In June 1781, Blalock received a commission as a Lieutenant, again serving under Captain Bynum. They joined the forces of LaFayette at Point of Fork, Virginia. After a skirmish with the British at Jamestown, they joined up with General Washington, taking part in the siege and surrender of the British at Yorktown in October, 1781. After the surrender, now as a Captain, Blalock took part in escorting and guarding the British prisoners being transferred to Albemarle barracks near Charlottesville, Virginia.

Summary of Later Life:

*There are documents in Burke County, North Carolina witnessed by a John Blalock in 1782 and 1783. *

John Blalock continued to live in Brunswick County, Virginia until ca. 1798, when he moved to Burke County, North Carolina, western portion, that later become Mitchell and Yancey Counties. * He lived in western North Carolina until about a year before he was pensioned, moving to Carter County, Tennessee. John Blalock was pensioned in Carter County, Tennessee, receiving an annual amount of $160.00.

Later, he moved back to North Carolina, so as to be near

his children. John Blalock died March 10, 1846. His widow, Polly Blalock died October 7, 1856. He and his wife were buried near Spruce Pine, Mitchell County, North Carolina. John and Polly Blalock had the following offspring:

Samuel b. 1798 m. Elizabeth Ballew
Jesse b. 1814 m. Eva Hipps
Mary B. 1802 m. Austin Coffey
John C. b. 1816
Tilman b. 1804 m. Sarah Wilson
David b. 1822 m. Minive Phillips
Elizabeth b. 1807 m. Thomas Vance
Matilda b. 1826 m. John Wiseman
William b. 1912

Land Holdings and Transactions:

    1815 Burke County Tax Lists show John Blalock with 100 acres on Beaver Creek, a tributary of Toe River (now Mitchell County NC, at Spruce Pine). Polly Blalock, in 1856, received a federal bounty warrant for 160 acres by the Act of 1855.

Census Locations:

1810 Burke Co NC and 1815 tax lists Burke Co NC
1820 Burke Co NC and 1815 tax lists Burke Co NC

References:
US National Archives Pension Data W1807.
Huggins, Edith W. Miscellaneous
        Burke Records in 4 volumes.
Pittman, Betsy D. "Burke County NC 1815 Tax Lists" (1990ed.) p. 103
Bailey, Lloyd. Article on John Blalock in Toe River Heritage.
Biggs, Robert. Chicago   Data submitted to author, Nov. 2004.

Bowman, Marshall

Summary of Early Life:

Marshall Bowman was born on October 13, 1760 in Amherst County, Virginia. At the beginning of the American Revolution, his father and family moved to Burke County, North Carolina, settling on the south side of the Catawba River near Lovelady Shoals. At that time, Marshall Bowman was age sixteen years. Burke records seem to indicate that he may have been the son of Edward Bowman and brother of Groves, Gilbert, and Sherwood Bowman.

Summary of Partisan Activity:

Marshall Bowman first entered military service at age nineteen years in 1779 (probably 1780). He served in Captain Mordecai Clarke's Company. He relates, in his pension declaration, how he marched with Greene's Army across the Pee Dee River to Cheraw Hills. There the army went into winter quarters. After three months duty, he was discharged (early 1781).

In the summer of 1781 he served as a militiaman in Charles McDowell's Burke Regiment and served at Woffords Fort on the North Catawba.

In the fall and winter of 1781, Bowman served in the Wilmington Expedition, headed up by Army Brigadier General Griffith Rutherford and Colonel Charles McDowell, along with Major Joseph White. Bowman served in Captain James McFarland's company of McDowell's Burke Regiment. It was here that news of Cornwallis' surrender was received. He and his company then returned home and were discharged.

Summary of Later Life:

Marshall Bowman, after the Revolution, remained a short while in Burke County and then moved back to Armherst County Virginia for five or six years. From there he moved to Kanawha

County, Virginia (later West Virginia). He lived in the Coal River area.

As a resident of Kanawha County, Virginia, Bowman applied for Revolutionary War pension benefits in October 1833. He was awarded an annual pension of $30.00 per annum. Bowman remained in Kanawha County until 1840. He then moved to Benton County, Missouri. He stated that his children had all moved to Missouri and that he had no way of support at home. Date of death not on pension records.

Land Holdings and Transactions:

In 1796, Marshall Bowman signed over his land inheritance to his brother Sherwood Bowman (on the death of Edward Bowman.) This was property on the south side of Catawba, adjacent to John McGalliard and on Bridge Creek (now present day Valdese – Rutherford College, NC).

Census Locations:

1790 (Edward Bowman Burke County, NC 2nd Company)
1810 Kanawha County, Virginia
1820 Kanawha County, Virginia
1830 Kanawha County, Virginia ("Martial Borron" pg. 26)

References:
US National Archives, Pension Statements; #S16651.
Felldin, Jeanne R. Index to the 1820 Census of Virginia GPC 1976 ed.
Crichard, Madeline W. Index to the 1810 Virginia Census, Parsons, West
        Virginia 1971 ed.
AIS (Salt Lake City UT) 1790 NC Census 1978 ed. Reprint.
AIS (Bountiful UT) 1976 ed. VA 1830 Census Index.

Bradford, Joseph <u>Bennett</u>

Summary of Early Life:

Bennett Bradford, son of John Bradford, was born in Fauquier County, Virginia on November 14, 1738. Tennessee records show Revolutionary soldiers Henry, John and William Bradford living in Tennessee – all originally from Fauquier County, Virginia and who had served in Virginia troops, relationship to Bennett Bradford not definitely known.

By the mid 1760's, Bennett Bradford had moved from Virginia to Guilford County, North Carolina and was living on South Buffalo Creek. Records also indicate an earlier marriage in Virginia (_____ George). He married Margaret Wilson in 1762 (of Burke County?). Since he did not receive a Burke land grant in the 1778-1779 period, it is assumed that he was still residing in the Guilford County area during the Revolutionary War.

Summary of Partisan Activity:

Several entries in the North Carolina Revolutionary Army accounts verify that Bennett Bradford served in the North Carolina militia and also furnished provisions.

Hosea Bradford, son of Bennett Bradford, later showed to his son a mahogany clothes brush presented to Bennett Bradford by General Thomas Sumter of South Carolina. Inscribed on the brush was "present from General Sumter to Bennett Bradford 1781". He stated to his son that the brush was for bravery exhibited at the Battle of Guilford Court House on March 15, 1781, where Bradford served on General Sumter's staff.

The author is convinced that Bennett Bradford served in the American Revolution – possibly at Guilford Court House (as he was residing in the area) and possibly under *General Sumter. If he served under Sumter, then the service more than likely was in South Carolina, not North Carolina. General Sumter was not at Guilford Court House, but actively engaged in South Carolina on the Congaree River at the time. South Carolina General Andrew Pickens and his troops were at Guilford Court House.

(Bradford was later a neighbor of William Sumter of Burke (later Caldwell County), brother of General Sumter.

Summary of Later Life:

As mentioned in earlier notations, Bradford moved from Virginia to central North Carolina some ten or fifteen years prior to the Revolutionary War. He appears to have come to Burke County (now Caldwell County) sometime after the war. He was married to: (1) _____George (2) Margaret Wilson, and children by one or both of these marriages were:

Hannah b. 1764 m. Jacob Headrick
Mary b. 1766 m. (1) John Tipton (2) Thomas Greer
Sarah b. 1770 m. Rice Coffey
John b. 1771 m. Ann Goodwin
Benjamin b. 1774 m. Mary McFarland
Henry b. 1776 m. Rachel McFarland
James b. 1777 m. Catherine Keith
Nelly b. 1781 m. William Daughery
Milton b. 1783 m. Jane Hill

Bennett Bradford married (3) Susanna Bush Jones, widow of Revolutionary soldier William Jones, who died in1798. By this union were born twins (1) Hosea b. September 20, 1803 m. Mary Coillier, or Collies, and (2) Susan b. September 20, 1803 m. Cannon Lowdermilk.

Burke County records show Bradford active in community and civic affairs. The soldier Bennett Bradford died November 14, 1828 in Burke County, now Caldwell County, North Carolina.

By occupation he appeared to have been a blacksmith and lived near Bradford Mountain, a well know Caldwell County eminence, just south of present day Lenoir, North Carolina.

Land Holdings and Transactions:

 Burke County Tax lists show Bennett Bradford with fifty acres land initially and later with 100 acres. State grants in Guilford Co. North Carolina:

1. 199 acres S. Buffalo Cr. Bk. 33 p.148 (13 Nov 1779).
2. 499 acres on on both sides of Paddy Creek, a tributary of Deep River. Bk 33 p.381. (Mar 1780).
3. 100 acres S. Buffalo Cr. Bk. 33 p. 408 (1 Mar 1780).
4. 330 acres on both sides of fork of Deep River Bk. 33 p. 435. (1 Mar 1780).

Census Locations:

1790 Burke County, North Carolina 7th Company
1800 Burke County, North Carolina
1810 Burke County, North Carolina
1820 Burke County, North Carolina

References:
DAR Miscellaneous Records relative to Bennett Bradford, Revolutionary Soldier.
DAR Patriot Index (1996 ed. Washington DC).
AIS Census indices NC 1790, 1800, 1810.
Potter, Dorothy Williams. 1820 NC census data.
TN DAR records ed. by Marsh, Helen C. 1979 (originally by Bates Lucy W.) p. 20.
Gibson, Randy. personal communication with author, 1990. (Caldwell Co. NC).
White, Virgil. General Abstracts Revolutionary War Pension Files. Vol. II. (1991) p. 1885.
Huggins, Edith. Miscellaneous Burke Records.
North Carolina Revolutionary Army Accounts (from printed Editions by Haun,Wynette P., Durham NC Parts I – XII), Vol. IX P39 #5492, Vol. IX S26 #526, Vol. VII, 443 Bk 26 p. 25, Vol. VII/ 469 BK 26 p. 51,Vol. V / 175 BK 28, Vol. IV G p. 354 #28.
Hofmann, Margaret M. "North Carolina Abstracts of State Grants. Vol. I. 1998 ed.

Brandon, Thomas

Summary of Early Life:

It appears that Thomas Brandon was living in Rowan County, North Carolina in 1761, the birth date of his son Josiah (as given in Josiah's Revolutionary War Pension application, 1832). During the Revolutionary War period, he was living on Crooked Creek in western Burke County, North Carolina (now McDowell County). What, if any, relation he was to Thomas Brandon on Grant's Creek, Rowan County, North Carolina, is not known.

Summary of Partisan Activity:

Thomas Brandon was a loyalist officer of Burke County and who commanded a company of men at the battle of Kings Mountain on October 7, 1780. His superior officer was Colonel Veazey Husbands of Burke County (he may have served under Colonel Ambrose Mills of Tryon County also). Captain Thomas Brandon was killed in action at Kings Mountain. His son, Josiah, fought also at Kings Mountain and was captured, later paroled.

The court martial records of Colonel Charles McDowell related the confiscation of a horse from Brandon's widow (as Tory property) and selling it to Captain Daniel Smith at about half its appraised value.

Other Brandon's in the area included Thomas (son?), Martin Brandon (?), and son Josiah Brandon.

Land Holdings and Transaction:

It appears that Thomas Brandon possessed two tracts of land on Crooked Creek in western Burke County, North Carolina (now McDowell County). One was his place of residence, and another was a nearby tract purchased from Lodwich Ray (or Wray). A road connected the two tracts (See entry by Captain James Forgy #578).

References:

Brandon, Josiah. US National Archives Pension declaration given in application #W335 (1832).

Huggins, Edith W. Miscellaneous Burke County Records, in four soft back volumes, multiple sources - indexed.

Land Grant Records. Burke County Library, Morganton, NC.

Braswell, William Jonas

Summary of Early Life:

William Barjonah or Jonas Braswell was from eastern North Carolina, possibly Edgecombe County. He was born ca 1755.

Summary of Partisan Activity:

Jonas Braswell, according to family traditions, had moved to the Burke County, North Carolina area during the Revolutionary War. Another source says Johnston County. Still another source states that he served in the militia, was in the Battle of Cowpens (January 17, 1781), and suffering from a wound from which he never fully recovered. The only North Carolina units to serve at Cowpens were from Burke County.

Summary of Later Life:

Jonas Braswell married Nancy _____ ? in 1798. Their children were as follows:

William Blackstock b. 1795 m. Margaret Shell
Nancy b. 1799 m. James Barber
Ryan Edward b. 1800 m. Ann Beard
Wiley b. 1802 m. Obedience Barber
Suzie

It seems that Braswell lived in the Lower Creek area of Burke (Caldwell) County and often hunted on Upper Creek and in the mountains. William Braswell died while on a visit to the mountains, possibly of exposure. He died 1825 on Three Mile Creek, Avery County, North Carolina.

References:
Braswell, Fred and Linda. Rutherford College, NC, Conversations with author
         2000-2004.
Internet access.

Bright, Samuel

Summary of Early Life:

Samuel Bright, like contemporaries Daniel Boone and Hunting John McDowell, was fully a western North Carolina "pathfinder". By living and trading in the vicinity of Native Americans, he became their friend. Bright had secured a North Carolina Crown Patent for land in western Tryon County. Other grants nearby already described the western trail known as "Bright's Path" or "Bright's Trail". By the time of the American Revolution, Bright had settled high in the Blue Ridge Mountains midway between the Watauga Valley (now East Tennessee) and the western Catawba and Broad River Valleys of North Carolina. The trail came into prominence in September 1780 as the Overmountain men marched over it during the King's Mountain Campaign.

Summary of Partisan Activity:

Samuel Bright was considered a loyalist by those who knew him and were associated with him. This may have stemmed from his friendship with the Cherokees, who eventually became allies of the British during the Revolutionary War. In March 1777, he was brought to court at Salisbury and was made to sign an oath of allegiance. He was brought to court to "answer a charge of having committed sundry misdemeanors against the state by encouraging the enemies of the state ". See data by Bailey, in Toe River Valley Heritage I/87. (1994 ed.). (Perhaps these enemies were the Cherokees??).

Summary of Partisan Activity:

Interestingly, Bright's name does not appear on the well-known "Tory List" of 1782 (court docket relating to Confiscation Acts passed by NC legislature) in Burke County. His name is not listed in the Court martial evidence in the trial of Colonel Charles McDowell (many Loyalists were enumerated). The North Carolina Revolutionary Army accounts list a certificate given to

Bright. These were usually for patriotic services, such as supplies, etc.

Summary of Later Life:

Burke County documents show that Samuel Bright was active in civil transactions from the close of the Revolution until the turn of the century. He is listed in various court cases, land juries, petitions, etc. He was in both the 1790 and 1800 census of Burke County. He had several tracts of land, mainly on Toe River and several cabins. One land entry document states that he had entered 640 acres of land on Toe River where "said Bright now lives on formerly named Lower Old Fields of Toe River" (ent. 18 Feb. 1778).

Bailey in his Toe River Valley Heritage, states that Bright left the North Carolina Mountains for Tennessee, along with members of a family named Grant.

Land Holdings and Transactions:

1. Burke County, NC. 360 acres on Toe River. The land lay adjacent to his upper entry. cc Thomas White; James Taylor White. Ent. 18 Feb. 1778, #240. Grant issued 15 March 1780, #172 Bk. 28, p. 71. The entry states land "on which he now lives".
2. Burke County, NC 640 acres on Toe River "being the place that said Bright now lives on". Known by the name of "The Lower Old Fields of Toe". The land lay on both sides of Toe River. cc Thomas White; James Taylor White, surveyed Aug. 10, 1778. Ent. 8 Feb. 1778 #239, Granted 15 March 1780 #108 Bk. 28 p. 108.
3. Burke County, NC 100 acres "on both sides of main Toe River". The land lay adjacent to that of Charles Deems. Ent. 29 Dec. 1792, #247 Granted 7 June 1799, #2609 Bk. 101 p. 101. cc William Bright, Jr., Joseph Cantest (?).

Census Locations:

1790 Burke County, North Carolina 10th Company
1800 Burke County, North Carolina

References:
AIS Census Books 1790, 1800 NC.
Material in vertical files, Burke County Library, Morganton, NC.
Land Grant data Burke County Library, Morganton, NC.
Bailey, Lloyd. Toe River Valley Heritage – Vol. I 1994 ed.article on Samuel
        Bright, p. 87.

Brown, Jeremiah

Summary of Early Life:

Jeremiah Brown was born near the Shallow Ford of the Yadkin River on May 8, 1759. At the beginning of the American Revolution, Jeremiah Brown was living with his father and family in Wilkes County, North Carolina. During the mid portion of the conflict, his family moved from Wilkes to Burke County, North Carolina, remaining until the close of hostilities.

Summary of Partisan Activity:

Jeremiah Brown first entered military service in 1780 as a volunteer militiaman in Colonel Benajamin Cleveland's, Wilkes regiment. Other officers under whom he served included Major Dula, Captain Elijah Clark, and Lieutenant Whitesides. With the Wilkes militia troops he marched to South Carolina and took part in the decisive battle of Camden on August 16, 1780 ("Gates' Defeat"). The American army was completely defeated in detail. He was discharged by Captain Clark a few weeks later at Saluda.

After moving to Burke County, Brown was drafted for a tour of six months and was sent to South Carolina and placed in a company commanded by Captain Patrick "Paddy" Carr; of Burke County, Georgia. Under Carr, they took part in the successful siege operation in and around Augusta, Georgia. Brown was present when the main garrison surrendered. Brown also served in the lower country of South Carolina and Georgia.

Summary of Later Life:

Jeremiah Brown, after the Revolutionary War, moved from North Carolina to Georgia and then to Tennessee (Jackson County, Bledsoe County, Powell Valley, Roane County, and back to Jackson County). Jeremiah Brown married (1) Elizabeth Floyd and (2) Jane Franklin. Jane Franklin was age 96 in 1870 and still living in 1874. Children by second wife (married 1800 Powell's Valley, East Tennessee) were Edmond, Barbara, William, John, and James.

Brown applied for federal pension in Jackson County, Tennessee on September 15, 1834, age 75 years. He was awarded a pension in the amount of $20.00 per annum.

Jeremiah Brown died in Jackson County, Tennessee on November 10, 1859, age 100 years. He is buried in New Hope Cemetery, west of Hidham and twelve miles east of Gainsboro, Tennessee.

Census Locations:

1790 Burke County, Georgia (?) 1790-1795 Headright Grant
1804, 1805 Grainger County, Tennessee (tax lists) (in that part
     that later became Union County?)
1820 Jackson County, Tennessee
1840 Jackson County, Tennessee

References:
US National Archives Pension Data #W 27542.
Sistler, Barbara and Byron. Early Tennessee Tax Lists. Evanston IL. 1977 p.
     24.
AIS Census Index 1820 TN.
DeLamar, M. and Rothstein E. The Reconstructed 1790 Census of Georgia.
     GPC 1985, p. 7.
Marsh, Helen C. "Soldiers and Patriots of the American Revolution
     Buried in Tennessee". (compiled by Lucy W. Bates), TN DAR
1974, p. 24.

Carrell, William

Summary of Early Life:

William Carrell was living in Amherst County, Virginia prior to the time of the American Revolution. He was born ca 1743-44. During the Revolutionary War, he was a resident of Wilkes County, North Carolina.

Summary of Partisan Activity:

William Carrell appeared to have been an officer in the American Revolution. A notice in the Raleigh Register and Raleigh Star states: "Died January 18, 1826. Captain William Carrell, a native of Amherst County, Virginia in the 82nd year of his age – a distinguished hero of the Revolution – at his residence in the County of Burke." The historian Gwathney gives a William Carroll as serving in Captain Jonathan Hamby's Company and a William Carroll serving in the 6th Regiment Virginia Continental Line. (See also statement of Adam Crum, a Revolutionary War soldier (this volume) concerning his service under a Col. Carroll, probably of Wilkes Co., NC.)

Summary of Later Life:

Carrell was living in Burke County after 1810 until his death in 1826 as shown by census records.

Census Locations:

1810 Burke County, North Carolina
1820 Burke County, North Carolina

References:
Neal, Lois S. op.cit. p, 115.
Gwathney, John H. Historical Records of Virginians in the American Revolution. 1938 Richmond, Va., pp. 132, 133.

Carruthers, Robert

Summary of Early Life:

Robert Carruthers was born ca 1762-63. He appears to have been living in Lincoln County, North Carolina during the Revolution. He was the son of Robert Carruthers Sr. and Margaret White Carruthers.

Summary of Partisan Activity:

Robert Carruthers served in a company of militia from Lincoln County commanded by Captain John Mattocks. With Mattocks, he participated in the Kings Mountain Campaign, ending with the American victory of October 7, 1780. Captain Mattocks was killed in this battle.

North Carolina Revolutionary accounts also record payment to Carruthers for Revolutionary War activity.

Summary of Later Life:

Robert Carruthers, in 1785, entered land on Mountain Creek in Lincoln County, North Carolina (now Catawba County). By 1790, he had moved into western Burke County. He appears as a foreman of a grand jury in 1790 in the Muddy Creek area. Robert Carruthers married Elizabeth Pattillo in 1785, a daughter of John Pattillo. The Pattillos were also associated with Lincoln County. They, along with Carruthers, moved to the western area of Burke County, now McDowell County.

Robert Carruthers was appointed a justice of the peace for Burke County in 1794 and 1796, presiding over several jury trials. He purchased 100 acres of land from David Vance. In 1799, he was located in Captain Thomas Hemphill's Company and owned 209 acres of land. He was listed in the 1800 census of Burke County.

In 1808, Robert Carruthers left Burke County and moved to

Maury County, Tennesse. He acquired land on Fountain Creek, a few miles southeast of present day Columbia, Tennessee. Robert Carruthers participated in civic affairs of Maury County. He lived there until his death in 1828. Robert and Elizabeth Carruthers had the following children:

> John Carruthers b. 1788, d. 1840
> Robert Carruthers b. 1791
> Susanna married John D. Lowe b. 1793, d. 1863
> Mary b. ? 1793 m. George Patton
> Samuel Carruthers b. 1798
> Elizabeth m. John D. Love (of Henry County, Tennessee)

Robert Carruthers will was recorded in Maury County, Tennessee in 1828.

Note: This Robert Carruthers not to be confused with Revolutionary War Soldier Robert Carruthers of Mecklenburg County, North Carolina, later living in Williamson County and Bedford County, Tennessee.

Land Holdings and Transactions:

1. Burke County, North Carolina, 30 acres on the Spring Branch, lying adjacent to his own land, formerly belonging to Brown. cc. Edward Jackson; Robert Coulter. Ent. 26 Oct 1796 #3207. Grant No. 2797, Iss. 2 June 1800, BK. 109, p. 37.

2. Maury County, Tennessee, David Lowe of Maury County, Tennesse to Robert Carruthers of Burke County, North Carolina deed dated 22 Feb 1808, registered 19 April 1808, 235 acres on Fountain Creek, including a portion of Hurricane Fort adjacent to land of Richard Dallum, Breckinridge and George Roland heirs. Maury County, Tennesse Deed BK. A-F (1807-1817).

3. Burke County, North Carolina, Robert and Elizabeth Carruthers receive 58 acres in Crooked Creek area (now McDowell County, NC) as their share of the estate of her father, John Petillo, Sr. (April 1809 session).

4. Burke County, NC, Robert Carruthers deeded 253 acres to his brother-in-law, Millington Pattillo. 13 May 1809 (this was in the time period of his removal to Maury County, TN).

Census Locations:

1790 Lincoln County, 9th Company
1800 Burke County, North Carolina
1816 Tax List Maury County, Tennessee
1820 Maury County, Tennessee

References:
Crosse, Melto C. <u>Pattillo, Patilo, Pettillo and Pittillo Families</u>. Ft Worth Texas
      1972, pp. 35-41.
Alexander, Virginia W. <u>Maury County Tennessee Deed Books A-F 1807-1817.</u>
      SHP 1981. pp 108-110; 4; 63.
NC Land Grant Data Morganton Library, Morganton, North Carolina.
NC Revolutionary Army Accounts.
Huggins, Edith W. Miscellaneous Burke County Records.
AIS Census Data NC 1790, 1800. TN 1820.
Sullivan, Kathy Gunter. "Burke County NC Deeds Registered 1804-1813".
Sistler, Byron and Barbara. <u>Early TN Tax Lists</u> 1977 ed., p 43.

Carswell, John (Creswell, Criswell)

Summary of Early Life:

     John Carswell and his family were living in Hunting Creek in Burke County, North Carolina during the American Revolution (near present day Morganton, NC). One source states that he may have moved from central North Carolina to the western part of the state.

Summary of Partisan Activity:

     In September 1780, on Cornwallis' first invasion on North Carolina, he detached Major Patrick Ferguson from the main army. Ferguson was to advance northward into western North Carolina, with the main objective of recruiting Tory sympathizers. As he entered Burke County, an ambush was planned by Colonel Charles McDowell at the head of Cane Creek, near present day Brindletown. Many of McDowell's militiamen were from the vicinity of Hunting Creek, Silver Creek and Muddy Creek, including John Carswell. Other soldiers included James Murphy, Peter Brank, and Samuel Woods.

     A skirmish occurred on September 12, 1780. McDowell's forces were scattered by the British. During the action, Peter Brank was killed and John Carswell was wounded. Most of the militiamen at Cane Creek followed McDowell into East Tennessee and eventually back across the mountains to Kings Mountain (Oct 7, 1780). It is not known as to whether or not Carswell was in this battle.

Summary of Later Life:

     From available data, it appears that John Carswell lived on Hunting Creek near Morganton and that he may have died at about the time of the first census in 1790-91. In the census, there are listed two females and four males. This would indicate a family of three boys and one girl. The only son listed in the records is a Robert or James Robert Carswell. Robert was the father of

William, Robert, Rankin, John, Samuel and Barbara Carswell. There is a possibility that the children in the 1790 census are those of Robert, who may have been the second adult male listed with John Carswell. Another researcher states that Robert Carswell was born in 1750 and died in 1790 and was married to Carolyn Brown.The genealogy of John Carswell is certainly subjective to a degree and more information is needed

Land Holdings and Transactions:

John Carswell entered 440 acres in Burke County, NC on Hunting Creek "where he now lives for complement". Entered 22 Feb 1778, ent. #183. Transferred to Charles McDowell, granted to McDowell on 9 Nov 1784. Grant #875 Book 57, p. 48. Surveyed by David Vance, the land after transfer was for 330 acres on Hunting Creek, including mouth of Long Branch, which flows into Hunting Creek. The land lay adjacent to land of John Hughes, William Welsh, and Hennessee. It also contained a portion of "Hennessee's Fork of Long Branch." cc William Walsh, John Hughes.

Census Locations:

1790 Burke County, North Carolina 13th Company
Note: a John Carswell is noted on several subsequent censuses, possibly John Carswell who married Jane Houck.

References:
AIS 1790 NC Census.
AIS Census Indices 1800-1830.
Land Grant Data in Burke County Library, Morganton, NC.
Huggins, Edith W. (SHP) Vol I-IV.
Ramsey, Juanita. Articles in Burke County NC Heritage (1981 ed) Vol. I, p 132.
Parsons, Ellen. Material in vertical file Burke County Library, Morganton, NC.
NC Revolutionary Army Accounts (A) VI/24/93 #3263 (B) TX/S-26/PrTX #145 from Haun, Wynette P. (Durham 2770A 1992 & 1995 Parts IV and VII).

Carter, William

Summary of Early Life:

William Carter was born in Albemarle County, Virginia on 2 April 1760. He was living in Albemarle County at the time of his initial entry into Revolutionary military service.

Summary of Partisan Activity:

William Carter first entered military service in Albemarle County, Virginia in September 1778, age eighteen. He was placed in Captain John Grayson's Company of Virginia militia and marched to Staunton in Augusta County, Virginia. Here he was placed in Captain Alexander Henderson's Company of Colonel William Boyer's Regiment. Their regiment marched to the Indian frontier on the Ohio River. Carter was for a while at Fort Redstone, then Fort McIntosh, and finally Fort St. Lawrence. At Fort St. Lawrence, he was placed in Captain Gibson's Company, and remained there about two months, then back to Fort McIntosh under Captain Henderson for the remainder of the tour, or about five months. He returned to Albemarle County and in 1780 moved to Burke County, North Carolina. There he volunteered for a tour of duty in Captain Moses Guest's Company of Colonel Benjamin Cleveland's Wilkes militia.

Under Captain Guest, they marched to Ramseur's Mill, but arrived there shortly after the Battle of June 20, 1780. They reconnoitered briefly in the area, but returned to rendezvous at Wilkes Court House. From here they, as mounted riflemen, marched to South Carolina where they fought in the great battle of Kings Mountain on October 7, 1780. Cleveland's men fought under the command of Colonel William Campbell of Virginia. Carter mentions the capture of 800-900 prisoners and 100 being killed in action, including their leader Major Patrick Ferguson. Carter was marched back to Burke Court House where he received a discharge from Captain James Shepherd. He had been placed in Captain Shepherd's company a few days before the battle.

In his pension affidavits he mentions fellow soldiers Michael Israel, James Ferguson, James Nailor, Richard Sorrels, George Carter, Joel Kirby, and lower rank officers, Thomas Ferguson, Thompson Epperson.

In a later clarification statement, Carter stated that he assisted in escorting the King's Mountain prisoners to the Moravian Towns (Winston Salem), and then to the Virginia line, where they were received by Virginia authorities. He was then discharged.

Summary of Later Life:

William Carter had moved to Burke County in 1780. He remained in Burke County, North Carolina for "ten or eleven years" and then returned to Virginia. He settled in Geenbrier County, that part which later became Monroe County, Virginia (now West Virginia).

William Carter applied for Revolutionary War pension in Monroe County, Virginia on February 18, 1833, age 73 years. He was awarded a pension of $33.33 per annum. Later his pension was suspended. After a considerable number of letters were written in explanation, his pension was re-instated. He was paid until September 4, 1837 (date of death?). Later correspondence gives a Kenyon Carter of Barber County, Kentucky, relation to soldier, if any, not stated. William Carter's last residence was in Nicholas County, Virginia (now West Virginia).

Land Holdings and Transactions:

1. Burke County, North Carolina 200 acres at head of Smokey Creek, a tributary of Catawba River on land previously entered by John Tabor. The land lay adjacent to that of Cooper. Ent. 23 Rt 1779 # 1699 Grant No. 1460, 4 Jan 1792. Bk. 75 p. 435 cc John Ussery; John Tabor.
2. Burke County, North Carolina 100 acres on Smokey Creek adjacent to his own survey and also adjacent to

John Tabor's old livery, Ambrose Jones, and William
Rippetoe. Ent. 28 October 1779 # 1669 Grant No.
1773, 7 July 1794 Bk. 85 p. 86. cc William Tabor,
James Ussery.
3. Burke County, North Carolina Tax Lists 1815
William Carter "300 acres on Waters of Caine Creek".
4. Burke County Court of Pleas and Quarter Sessions July
1796. "Deed from John Maxwell to William Carter for
150 acres land" dated October 1793. Proved by
William Peremon.

*Census records, court records, will and probated records indicate at
least three William Carters in Burke County. Neither "William Carter
Sr. nor William Carter, Jr." seems to be the soldier William Carter.
William Carter, Sr's. will probated in 1806. They may have been of
some relation to the soldier. William Carter, Sr. and William Carter,
Jr. appear on 1800 census of Burke County.*

Census Locations:

1790 Burke County, NC 7th Co. *see previous note under land records*
1800 Burke County, NC ("William Carter, Sr. and William Carter, Jr.)
1810 Monroe County, Virginia
1820 Monroe County, Virginia
1830 Monroe County, Virginia

References:
US National Archives Pension Data # S9133.
Burke County, North Carolina Land Grant Data, Burke County Library,
        Morganton, NC.
Pittman, Betsy Dodd. Burke County, North Carolina 1815 Tax Lists (1990) p.
        31.
AIS Census Records. (NC 1790; VA 1810, 1830).
Felldian, Jeanne R. Index to 1820 Census of Virginia. GPC 1976.
Minutes of Burke County NC Court of Pleas and Quarter Sessions (1795-1798).
        compiled by Daniel D. Swink (1987) p. 31.
Philbeck, Jr. Miles and Turner, Grace. "Burke County NC Surviving Will and
        Probate Records 1777-1910" (1983) #99.
Gwathney, John H. Historical Register of Virginians in the Revolution.
        Richmond 1938 (GPC Reprint 1996) p. 135.

Case, Thomas

Summary of Early Life:

It appears that Thomas Case was living in western Rowan County, North Carolina, later Burke County, prior to the American Revolution. He resided near White's Mill Creek, northwest of Morganton, North Carolina. Case was active in Rowan affairs and was appointed a Constable in 1772.

Summary of Partisan Activity:

As a member of the Burke militia, Case was severely wounded in a conflict with the Cherokee Indians on the Western North Carolina Frontier (the Cherokees were allied with the British cause). Case was permanently disabled by his wounds and unable to pursue a gainful occupation in later years.

In 1779, Case petitioned the North Carolina government for financial relief. An affidavit in his behalf signed by Colonel Charles McDowell (commanding officer of Burke militia) and by militia officers, William Moore, John Hardin, Alex Erwin, Joseph McDowell, William White and William Stuart.. Because of the early Revolutionary War data and the officers listed, the military action most likely was the Cherokee Expedition of 1776, headed by Brigadier General Grifffith Rutherford.

Summary of Later Life:

Case was active in Burke County civic affairs from 1782 thru 1800, and was appointed a Burke County Constable in 1793. He is listed on the1790 and 1800 censuses in Burke County, North Carolina. Later censuses list a Thomas Case in Buncombe County, but none in Burke. Other Cases in Buncombe include John, Sr., John, Jr., Thomas, Jr., William, Daniel, Laxton, and Leuallen. Whether this is the family of Thomas Case, the soldier, is not definitely known.

Land Holdings and Transactions:

1. Burke County NC 445 acres on Husband's Creek, a tributary of Lower Creek (which flows into Catawba River). The land also included portions of Sealey's (Celia's) Creek. The land lay adjacent to that of Colonel Christopher Beekman. Ent. 23 Aug 1778 #411, Granted 15 March 1780 #162, Bk. 28 p. 161.
2. Buncombe County NC Land Grants
    (a) 100 acres Clear Creek 26 Nov 1799
    (b) 100 acres Big Hungary Creek 30 Nv 1819
        additional grants 1825-1830, possibly Thomas Case, Jr.

Census Locations:

1790 Burke County, North Carolina 7th Company
1800 Burke County, North Carolina
1810 Buncombe County, North Carolina (?)
1820 Buncombe County, North Carolina (?)

References:
Huggins, Edith W. Miscellaneous Burke County NC Records Vol. IV. pp 136,143.
Burke County Court Records on microfilm.
Wooley, James E. Buncombe County NC Index to Deeds 1783 -SHP 1983 ed. pp. 84-86.
Various NC Censuses AIS, printed.
Burke County NC Land Grant Data, Burke County NC Library, Morganton NC.
Linn, Jo White. "Abstracts of the Minutes of the Court of Pleas And Quarter Sessions of Rowan County NC 1763-1774" Vol. II. Salisbury 1979. pp. 132, 150, 158, 164.

Collett, Abraham

Summary of Early Life:

Abraham Collett, according to family sources, was born ca 1743 possibly in Scotland. He was one of the earlier settlers of Rowan County, receiving a Granville Grant on Mountain Creek in 1761. By the time of the American Revolution, he was living on Upper Creek, Burke County, North Carolina, adjacent to the Quaker Meadows tract of Colonel Charles McDowell. He was one of the signers of a petition to create a new county from Rowan (ca 1771-73). Abraham Collett was active in Rowan and Burke County civil matters from 1761 to 1778, as indicated in court and other records.

Summary of Partisan Activity:

In 1781 or 1782, Abraham Collett was killed by the Indians on the western frontier (the Indians were allied with the British).

His death was confirmed by a report rendered by Colonel Joseph McDowell, commanding officer of the Burke regiment of militia (he had assumed this command in 1782). This report stated, "the people killed by Indians since the last proposal of treaty by the Indians." Then followed a list of approximately fifteen names, including that of Abraham Collett.

North Carolina Revolutionary army accounts verify Abraham Collett as being a member of the North Carolina militia.

Family Data:

According to the land records of Rowan County, Abraham Collett's (first) wife was named Ulah or Ula. Family data also gives a (second) wife as Margaret Wakefield. Children by these women included:

Elizabeth b. 1769 m. Thomas Church
Rachel b. 1770 m. _____ Inman

48

Charles b. 1772 m. Amelia Parks (Caldwell County NC)

Margaret seems to have died a year after Collett's death. Washington County, Tennessee lists an estate sale for Abraham Collett in ca 1783-84. Purchasers included Mary, Jacob, Ann, Ruth, and Isaac Collett (children by Ulah?). An Abraham Collett is listed on 1805 tax lists of Green County, Tennessee.

References:
Huggins, Edith. Miscellaneous Burke County Records Vols. I-IV. Multiple entries.
Linn, Jo White. Rowan County land records.
Richardson, Jan L. (Las Vegas, NV) Material in vertical file Burke County NC Library, Morganton, NC (1994).
Legislative Paper. L. P. 45, undated loose paper, NC Department Of Archives and History, Raleigh, NC (copied by author, 1978) (relating to the death confirmation of Abraham Collett).
Burke. NC DAR Roster of Soldiers from North Carolina in the American Revolution. Originally published 1932 GPC Report Copy p. 368, Vouchers #4495 (transcribed as Abraham "Collon").
Sistler, Byron and Barbara. Early Tennessee Tax Lists. 1977ed., p 40.
Phifer, Edward W. Jr. Burke   1982 ed. pp. 361-2.

Collins, Brice

Summary of Early Life:

Brice Collins was born in Maryland in 1758. Prior to the Revolutionary War, his father and family had moved to central North Carolina, now Orange County area. Brice Collins was the son of Brice (sometimes written as "Price"), and Elizabeth Bradley Collins.

Summary of Partisan Activity:

Brice Collins enlisted in the American Army initially as a substitute for his father.

One source says he served seven years and was in Baron de Kalb's Regiment at the Battle of Camden in South Carolina (August 16, 1780). He is said to have been an eyewitness to Baron de Kalb's death, and in later years, often referred to this event.

Summary of Later Life:

Following the close of the Revolutionary War, Brice Collins settled for a while in Hillsborough, Orange County near his boyhood home. In the 1790's, he moved to Salisbury in Rowan County. About 1794 he moved to Burke County, North Carolina. He remained in Burke County for the remainder of his life. Brice Collins became an outstanding public servant in Burke County. As a lawyer, he was active in many civic affairs. He served in the North Carolina legislature on eleven different occasions. Brice Collins was described as being a strong muscular man and with the appropriate nickname of "Ram".

Brice Collins was married to Jemima Moore (b. 1780), the daughter of James and Rebecca Moore. They were married ca 1803-1804. They had the following children:

Joseph LaFayette b. 1805 m. Elizabeth Truehart Johnson.
Mary Selina ("Polly") b. 1807 m. Peter Johnson.

Evelina b. 1810 m. Eli R. Shuford.
Elvina E. b. 1812 m. Major Andrew Hoyle Shuford
Brice Monroe III b. 1815 not married

The Revolutionary War soldier, Brice Collins, died on January 15, 1829. The Raleigh Register stated this about his death: "Died Jan 15, 1829 at his residence on John's River. Major Brice Collins entered the army at the age of fifteen years as a substitute for his father. A citizen of Burke County for 35 years and represented the County in the State Legislature."

Land Holdings and Transactions:

1. Burke County NC. Deed from David Baker to Brice Collins 476 acres, 29 Oct. 1794. Ack. By David Baker.
2. Burke County NC 1815 tax lists. Brice Collins 600 acres home place and 100 acres Jonas Ridge. Total 700 acres.
3. Orange County NC. 400 acres both sides of Owens Creek. Deed from John Swany to Brice Collins Jr. 4 April 1786. The land lay adjacent to that of James Garner, James Byrd and Samuel Actor.

Census Locations:

1790 Orange County, North Carolina
1800 Burke County, North Carolina
1820 Burke County, North Carolina

References:
Fletcher, Marjorie and Robert. Material accessed from internet source: http:/home.sprintmail.com-robtmarj/thecollins family.html.
Neal, Lois S. Abstracts of Vital Records from Raleigh NC   Newspapers 1820-1829 Vol. II. P. 142.
AIS Census Indices. NC 1790, 1800, 1810, 1820.
Swink, Daniel D. "Minutes of the Court of Pleas and Quarter Sessions". (Burke County NC), (1791-1795), and (1795-1798).
Pittman, Betsy D. "Burke County North Carolina 1815 Tax Lists". 1990 ed. p. 94.
Bennett, W. D. "Orange County Records Vol. II. Deed Books 1 and 2 abstracts. (1989 ed.), p. 59.

Connelly, Hugh

Summary of Early Life:

     Hugh Connelly was born in 1761, the son of Brian and Mary Connelly. The Connellys lived on Freemason's (also sp. Free Mason) Creek in what is now southern Caldwell County, Dry Ponds area.
See data on John and William Connelly, this volume, for further details.

Summary of Partisan Activity:

     The North Carolina Army accounts for Morgan military district verify the military service of Hugh Connelly as a militiaman. In Burke County, he would have served in Colonel Charles McDowell's Burke Regiment. McDowell's brother, Colonel Joseph McDowell, commanded the regiment after the formation of Morgan District in 1782.

Summary of Later Life:

     Hugh Connelly was married to Lucy Ballew. Their children were Hugh and Jesse.

     Hugh Connelly was active in Burke County civic affairs in the late 1700's into the early 1800's. At various times he served as a juryman. He also served on road and condemnation juries from time to time, and in 1792 served as a constable.

     Hugh Connelly lived on Freemason's Creek until about 1796. He disposed of his land and acquired land from John Montgomery in Western Burke County, now McDowell County. It was during this period that many of the Connellys and their kinsman, the Ballews, moved to the western area of the county.

     Hugh Connelly died ca 1820 and his will was probated in the July 1820 session of Burke County court. His wife Lucy was administratix.

Census Locations:

1790 Burke County, North Carolina 2nd Company
1800 Burke County, North Carolina
1810 Burke County, North Carolina

Land Holdings and Transactions: (*reflected in Burke County minutes*)

1. In 1792, Hugh Connelly received 100 acres from his father, Brian Connelly.
2. In 1793, Hugh Connelly conveyed 100 acres to his brother, John Connelly.
3. In 1795 he, along with other Connelly heirs, conveyed 117 acres to William Connelly.
4. In January 1796, Hugh Connelly received 361 acres from John Montgomery, in western Burke County.

References:
Article by Sarah Annis in Burke County NC Heritage 1981 ed. pp. 146-147.
AIS Censuses 1790, 1800, 1810.
NC DAR Roster of Soldiers from NC in the American Revolution (1967 reprint of 1932 ed.) p. 369.
NC Revolutionary Army Accounts Vol. VI. Bk 24 p. 5.
Pittman, Betsy D. Data on Connelly family in Burke County NC Library.
Vertical file Data Burke County Library, Morganton, NC.
Huggins, Edith W. Misc. Burke County Records in 4 Vol.
Swink, Daniel Abstracts of Burke County Court Minutes 1791-1803 in 3 ed.

Connelly, John

Summary of Early Life:

Several dates are given as John Connelly's birthdates (1740, 1744, 1750). John Connelly, according to recent data, appears to have been the son of Brian Connelly; born most likely in Ireland (another source says Pennsylvania). Other sources have stated that he was the son of a John O'Connelly. The Connellys, at the time of the American Revolution, lived in the Dry Ponds area of what is now South Caldwell County near Freemason's Creek, a tributary of the Catawba River. John Connelly's mother was Mary Connelly. John was the brother of Hugh, William and James Connelly and of Rebecca Gibbs. Their neighbors included the Ballews, Moores, Bowmans, and Murrays.

Summary of Partisan Activity:

Most of John Connelly's military service was in the mid and later phases of the American Revolution. He served as a Captain of militia in Colonel Charles McDowell's Burke Regiment. He served mainly on the western Catawba frontier, opposing the actions of the Cherokee Indians, then allied with the British. Verification of his service is given by the statements of three pensioned Revolutionary War Soldiers, John Gibbs, John Blackwell, and Jacob Gabbert. His service is also verified by the North Carolina Revolutionary Army accounts.

In late 1782, Connelly's name appears on a subpoena docket of suspected Tories. This was in relationship to the North Carolina Confiscation Acts. No action taken, as the war was to end in a few months.

Some sources mention his participation in the Cherokee Campaign (1776) and at Kings Mountain (1780).

Summary of Later Life:

John Connelly married Jane Ballew (1755-1851). m. ca

1770-1772. She was the daughter of Robert Ballew, Sr. (another source says Joseph and Elizabeth Ballew). By this union were the following children:

William b. 1774	Jane b. 1787
Mary b. 1776	George b. 1789
Elizabeth b. 1778	Joshua b. 1792
James b. 1782	Allen b. 1795
John b. 1784	Caleb b. 1798
Susannah b. 1785	Joseph b. 1801

John Connelly and his wife Jane continued to live at their home on Freemason's Creek. During the late 1790's and early 1800's, John Connelly was a prominent and busy citizen. Burke County court records verify his numerous duties as a public servant. He served on various juries, was a tax collector, census taker, and magistrate. He also served as Captain of a military judicial district, or precinct. He served as an administrator in the estate matter of Samuel Davidson. One researcher says there is no evidence that John Connelly lived anywhere but on Freemason's Creek and may be buried in a small cemetery there. He died on July 16, 1826. His widow, Jane Ballew Connelly later moved to McDowell County North Carolina, near her youngest son, Joseph Connelly. She died in 1851.

Land Holdings and Transactions:

1. 235 acres Burke County NC lying on North side of Catawba River and adjacent to his own land and that of James Moore and Brian Connelly. Ent. 15 Aug 1778 #290 Grant No. 428 Iss. 28 Oct 1782 Book 44 p. 178. cc (James Moose, James Connelly)
2. 400 acres Burke County NC lying just North of above survey and adjacent to land of James Moore. Ent. 20 Jan 1793 # 892 Grant No. 1793 Iss. 7 July 1794 Book 85 p. 94. cc (James Moore, William Connelly).
3. 100 acres Burke County NC on North side of Catawba River adjacent to his own land and that of James Moore.

Ent. 25 Jan 1803 #4549 Grant No. 3356 Iss. 28 Nov 1805
Book 119, p. 205 cc (John Connelly, Jr., Philip Killian).

Census Locations:

1790 Burke County, North Carolina 2nd Company
1800 Burke County, North Carolina (from 1799 tax lists)
1810 Burke County, North Carolina
1820 Burke County, North Carolina

References:
AIS Census Indices 1790-1820.
Pittman, Betsy. Data on Brian Connelly and Connelly family in Vertical files
        Morganton NC Burke County Library.
Swink, Daniel. Minutes of Burke County Courts of Pleas and Quarter Sessions
        (1791-1803). In 3 iss., Lawndale, NC.
Land Grant Data Burke County Library, Morganton, NC.
Whitley, Edythe Rucker. Membership Roster and Soldiers (TN Soc DAR)
        1961.
Jackson, Okey H., Jr. Material in vertical files. Burke County
        Library Morganton.
DAR Patriot Index (Nat. Society of DAR 1966 ed.) p. 149 Washington DC.
US National Archives Pension data on John Gibbs, John Blackwell , and
        Jacob Gabbert.
NC Revolutionary Army Accounts (as given in Haun, W. op.cit.) Vol. VI Bk 24;
        Vol. IX Bk. 14 Vol. VIII – F/1.
"The Conely Family of Crockett County, Tennessee". as given in vertical files
        Burke County Library.

Connelly, William

Summary of Early Life:

William Connelly was born August 5, 1764, the son of Bryan and Mary Connelly.

The Connellys came first to Rowan County, obtaining granted land on Mulls Branch of Elk Creek (now Catawba County) in 1767. Having disposed of their land the same year, the Connellys then moved to the north bank of the Catawba. This was in Burke County during the Revolutionary War, now South Caldwell County, and lay mainly in the vicinity of Freemason's Creek, which flowed south into the Catawba River.

Summary of Partisan Activity:

Late in the American Revolution, William Connelly became an officer in the Burke County militia, with the rank of Ensign. He served in a company commanded by Captain Mordecai Clark and Lieutenant James Nicholson. In early 1781, they marched into Mecklenburg County, joining the units commanded by Lieutenant Colonel (Brigadier General of militia) William L. Davidson. This was the time of Cornwallis' second invasion of North Carolina. They advanced from Twelve Mile Creek to Tuckaseegee Ford on the Catawba River. They were scattered by the British troops, with General Davidson being killed during one of the encounters. Clark's company then returned to Burke County and was stationed at Wofford's Fort on the North Catawba River. There they guarded against the incursion of the Cherokee Indians (from pension data of Benjamin Spencer, who served under William Connelly).

Summary of Later Life:

William Connelly married Mary Sanor Cooper. They had the following offspring:

John (Dutch John) b. 1783 m. Elizabeth Wakefield

Bryant
Elizabeth
William, Jr. ("Big Bill") m. Sara Massey Moore

William Connelly was active in Burke County civic affairs until after the turn of the century. Burke County Court records show him serving on juries, road juries, etc. The records indicate he was living in the Freemason Creek area, probably near his father's property. Following the death of his father, he received the property from the heirs of Brian Connelly in 1796, and then conveyed it to his niece and nephew (Groves and Mary Bowman) in 1797. The same year he received a deed from David Rutherford of 143 acres in western Burke County, later McDowell. This seems to indicate a proposed move to western Burke (along with other members of the family). William Connelly died in 1807. His widow, who lived to age ninety-nine years, continued to live in western Burke County with her son, William Connelly, Jr.

Land Holdings and Transactions:

1. The receipt of property from the heirs of Brian Connelly is abstracted in Huggins, Edith W. "Burke County NC Records" Vol. IV, p. 26. (SHP 1987 ed.)
2. The transfer of land from David Rutherford to William Connelly is abstracted in Swink, Daniel "Minutes of the (Burke County, NC) Court of Pleas and Quarter Sessions 1795-1798". (Lawndale NC 1987 ed.) p. 56, Apr. 1797.
    The land above is most likely the same tract as given in Huggins under "Daniel Rutherford" 142 ac 1795 Captain Morrison's Company. (in Western Burke, later McDowell County, NC.)

Census Locations:

1790 Burke County, North Carolina 2nd Company
1800 Burke County, North Carolina

References:
US National Archives Pension Data. Benjamin Spencer (W6158).

US Revolutionary Army Accounts.

AIS Censuses 1790; 1800.

Swink, Daniel. Abstracts of Burke County NC Courts of Pleas and Quarter
  Sessions. 1791-1803 in 3 editions.

Connelly, Robert L., Jr. Article in Burke County NC <u>Heritage</u>. Vol. I, pp 147-
  148. 1981 ed.

Pittman, Betsy D. "Sightings of Bryan Connelly (with various
  spellings) April 1994. copy in Burke County NC Library.

Winters, Clarence. "Deaths Recorded" Burke County Court of Pleas and
  Quarter Sessions 1791-1834. 1997 ed. Burke County Library.

Connelly family data in vertical files Burke County NC Library.

Cooper, Jacob

Summary of Early Life:

Jacob Cooper was born ca 1734-1735. He was age 98 when applying for Revolutionary War pension in 1832. At the beginning of the Revolutionary War, he was living near Swan Ponds, Burke County, North Carolina, near present day Morganton.

Summary of Partisan Activity:

Jacob Cooper first entered military service as a militiaman in Captain William Moore's Company of Colonel Christopher Beckman's 2nd Rowan Regiment (later to become Charles McDowell's Burke Regiment). Under Captain Moore, he was marched to Cape Fear. This was the expedition of March 1776, following the Battle of Moore's Creek Bridge. Cleanup operations were carried out against the Scotch Tories.

Later Jacob Cooper enlisted as a militiaman in Captain Thomas Kennedy's Company of McDowell's Burke Regiment. He stated in his pension declaration that he was in the actions on Broad River. This probably represents the South Carolina actions of McDowell culminating in the Battle of Musgrove's mill. He was then marched to Wofford's Ironworks. He later returned to North Carolina and was discharged.

His last tour of duty was under Captain Joseph McDowell. This duty consisted mainly of scouting duties against the hostile Cherokee Indians.

Summary of Later Life:

Jacob Cooper mentions that his home was burned, along with his Revolutionary War papers, documents, etc. Jacob Cooper left Burke County and eventually settled in Adair County, Kentucky. A 1798 Kentucky land grant was issued to him on waters of Cumberland River. He may have been living later in adjacent Tennessee, Overton and Fentress Counties.

Land Holdings and Transactions:

1. Burke County, NC. 200 acres, south side of the Catawba River, "above the Swan Ponds" and adjacent to land of James Locke, Joseph Dobson. Ent. 10 Oct. 1778, #428, Grant #278. Issued: 15 March 1780. Bk. 28, p. 277. cc Daniel Gowan, Jacob Cooper.
2. Lincoln County, KY. 200 acres on Cumberland River. Bk. 1, p. 543.

Census Locations:

1800 Jefferson County, Tennessee?
1820 Overton County, Tennessee?
1830 Fentress County, Tennessee?

References:
US National Archives Revolutionary War Pension Data #S12604, Burke County NC Land Grant material, Burke County Library, Morganton, NC.
Jillson, W. R. The Kentucky Land Grants Vol. I, GPC Baltimore (Reprint, 1971)., p. 291.
Bentley, Elizabeth P. Index to the 1820 Census of Tennessee GPC, 1981 ed.
Sistler, Byron and Associates. 1830 Census East Tennessee. Evanston, Ill., 1973 ed.

Coulter, Martin Jr.

Summary of Early Life:

Martin Coulter, Jr. was born in North Carolina in 1759. He was the son of Martin and Catherine Rosannah Coulter. The Coulters were from near the German/ Swiss border. They came to America ca 1749 and migrated to the Catawba Valley of North Carolina. Martin Coulter, Jr. was a brother of Philip Coulter.

Summary of Partisan Activity:

Martin Coulter, Jr. first served as a militiaman on the western North Carolina frontier in 1776. For a few days he was a member of a scouting party commanded by Captain (William) Moore. He also accompanied wagons containing provisions for General Griffith Rutherford's Army (July and August, 1776).

In 1778, as a drafted militiaman, he again spent a three-month tour of duty on the western Catawba frontier. He was in a company commanded by Captain William Davidson. He was stationed at different times at the Upper Forts ,commanded by Sergeant, later Captain, James Forgey, at Davidson's Fort and at Cathey's Fort.

Coulter's next tour of duty was as a drafted militiaman in November 1780. He was placed in Colonel Francis Locke's regiment in a company commanded by Captain James Byers and Lieutenant Gailbreth Neill. Later Captain Caleb Phifer replaced Captain Byers. George Henry Barrier (Barringer) was Major. He joined the regiment at Rocky River and later took part in the skirmishes that preceded Cornwallis' withdrawal into South Carolina. Coulter was in a small skirmish in which the "British soldiers gave way and fled", leaving behind a few prisoners and some arms. He marched with his company through Charlotte to the Providence area. Shortly before his discharge, he was afflicted with a febrile illness and went on a fourteen-week furlough. During this time General Smallwood and Colonel (William) Washington came through the area, eventually headed toward

Cowpens. Coulter also mentions Cornwallis' second advance into western North Carolina and the skirmish in which General William Davidson was killed (February 1781). His discharge was sent to him by Captain Byers.

Martin Coulter, Jr. was cited to Burke County Court in late 1782 on charges of being a Tory. The case was never resolved, as peace with Great Britain came a few months later.

Martin Coulter is a good example of a soldier who was on both sides of the fence. The usual "1780 hiatus" was present; in other words, no mention of any military activity from the fall of Charleston (May 1780) until Kings Mountain (Oct. 1780). These were critical days militarily and most able-bodied men participated in some way.

Summary of Later Life:

Martin Coulter, Jr. was married to Elizabeth "Betty" Aydelotte of Guilford County in 1787. Children were:

John b. 1788 m. Barbara Ramsuer
Henry b. 1790 m. Elizabeth Alexander
Ephriam b. 1793 d. infant
Rhoda b. 1794 m. David Shuford
Catherine b. 1797 m. Maxwell Warlick
Elizabeth b. 1800 m. Andrew Hoke
Jedadiah b. 1803 m. Rachel Moore
Elkanah b. 1806 m. Malinda Wilson
Caleb b. 1809 m. Hannah Martin
(from article by J. E. Hodges 1953 vertical files Catawba County Library)

Martin Coulter, Jr. applied for federal pension for his Revolutionary War services in Lincoln County, NC on January 24, 1833, age 73 years. He was awarded a pension in the amount of $21.56 per annum.

The Coulter family operated a mill near the confluence of Jacobs Fork and Henry River in what is now South East Catawba County.

Martin Coulter, Jr. died in 1847. Elizabeth Coulter died two years later in 1849. They are thought to be buried at the Coulter family cemetery, near the mill location. Martin Coulter's will probated April Session 1847, Catawba County Court.

Land Holdings and Transactions:

Burke Co. NC   Land entry data.   # 1062   400 acres S. Fork of Catawba River, adjacent to his own land.

Census Locations:

1790 Lincoln County, North Carolina 4th Company
1800 Lincoln County, North Carolina
1810 Lincoln County, North Carolina
1820 Lincoln County, North Carolina
1830 Lincoln County, North Carolina
1840 Lincoln County, North Carolina

References:
US National Archives Pension Data #R2363.
Watkins, Jim. "The Coulter Family", article in Catawba County Heritage Vol I
        (Winston Salem 1986) p. 118-119.
AIS Censuses and Indices, NC.
Preslar, C. J.   A History of Catawba County. (Salisbury NC 1954) Includes
        Yoder's 1886 map of Catawba County.
Revolutionary Army Accounts. Vol. VII Bk 90 Folio 286.
Dittman, Catherine and Brown, Mary. Article in Catawba County NC Heritage
        Vol. I op.cit. p.119.
Sherrill, Elizabeth Bray. "Catawba County NC Will Search I" (Heritage Books,
        OA, MD. 1994) p. 31.

Coulter, Martin Sr.

Summary of Early Life:

Martin Coulter, Sr. was born ca 1728 near the Swiss – German border. He immigrated to America in 1749 and shortly afterwards was married to Catherine Rosannah Boone, born 1733, a relation of Squire and Daniel Boone. By the early 1750's, Coulter was in Piedmont North Carolina. The Coulter family settled in what is today Catawba County, previously Anson, Rowan, Burke and Lincoln counties. During most of the Revolutionary War, the region lay within Burke County.

Summary of Partisan Activity:

During the Revolutionary War, Martin Coulter was a Loyalist, as were other members of the family. In 1782 he was cited (along with two of his sons) to Burke County Court on charges of being a Tory. He was to show cause as to why his property should not be confiscated, for being inimical to the American cause. The case was never resolved, due to the end of the Revolutionary War a few months later.

Summary of Later Life:

Martin Coulter, Sr. and his family operated a milling business near the origin of the South Fork River. He is also listed as a tailor by profession in Lincoln County records.
Martin and Rosannah Coulter had the following offspring:

> Catherine (1753-1831) m. Isaac Lawrence
> Martin Coulter, Jr. (1759-1847) m. Elizabeth Aydelotte
> John m. Sarah Horton
> Philip m. Clara Wise

Martin Coulter, Sr. and Rosannah Boone Coulter are thought to be buried in the old Coulter Cemetery near their home site.

Land Holdings and Transactions:

1. Anson County NC 400 ac. deeded to Coulter by John Clark 1753.
2. Mecklenburg County NC Crown Grant 520 ac on South Fork of Catawba River adjacent to Henry Whitener and James Robinson, 6 April 1765. (now Catawba County) Patent Book 18 p. 143.
3. Martin Coulter sold 25 acres on South Fork to George Wilfong 1788 Bk 3 p. 432.

Census Locations:

1790 Lincoln County, North Carolina 4th Company

References:
Watkins, Jim. Article, "The Coulter Family" in Catawba County. Heritage Vol. I. (Winston Salem NC 1986) pp. 118-119.
AIS Census Data NC.
Hofmann, Margaret M. Colony of North Carolina. 1765-1775.
Abstracts of Land Patents. Vol. II.

Coulter, Philip

Summary of Early Life:

Philip Coulter was born in Rowan County, North Carolina in 1763. He was the son of Martin and Rosannah Coulter and a brother of Martin Coulter, Jr. *(See separate biographies, this volume).*

Summary of Partisan Activity:

In 1782, Philip Coulter, along with his father and brother, Martin, Jr. were cited to Burke County Court on charges of being Tories. They were to show cause as to why their property should not be confiscated. *(See biographies, Martin, Sr. and Martin, Jr.)*

Summary of Later Life:

Philip Coulter was married to Clara Wise, born ca 1764. They had the following offspring:

    Catherine
    Henry m. Polly Rader
    Mary m. John Fry
    Daniel m. Nancy Ann Stilwell
    Elizabeth
    David
    Anna m. Henry Smith

Philip Coulter lived just north of his fathers grant. His home was still standing as late as 1960.

Census Locations:

1790 Lincoln County, North Carolina 4th Company
1800 Lincoln County, North Carolina
1810 Lincoln County, North Carolina
1820 Lincoln County, North Carolina
1830 Lincoln County, North Carolina

References:

Watkins, Jim. Article in Catawba County <u>Heritage</u> Vol. I (1986) pp.118-119.
Dittmann, Catherine, and Brown, Mary. <u>Ibid.</u> p. 119.
AIS Census Data.
Huggins, Edith. Burke County NC miscellaneous records.

Cronkelton, Joseph (Crunkelton)

Summary of Early Life:

Joseph Cronkelton, his wife Margaret and family came to Rowan County (later Burke, Lincoln and then Catawba County) ca 1770, acquiring land on Mountain Creek, a tributary of the Catawba River. The property was purchased from Francis Beatty of Mecklenburg County. It was part of Burke County during most of the Revolutionary War.

Summary of Partisan Activity:

The North Carolina Revolutionary Army Accounts show that Joseph Cronkelton, on several occasions contributed patriotic services and supplies for the American cause.

Summary of Later Life:

Joseph and Margaret Cronkelton continued to live on their Mountain Creek property until Joseph's death ca 1789.

Children include Joseph Cronkelton, Jr. and John Cronkelton. Joseph Cronkelton, Sr. had deeded his Mountain Creek property to his sons Joseph, Jr. and John in 1787.

Land Holdings and Transactions:

1. Rowan County NC – John Lytle and wife to Joseph Cronkelton 347 acres on Mountain Creek adjacent to land of Moses Perkins. 4 Jan 1771.
2. Rowan County NC – Francis Beaty of Mecklenburg County NC to Joseph Cronkelton 254 acres Mountain Creek adjacent to land of Moses Perkins and Fleming. May 1771.
3. Burke County NC – Joseph Cronkelton entered 200 acres middle fork of Drowning Creek. 11 Dec 1778.
4. Burke County NC – Joseph Cronkelton entered 200 acres on branch of Beaver Creek. 19 June 1778.

References:
NC Revolutionary Army Accounts (as given in Haun, Wynette P. Durham NC).
1. Vol. IX Book 5-26 Part VII #710
2. Book IX Book 14 Part VII Folio 97 #50.
3. Vol. VI Book 25 p. 35 #1104
4. Vol XII Book 8 Part XI Folio 25 #181
Linn, Jo White. "Abstracts of the Deeds of Rowan County NC 1753 – 1785".
Salisbury 1985 ed. pp. 108, 109, 119, 120.
McAllister, Ann W, and Sullivan, Kathy G. "Lincoln County NC Courts of
Pleas and Quarter Sessions (April 1789-1796) 1987 ed. p. 13 (estate
records).
Pruitt, Dr. R. B. "Abstracts of Deeds; Lincoln County NC 1786-1793". # 426-
427.
AIS Census records NC 1790; 1800.
Huggins, Edith. Miscellaneous Burke Records Vol. I. pp. 45, 106.

Crosson, Robert

Summary of Early Life:

Robert Crosson was living in Virginia at the beginning of the American Revolution. He later enlisted in the "German" regiment, which was composed of those men recruited in northern and western Virginia (this company was raised in Fincastle and Dunsmore counties). Robert Crosson was born ca 1740.

Summary of Partisan Activity:

Robert Crosson entered military service in Virginia in 1776 (Millerstown, in northern Virginia) as a member of the 8th Regiment, Virginia Continental Line. The regiment was commanded by Colonel (Peter) Muhlenberg. He was placed in a company of riflemen under Captain (John Richard?) Campbell. His regiment marched to South Carolina and assembled in the defense of Charleston at Fort Moultrie. The British were repulsed (July 1776). Many of the Virginia troops remained in South Carolina after the siege. He was discharged at Fort Moultrie. Crosson next re-entered the service in the 5th Regiment South Carolina Continental Line commanded by Colonel Isaac Huger. His company was commanded by Captain Alexander Keith. Crosson remained in this unit until the summer of 1779, at which time he was discharged. He re-enlisted a second time in the 1st regiment of the South Carolina Continental Line, commanded by Colonel Charles Pinckney. His company was headed up by Captain John Turner.

In May 1780, Colonel Pinckney's 1st Regiment took part in the defense of Charleston, under siege by the British. On the fall of Charleston in May 1780, Crosson was taken prisoner. Colonel Pinckney was also captured. Later released, Crosson again rejoined his unit and was at the battle of Eutaw Springs on September 8, 1781.*Shortly afterwards he was discharged at Statesboro, South Carolina. In his pension declaration, he stated that he took part in the battle of Norfolk, probably prior to his march to South Carolina in 1776.

Crosson stated he was discharged "after the battle of Eutaw Springs". It is not clear as to whether he actually participated in the battle itself.

Summary of Later Life:

Some time after the Revolutionary War, Robert Crosson had moved to Burke County North Carolina. There, he applied for pension in 1818 and in 1820. He described himself as being eighty years of age, in poor circumstances, and with a wife age sixty-four years who was "sickly". He was awarded a federal pension of $8.00 per month. A note with his papers, torn, gives a date of February 7, 1821 (death date?).

Census Locations:

On the 1810 Census of Burke County (census Index by AIS), there is a "Robert Croping" listed, possibly representing Robert Crosson.

References:
US National Archives. Pension Data # S 41498.
1810 North Carolina Census AIS (Index) p. 32.
Moss, Bobby G.   Roster of South Carolina Patriots in the American Revolution (GPC 1983 ed.) p.220.

Crum, Adam

Summary of Early Life:

Adam Crum was born in Augusta County, Virginia on October 5, 1756. In his pension statements, Crum stated that he spoke with a German accent, and that he had at times, difficulty in understanding his English-speaking officers.

Summary of Partisan Activity:

Adam Crum first entered military service in Burke County North Carolina in May or June 1776. He was drafted into a regiment commanded by Colonel Cocke. His company commander was Captain Brown. They then marched across the mountains where they joined forces with General "Christy" (Colonel William Christian of Virginia). There they embarked on a campaign directed against the Cherokee Indians. They relieved a fort on the Tennessee River that was being assaulted by the Indians. The Indians fled to the vicinity of Lookout Mountain (near Chattanooga, Tennessee). The Americans then burned their crops and destroyed their villages. This campaign was part of an overall offensive led by General Christian of Virginia, General Rutherford of North Carolina, and General Williamson of South Carolina. Most of the action was in July and August of 1776. Crum served six months on this tour, being discharged at the Long Island of the Holston River (Kingsport, Tennessee) in December 1776.

Crum next volunteered for a tour of duty in 1778 in Burke County North Carolina. He served in Captain (later Major) Joseph Whitener's company of Colonel Charles McDowell's Burke regiment. They rendezvoused at Quaker Meadows (Morganton, North Carolina) and marched through Swannanoa Gap of the French Broad River. The Indians supposedly were planning to join the "British and Tories". They soon surrendered. The Americans burned their corn and two of their towns. They took "some of their squaws". After this action, he was stationed at a fort on the western Catawba until January 1779. At this time he was

73

discharged after a six months tour. Crum then said, "about this time" Colonel Benjamin Cleveland was taken prisoner and was spared from hanging after giving his captors a pass, stating they were "good Whigs".

In July 1780, Crum enlisted for a three-month tour of duty in McDowell's Burke Regiment. His company was commanded by Captain Lemon and Lieutenant Hawson (Colonel Carroll's regiment). Crum then took part in the Kings Mountain campaign and battle (October 7, 1780). He describes the battle and the death of Ferguson.

In May 1781, Crum moved to the Clinch River Valley of Washington County, Virginia. There he enlisted in a company commanded by Captain Snoddy and Lieutenant R. Robertson. Crum served as an Indian spy, or scout. He served in the vicinity of Powell's Valley guarding against incursions of the Shawnee Indians. He was discharged in October 1781.

Summary of Later Life:

Adam Crum had moved from Burke County North Carolina to Washington County, Virginia in 1781. From there he moved to Floyd County, Kentucky, remaining there until the mid 1820's. Kentucky land grants were obtained for land on the fork of Rockcastle River in Lawrence County, Kentucky. He remained in Lawrence County for the remainder of his life.

Adam Crum married Barbary Horn. Other Crums listed by land records of Floyd and Lawrence counties; include Henry, Michael, David, and John Crum. These were presumably descendents of the Revolutionary War soldier Adam Crum. Adam Crum applied for a Revolutionary War pension in Lawrence County, Kentucky on March 13, 1834, age 77 years. He was awarded a pension of $50.00 per annum. Adam Crum died on October 10, 1851, age 95 years. Further family records available in DAR files.

Land Holdings and Transactions:

1. Kentucky Land Warrants:
    (a) 50 acres Lawrence Co Ky. . Rockcastle R.
        15 Jan 1824
    (b) 50 acres Lawrence Co Ky. Rockcastle R. 11
        Sept 1826
    (c) 50 acres Lawrence Co Ky. Turkey Creek
        29 Feb 1828

Census Locations:

1810 Floyd County, Kentucky
1820 Floyd County, Kentucky
1830 Lawrence County, Kentucky

References:
US National Archives Pension Data # S 8260.
Jillson, Willard R. The Kentucky Land Grants. GPC 1971 (orig published
        1925), Part I p. 521-522.
AIS Census Index Kentucky 1810.
1820 Kentucky Census. Volkel, Lloyd. Thomson, IL. 1975.
1830 Kentucky Census. Smith, Dora W. Thomson, IL 1974.
DAR Patriot Index National Society DAR Washington DC 1966 ed. p. 167.

Crye, William (Cry)

Summary of Early Life:

William Crye was born on the Isle of Man (an island in the Irish Sea, 220 square miles, midway between England and Ireland) in the year 1754. Before the American Revolutionary War, Crye had come to America and settled in Chester County Pennsylvania. Before the advent of hostilities, he had moved to Mecklenburg County North Carolina. He continued to live in Mecklenburg County throughout the duration of the war.

Summary of Partisan Activity:

William Crye first entered military service in Mecklenburg County North Carolina for a three month tour of duty. He served in William Hagan's Company of Colonel Adam Alexander's Volunteer Regiment (Alexander was a signer of the Mecklenburg Declaration of Independence). Joining the forces of Colonel (Alexander) Martin, they served in the Wilmington area, most likely relating to the Moore's Creek Bridge Campaign of 1776. Crye served with the commissary wagons.

During the Cherokee Wars of 1776, Crye joined in with South Carolina troops under the overall command of General Andrew Williamson. He served near Prince's Fort and Wofford's Fort (Spartanburg area in South Carolina).

Crye served in Captain John Drummond's company of Colonel Thomas Neal's South Carolina Regiment. In 1780 Crye was drafted to serve in General Gates' army during the Camden Campaign. He hired a substitute to serve in his place. He was drafted again (probably in 1780) and served as a horseman under Captain John Foster, who along with the company of Captain Robert Davis, "scoured" the country in search of Tories (three months tour). These were South Carolina Troops. His final tour of duty was under Colonel Erwin, and Major Harris of Mecklenburg County. He served in the Wilmington Expedition of the fall and winter of 1781(Wilmington was occupied by the Americans after the British had departed).

Summary of Later Life:

William Crye was still in Mecklenburg County at the time of the 1790 census. By 1791, he was in Burke County, North Carolina, where his name appears on various court records. He continued to be active in Burke County civic activities until the turn of the century. He was selected as a Burke County militia officer but an amendment stated he "had moved away".

William Crye was married to Sarah Hagans or Higgins (age 77 in 1839) on April 8, 1779. By this union were the following children:

Catron b. 1780	Mary b. 1794
William b. 1782	John b. 1796
Hugh b. 1784	Isabel b. 1798
Mary b. 1785?	James b. 1796
Joseph b. 1789	David b. 1803
Sarah b. 1791	Jonathan b. 1804

William Crye later moved to McMinn County, Tennessee where he applied for federal Revolutionary War pension on June 4, 1833, age 76 years. He was awarded a pension in the amount of $29.16 per annum. The Revolutionary War soldier died in McMinn County, Tennessee only a few years later, on July 4, 1834 (another source says 30 Aug 1835). His widow applied for and received continuation of his pension amount. Jesse Anderson and John Madrus stated under oath that they were well acquainted with William Crye, a Revolutionary War soldier, and that he died in McMinn Co. TN on 30 August 1835, leaving a widow Sarah. (1 Jan 1837).

Land Holdings and Transactions:

Burke County North Carolina 100 acres on Coldarse Creek adjacent to land of Paul Cochran. Entered 11 Nov 1800 #399A Grant no. 3060 Iss. 17 Dec 1801, Bk. 114 p. 356 cc William

Crye, Joseph Cry. There is mention of land obtained earlier from William James.

Census Locations:

1790 Mecklenburg County, North Carolina
1800 Burke County, North Carolina
1810 Burke County, North Carolina

References:
US National Archives Pension Data #W6757.
AIS Census Indices NC 1790, 1800, 1820.
From "Wills and Estate Records of McMinn County Tennessee 1820-1870",
        copy by Reba B. Boyer 1966 p. 42   SHP.

Dellinger, John

Summary of Early Life:

John Dellinger was born ca 1740, the son of John Philip and Mary Dellinger. The Dellingers originated in Germany (Baden Province) and came to American ca 1750. By the end of the French and Indian War, John Philip and his son John had settled on Leeper's Creek in what is now southeast Lincoln County. Land records indicate that John Dellinger may have moved to southwest Lincoln County on Indian Creek, then Tryon County. There is no mention of family at this time.

Summary of Partisan Activity:

John Dellinger became a prominent member of the early Revolutionary movement in Tryon County. He was selected as a member of the Tryon County Committee of Safety in 1774-75 and was a signer of the Tryon Association Declaration of Independence. By early 1776, he was a Captain in the Tryon militia and commanded companies of both footmen and light horse (the North Carolina Revolutionary Army Accounts verify his rank and command).

In February and March of 1776, Dellinger and his command were part of the Cross Creek Expedition under Brigadier General Rutherford of the Salisbury district. This expedition was the final portion of the Moore's Creek Bridge Campaign. The Salisbury militia assisted in clean up operations, conveying prisoners, etc.

Data given relative to later federal pension awards mentioned that Dellinger served as a Captain of militia at Ramsour's Mill (June 20, 1780), Kings Mountain (Oct. 7, 1780), and Cowpens (Jan 17, 1781). A pension statement of a soldier who served as a mounted militiaman under Dellinger, says that he was with Dellinger in December 1780, just prior to Cowpens. (Seymor left the unit at this time because of illness.)

There are numerous entries in the North Carolina Revolutionary Army Accounts verifying Dellinger's military service throughout the conflict.

Summary of Later Life:

Sometime during the Revolutionary War, ca. 1778 or 1779, John Dellinger married Barbara Whitener, daughter of Henry and Catherine Mull Whitener, Sr. of Henry Fork, then Burke County (later Lincoln, now Catawba County). Whitener served in the Burke militia under the McDowells, until the close of the war. At about the time of his marriage, he appears to have moved from Indian Creek to Henry River, where most of the Whiteners had settled.

After the war, Dellinger (now in Lincoln County) was active in civil matters, frequently serving as a juror or magistrate. By his union with Barbara Whitener, there were the following children:

Henry Dellinger b. 1779 m. Katherine Setzer
Joseph Dellinger b. 1787 m. Margaret Sigmon
Katherine Dellinger b. 1782 m. Jacob Yoder
John Dellinger b. 1784 m. Elizabeth Shuford
Barbara (or Barbary) Dellinger b. 1790 m. Henry Sigmon
Jacob Dellinger b. 1798? m. Sally (Sarah) Setzer

The Revolutionary soldier John Dellinger died ca November 4, 1826 at age 86. Barbara Whitener Dellinger, by data in pension applications, died on February 8, 1840.

Descendants of John and Barbara Dellinger applied for retroactive pension monies due the soldier and his widow. An award of $285.33 per annum was made extending from 1831 through February 8, 1840.

Land Holdings and Transactions:

1. Tryon County NC 100 acres Leeper's Creek adjacent to his own land and Shulls's land. May 20, 1772. Grant # 3661 (Crown Grant)
2. Tryon County NC Crown Grant 200 acres both sides Henry Dellinger's branch of Hoyle Creek (tributaries of South Fork Catawba River,) adjacent to land of Henry Dellinger and Jacob Rine. 28 Feb 1775.
3. Tryon County NC Crown Grant 230 acres on both sides of Shole Branch adjacent South Fork of Catawba River adjacent to Phifer's corner and Sipes line 28 Feb 1775.
4. Tryon County Land Patent 100 acres Dec 10, 1770.
5. Tryon County Land Patent 250 acres 1774.
6. Tryon County Land Grant 200 acres Little Branch of Indian Creek, a tributary adjacent South Fork of Catawba River adjacent to land of John Alexander and to his own land Jan 1, 1779.
7. Tryon County 200 acres on Indian Creek adjacent to land of Peter Carpenter. Jan 1, 1779. Land Grant.
8. Tryon County 60 acres Land Grant North side of Indian Creek adj. to John Alexander and Pete Carpenter. April 20, 1779. Lincoln County NC 200 acres South Fork adjacent Catawba River on Mountain Creek that flows into Henry River in Wilfongs ("Lickblock") Granted. Jan 5, 1786.
9. Lincoln County NC grants adjacent 100,100 and 60 acres on Indian Creek adjacent to land of George Icard and Peter Carpenter Apr 5, 1786.
10. Lincoln County NC 150 acres adjacent to Michael Whitener, Jacob Weaver, Conrad Yoder March 30, 1787.
11. Lincoln County NC 100 acres adjacent to George Icard Mar 30, 1787.

Census Locations:

1790 Lincoln County, North Carolina
1800 Lincoln County, North Carolina
1810 Lincoln County, North Carolina
1820 Lincoln County, North Carolina

References:

US National Archives Federal Pension Data #W 19180.

Dellinger, Paul H. "Dellinger Genealogy". Lincolnton NC 1898.

Sullivan, Mrs. John T. "Dellinger Family" in Heritage of Catawba County County NC. 1986 ed. Vol. I p. 133.

AIS Census Indices.

Catawba County Library Newton NC, Miscellaneous data from vertical files under able supervision of Mrs.Rhodes, curator of genealogical section.

Land Records from: Burke County Land grant data in Burke County Library, Morganton, NC

Hofmann, Margaret M. Colony of North Carolina 1765-1775. Abstract of Land Patents. Vol II. Weldon NC 1984. pp. 279, 676.

Haun, Weynette Parks. "NC Court of Claims; Records of Patents Granted". 1740-1775. Durham NC 1996. pp. 166, 193.

Rouse, J. K. Another Revolutionary War Hero Dies. Kannapolis NC 1978. (from Western Carolinian Nov 21, 1826 ed.)

Doty, Azariah

Summary of Early Life:

Azariah Doty was age eighty-seven when applying for federal pension in 1832. This would place his birthdate ca 1745. Another source says 1741. He was born in Piscatony, New Jersey, the son of Isaac Doty and ____Reyno Doty. Azariah Doty was living in Burke County, North Carolina shortly before and during the early part of the American Revolution.

Summary of Partisan Activity:

Azariah Doty served as a militia "minuteman" in 1775. He served in a company commanded by Captain William Moore and Sergeant (Noah) Hawthorne. According to Doty, "they scouted Burke County to keep down the Tories and keep off the Indians". He stated that Burke County was a frontier County and was frequently "annoyed" by the Cherokees. This tour of duty lasted three months. As the Indian menance subsided in Burke County, Doty decided to move to Washington County, North Carolina, later Tennessee. Doty settled in that section, which later became Greene County, Tennessee.

In Tennessee, Doty was drafted for a three month tour of duty. He was sent to South Carolina. This was in September 1781. He served under Colonel John Sevier, Captain John Patterson, and Sergeant Flippen. They marched through Morganton and Charlotte into South Carolina. They reached the High Hills of the Santee, and then west to the Santee Swamps, joining with the troops of General Francis Marion. During this tour, Doty served in the mounted troops. He was not in any battle or skirmish. After serving his three month tour, he returned home to Washington County.

In Washington County, he served several short tours of duty "going after the Indians". He served one tour under Captain Whitson and another, in Blount County, under Captain Wear.

Summary of Later Life:

Azariah Doty continued to live in Greene County, Tennessee for the remainder of his long life. He was married to Sarah Tucker and had the following children:

Bowser	Mary
Sarah	Hannah
Susannah	Ephraim
Nancy	Jesse
Isaac	Enoch

Azariah Doty applied for federal pension in Greene County, Tennessee in 1832, age eight-seven years. He was awarded an annual pension of $21.66. Azariah Doty, the Revolutionary War soldier died on June 7, 1851, age 106 years.

Land Holdings and Transactions:

1. Greene County, Tennessee. A 1783 tax list shows Azariah Doty as being in Captain Morris' district with 200 acres land.

Census Locations:

1783 Greene County, TN (tax list)
1797 Greene County, TN (tax list)
1805 Greene County, TN (tax list)
1830 Greene County, TN
1840 Greene County, TN (in household of Ephraim Doty)
1850 Greene County, TN

References:
U.S. National Archives Rev. War Pension Data   # S 1804.
AIS Census Indices TN 1830-1850
Tennessee Tax Lists Greene Co.

Douglass, David

Summary of Early Life:

David Douglass, during the American Revolution, was living on Jacob's Fork, a tributary of the South Fork, Catawba River.

Summary of Partisan Activity:

In 1782, David Douglass was on a list of suspected Tories of Burke County North Carolina. Later his name was on the court docket. Witnesses in his case included Major Daniel McKissick and Captain George Walker.

A David Douglass is listed as receiving payment for Revolutionary services in Guilford County North Carolina. Another David Douglass is listed as a member of a Regiment of South Carolina (Loyalists). It is doubtful that either of these represents the David Douglass of Burke County.

Summary of Later Life:

David Douglass apparently died just at the conclusion of the Revolutionary War (circumstances not known). Administrative papers were filed in Burke County North Carolina 1783. Administrative bonds by Robert Oliphant, James Neil and John Robinson.

Land Holdings and Transactions:

1. 100 acres Burke County NC on both sides of the Middle Creek on North side Jacob's Fork of South Fork of Catawba River adjacent to land of Henry Whitener. Entry states "improvements whereon he now lives". Ent. 31 Dec 1778 #1333 Grant no. 550 Iss. Oct 11, 1783 Book 50 p. 194 c.c. (William Orr, Henry Machelroy).

References:

Huggins, Edith W. Miscellaneous Burke County, NC Records Vol. II.
      pp.151,154,164,

NC Revolutionary Army Accounts. Vol. IX Book 14 Part VII 1785.

Clark, Murtie June. <u>Loyalists in the Southern Campaign</u>. Vol. I GPC Baltimore
      1981. pp. 203, 208.

NC Land Grant Data. Burke County Library, Morganton, NC.

Dowell, John

Summary of Early Life:

John Dowell was born in 1764, Albemarle County, Virginia. At the beginning of the American Revolution, he was living in Burke County, North Carolina. He was a brother of George Dowell, also a Revolutionary War soldier.

Summary of Partisan Activity:

John Dowell first entered military service in December 1779 as a volunteer militiaman, for a tour of three months. He entered the company commanded by Captain Peter Ford of McDowell's Burke Regiment. Under Captain Ford, he marched to the vicinity of Charleston, South Carolina, then under siege by the British. His main duty was cutting and hauling pine timber for use in defensive breastworks. In March 1780, Dowell was discharged after serving out his tour of duty. He therefore escaped being captured, as the British were soon to surround the entire city, forcing its eventual surrender in May 1780.

After returning to Burke County, Dowell enlisted for a ten month tour of duty. He was placed in Captain John Sumter's company and marched to South Carolina on Wateree River. There he was transferred to South Carolina authorities. He was placed in Captain McKenzie's Company of Colonel Wade Hampton's regiment. They were marched to the area near the confluence of the Congaree and Wateree Rivers. Here they were mainly engaged in anti-Tory activity. He was not in any major battle or campaign. He was discharged by Colonel Hampton after serving out his full ten month tour. This ended his Revolutionary War service.

Summary of Later Life:

After the Revolutionary War, John Dowell lived in Burke County, North Carolina. Later he moved to Cumberland County, Kentucky, Overton County, Tennessee, Smith County, Tennessee, and Jackson County, Tennessee.

John Dowell applied for Revolutionary War pension in Jackson County, Tennessee in 1851, age 87 years. Due to the lateness in filing for a pension, his application was rejected.

Census Locations:

1820 Bracken County, Kentucky
1840 Jackson County, Tennessee

References:
US National Archives Pension Data, #R3059.
Sistler, Byron and Barbara. 1840 Census Tennessee. Nashville, TN, 1986 ed.
Felldin, Jeanne and Inman, Gloria. Index to the 1820 Census of Kentucky.
        GPC 1996.
Moss, Bobby G   Roster of South Carolina Patriots in the American Revolution.   GPC 1983 ed. p. 2

Eberhart, Jacob (Everhart)

Summary of Early Life:

Jacob Eberhart was born in North Carolina in 1756. He was the son of Jacob Eberhart, Sr. and a brother of David Eberhart (see Vol. II this work). The older Eberhart had received an earlier land grant in Mecklenburg County in 1765 on branches of Clark's Creek (later Lincoln County North Carolina). Burke County records show a Jacob Eberhart, Sr. living on Silver Creek, most likely the same one living earlier on Clark's Creek, though this could have been Jacob Eberhart, the Revolutionary War soldier.

Summary of Partisan Activity:

The statements relating to military service as given by the pensioner Jacob Eberhart are somewhat indistinct. Though giving the details of duties and listing officers, his data is mixed and lacks specific dating – probably the effect of aging (76 years at time of application). He lists several short tours of duty beginning in 1776 and extending to 1780 or 1781.

He first describes a two-month tour of duty under General Griffith Rutherford and Captain John McDowell of Burke County (then Rowan) along with Lieutenant James Donnahue. This was probably the Cross Creek Expedition of March 1776, the sequel of the Moore's Creek Bridge Battle of February 1776. Next he mentions the Charleston Campaign resulting in the surrender of 10,000 American troops (May 1780). He was serving under Colonel Charles McDowell and correctly states that they were not involved in the surrender (McDowell commanded troops on the outskirts of Charleston and unsuccessfully attempted to break the siege). Other officers listed were Major Joseph McDowell and Captain John (Robert?) Holmes. He also states that "General Washington" was there. This was probably Lieutenant Colonel William Washington, a relative of the Commander in Chief.

Eberhart next describes a three month tour to Camden area under Colonel Malmedy (a "Frenchman"), Captain Thomas Lytle and Major James Donnahue.

This appears to be the action at Eutaw Springs, South Carolina in September 1781. Malmedy commanded the North Carolina militia. North Carolina militia had gathered earlier at Camden. Eberhart then describes a short tour of duty on the Catawba frontier at George Capps (Cathey's?) station under Colonel Joseph McDowell, Captain John Carson and Lieutenant Rowland Alexander, guarding against Cherokee Indians.

Following this duty, Eberhart took part in the Kings Mountain Campaign and Battle of September and October 1780. He served under Colonel Charles McDowell, Colonel Isaac Shelby, Colonel Benjamin Cleveland, and Captain Thomas Lytle. He mentions the death of Major Patrick Ferguson, the capture of the British troops and their conveying them to the Moravian Towns (Winston Salem, North Carolina).

Summary of Later Life:

Eberhart, shortly after the Revolutionary War moved from Burke County, North Carolina to Georgia. He appears to have still been in Burke County in 1787 as court records mention jury duty (his father maybe?). A Jacob Eberhart also in 1787 appears on Wilkes County, Georgia records. Still later, a Jacob Eberhart received land grants in Elbert County in 1789-92 (Elbert County was created from Wilkes County in late 1790). He is listed in Oglethorpe County, Georgia in 1820, Madison County in 1830 (all of these counties join one another). It is possible that he lived at only one locale.

Jacob Eberhart applied for Revolutionary War pension in Oglethorpe County, Georgia on November 5, 1832. He received an annual pension of $43.33. In a letter to the pension agency, a lineal descendent of Jacob Eberhart, Sr. stated that Jacob Eberhart, Jr. was a bachelor. Jacob Eberhart, the Revolutionary War soldier, died (according to DAR records) on March 2, 1848.
Land Holdings and Transactions:

1. Mecklenburg County NC (later Lincoln County) 30 Oct 1765   400 acres on branches of Clark's Creek (Jacob Eberhart, Jr.)
2. Burke County NC   300 acres Silver Creek ent 1778 (19 Feb) later conveyed to Henry Martin 1796. (Jacob Sr. or Jacob Jr.)
3. Elbert County GA   Documents in Deed Book "A" 1789-1792.

Census Locations:

1789-92   "Reconstructed" 1790 Census of Georgia
1820   Oglethorpe County, Georgia
1830   Madison County, Georgia (?)

References:
US National Archives Pension Data   #S31661.
Reconstructed 1790 Census of Georgia. Lamar, M. and Rothstein, E. (1985).
AIS Census Indices. Georgia 1820; 1830.
White, E.R. Vol. II this work p. 109 "David Eberhart" (1988).
Hofmann, Margaret. Colony of NC 1765-1775. Abstracts of Land Patents
        Vol II, #504.
Revolutionary War Accounts. (NC) Vol. VI, Bk. 23, p. 5   #34.
DAR Patriot Index. Washington D.C. 1966 ed. p. 225.
Swink, Daniel. Burke County NC Minutes of Court of Pleas and Quarter
        Sessions 1795-98. (1987) p. 39.
Huggins, Edith. Miscellaneous Burke Records Vol. I, p. 24.
Moss, Bobby G. The Patriots at Kings Mountain. Blacksburg, SC   1990. p.
        74.

Edmisten, William

Summary of Early Life:

William Edmisten was born ca 1760 (he was age 84 in 1844). He was the son of James Edmisten and brother of Robert Edmisten. William Edmisten, at the time he entered Revolutionary service, was living in Amherst County, Virginia, at the headwaters of Pedlar Creek (now Pedlar River, westernmost Amherst County).

Summary of Partisan Activity:

William Edmisten enlisted as a volunteer militiaman in Amherst County and served in Captain John Jacobs Company of Colonel Taylor's Regiment. He acted as a guard at the Albemarle Barracks, guarding prisoners taken earlier at Saratoga. He served another tour in October 1780, as a substitute for his brother, Robert Edmisten. He was in a company commanded by Captain Samuel Higgenbotham and Lieutenant Joseph Higgenbotham Morrison. He served in the vicinity of Richmond. In March 1781, he moved to Lower Creek, Burke County North Carolina (now Caldwell County). He became a Sergeant in Captain William Sumter's Company of Colonel Charles McDowell's Burke Regiment. James Blair was Lieutenant. He served a six-month tour of duty on the Catawba frontier, guarding against local Tories and Cherokee Indians. In September 1781, he moved back to Amherst County and was serving in Captain Richard Ballenger's Company, when they received news of Cornwallis' surrender. This ended his military service.

Summary of Later Life:

At the close of the American Revolution, William Edmisten moved back to Lower Creek (September 1782). He was married and had 13 children as follows:

Susannah m. Blair	Allen	Lucy	Southard	
Betsy	Sally	Abraham	Emanuel	
Belinda	Robert	Thomas	William	John T.

William Edmisten was active in Burke County matters and served as a juror on numerous occasions. He continued to live in Burke County until 1841, when he moved to Wilkes County North Carolina.

William Edmisten died in Wilkes County NC, October 21, 1847 age 88 years. His application and claims for Revolutionary War pension was rejected on grounds that he did not serve six months in an organized unit.

Land Holdings and Transactions:

1. Burke County NC Thomas Hays conveyed 100 acres land to William Edmisten 6 July 1798.

Census Locations:

1790 Burke County, North Carolina 5th Co.
1800 Burke County, North Carolina
1810 Burke County, North Carolina
1820 Burke County, North Carolina
1830 Burke County, North Carolina
1840 Burke County, North Carolina

References:
US National Archives Pension Data #R3243.
Swink, Daniel. Minutes of Burke County NC Court of Pleas and Quarter
        Sessions 1791-1795; 1795-1798. Lawndale, NC 1986, 1987.
Huggins, Edith. Burke County Miscellaneous Records Vols. I-IV.
Federal Records Center, Atlanta, Georgia. (microfilmed pension records, census
        data).
AIS Census Indices NC. 1790-1840.

Egner, Matthias (Egnor)

Summary of Early Life:

Matthias Egner was born in 1763 or 1764 in western North Carolina on Clark's Creek, later Lincoln County North Carolina (now Catawba Co.). There was a Jacob Egner living on Clark's Creek, near Peter Icard, possibly his father.

Summary of Partisan Activity:

Matthias Egner, as a fourteen year old, was taken along by his father and joined the British Army, then in South Carolina. In Charleston, he ran away from his father, returned to Burke County North Carolina, where he sought protection by the military authorities (Colonel Charles McDowell). In the summer of 1782, he was placed in the eighteen month Continental Line service. At that time he was described as being five feet - six inches tall, gray eyes, brown hair, fair complexion, and eighteen years of age. He was marched to the Ramsour's Mill Battle site, where he was placed in the 3rd Regiment North Carolina Line. His company commander was Captain Alexander Brevard. Captain Brevard then marched his company through Charlotte into South Carolina to the High Hills of Santees. There they were placed in the Regiment commanded by Colonel Archibald Lytle of the North Carolina Line. His new company commander was Captain (Peter) Bacote. The overall commander was Major General Nathaniel Greene.

From the High Hills, the army crossed the Santee River, taking 200 British soldiers as prisoners. Advancing further to Monck's Corner, there was a skirmish. They proceeded then to Dorchester, where there was another skirmish. His units then advanced to the outskirts of Charleston and later to James Island. They took possession of an abandoned fort on James Island. There they were joined by troops of the Pennsylvania and Maryland Lines.

As a volunteer in General Francis Marion's Brigade, he

94

took part in an engagement at Parker's Ferry against British troops of Colonel Fraser. He returned to his regiment at James Island where he remained until December 1783. He was discharged home after serving his tour of duty.

Summary of Later Life:

In his pension statements, Matthias Egner, stated in 1840 that he had always lived in Lincoln County NC since the war. Matthias Egner applied for Revolutionary War pension benefits in Lincoln County, North Carolina in 1840. His pension decision was delayed, probably due to his earlier service with the British. Also, those applying later received more suspicious scouting (most applied 1832-1834).

Matthias Egner died February 8, 1844. His wife had predeceased him (d. 1807). His pension was posthumously approved, after his descendants had re-applied in Union District South Carolina in 1852. There were supporting statements from William Hill, Secretary of State in North Carolina, and from the North Carolina Comptroller, William S. Clark, verifying Mathias Egner's service in the Continental Line and stating that he had received a military warrant for 640 acres of land.

Matthias Egner in his 1840 statements, mentioned a son that had predeceased him. Pension data list the following daughters:

Elizabeth m. Joshuha Chapman
Mary m. William Hanlerton
Sarah m. Jesse Graham

References:
US National Archives Pension Data #S21745.
Huggins, Edith W. Miscellaneous Burke Records in 4 Vol. Vol. II p. 156.
Roster of Soldiers from NC in the American Revolution. NC DAR GPC reprint
        of orig. 1932 copy. P. 252.
NC Revolutionary Army Accounts as published by Haun, Wynette P. Durham
        NC. Part XV (1999) Military Land Warrant Book warrant #950.
        pg. 2033.

Erwin, Arthur

Summary of Early Life:

According to DAR records and data of McCall, Arthur Erwin was born in Ireland in 1738. He was the son of Nathaniel Erwin (1712-1792-94) of Bucks County, Pennsylvania, who migrated to York County South Carolina and who was married to Leah Julian. (More clarification is needed in the Nathaniel Erwin connection to Arthur and Alexander Erwin.) Arthur Erwin was a tailor by occupation and an older brother of Alexander Erwin of Burke County North Carolina. By 1770 he had established his residence in Rowan County on Crane Creek, east of Salisbury. He was living in Rowan County as early as 1766, as indicated in court records.

Summary of Partisan Activity:

Arthur Erwin was a member of the Rowan militia and early in the war received a Captain's commission. He appears to have served in the Cross Creek Expedition in early 1776. His Revolutionary War service is confirmed by the Revolutionary Army Accounts. No later military service is documented, but being an experienced tailor, he was probably busy enough on the home front, as Salisbury was the headquarters of Salisbury military district and a center of logistical activity.

Summary of Later Life:

Arthur Erwin, in 1770 and 1772, acquired property on Crane Creek, east of Salisbury and in proximity to the well know Trading Ford. His land was adjacent to that of John Brandon, his father-in-law.

Arthur Erwin was married to Margaret Brandon, daughter of John Brandon. At this time, he was residing in Rowan County. Alexander, his younger brother, was associated with the residents of eastern Burke County and later moved to Upper Creek, near Morganton.

After the close of the Revolution, Arthur Erwin and his family decided to leave Rowan County and settle near his brother Alexander, on Upper Creek. In 1784 and 1785, he had acquired land on Upper Creek previously owned by Martin Deadwiler. The estate was called "Belvidere". At the same time, he was dispensing of his Crane Creek lands in Rowan County. The Rowan deed records clearly state that the Arthur Erwin of Burke was the same person who earlier had resided in Rowan. By his marriage to Margaret Brandon, the following children were born:

William Willoughby b. 1764 m. Matilda Sharpe, daughter of
    William Sharpe of Iredell County -16 children
John b. 1767 m. Catherine Erwin, a cousin - 6 children
Frank
Arthur
Alexander
(Polly) m. Joseph Patton
James m. Mary Midler - 6 children

Arthur Erwin lived in Burke County for the remainder of his life. He was an active public servant. He served as a processioner, as a jurist and as County Treasurer. He was also a judge of the Congressional Elections of 1793. He acted as security on several estate matters and as security for his nephew James Erwin, Clerk of Burke County Court.

Arthur Erwin's will was made in 1819 and underwent probate in 1821. His wife, several children and grandchildren are listed. His tombstone dates were 1738-August 21, 1821. Arthur Erwin was buried on his Belvidere estate. His wife, Margaret Brandon Erwin (b. 1740 d. December 26, 1832) was also buried at Belvidere.

Land Holdings and Transactions:

1. Burke County NC 200 acres on both sides of Swannanoa River. Ent. Aug 1783 #30 Grant #956 Iss. Aug. 7, 1787 Bk. 65 p. 370. The land lay adjacent to that of Samuel Davidson. Deeded to John Patton.

2. Burke Co NC 100 acres. This land lay adjacent to his own land and to that of Paul Anthony and John Lawrence. Ent #3609 17 Apr 1799 Grant #2680 Iss. 6 Dec 1799 Bk. 107 p. 56.
3. Deadwiler Tract. (300 acres) Upper Creek Cherry fields – Belvidere]
4. Acquired from John Patton Muddy Creek (300 acres)]
5. Rowan County NC John McConnell to Arthur Erwin 114 acres on Middle Fork Crane Creek Aug 1770. (sold to Abraham Hill Aug 1782)
6. Rowan County NC land acquired from Matthew Locke of Rowan County 585 acres Crane Creek adjacent to Francis Johnston and John Brandon 28 Sept 1772
7. Rowan County NC 74 ac on Crane Creek adjacent to Johnson, Thoman Hill, John McConnell. Oct 1783. (sold as 80 acre tract to Abraham Hill Aug 1784)
8. Rowan County Arthur Erwin to John Erwin of Rowan County 238 acres on Middle Fork Crane Creek Aug 1785.

Census Locations:

1790 Burke County, North Carolina 3rd Co.
1800 Burke County, North Carolina
1810 Burke County, North Carolina
1820 Burke County, North Carolina

References:
NC Revolutionary Army Accounts Vol. VIII Book F-2 Part VI #2064 as given in Haun, Wynette P. NC Revolutionary Army Accounts Part VI. (Durham NC 1995 p, 801).
McCall, Ettie Tidwell. Rosters of Revolutionary Soldiers in Georgia and Other States. (gen. Publ. Co. Baltimore 1968) pp. 49-50.
Winter, William Elliott Jr. M.D. Article in Burke Heritage Vol. I #238 pp. 171-174. 1981 ed. Morganton, NC.
Burke County NC Court minutes. On microfilm in possession of author.
Turner, Grace and Philbeck, Miles. "Burke County NC Surviving Will and Probate Records" 1777-1910. Chapel Hill 1983   #172.
Land Grant Data Burke County Library, Morganton NC.
Linn, Jo White. Abstracts of the Deeds of Rowan County NC Salisbury NC 1983 ed. multiple listings.
Pittman, Betsy Dodd. "Burke County NC 1815 Tax Lists". 1990 ed. p. 91.

AIS Census books and indices 1790-1820.
Moss, Bobby G. <u>The Patriots at Kings Mountain</u>. Blacksburg SC 1990. p. 79.

Eslinger, George

Summary of Early Life:

George Eslinger and his wife Fanny came to the Catawba Valley in the 1770's after having purchased tracts of land on Lyle Creek and Elk Creek in what is now Catawba County. During the American Revolution, it was part of eastern Burke County. According to entry records, he lived on the Elk Creek tract.

Summary of Partisan Activity:

During the Revolutionary War, George Eslinger was a militiaman in Charles McDowells' Burke Regiment. In 1782, he was called in as a witness in the court martial proceedings involving Colonel McDowell. Most of the militiamen from the area served under Captain Mordecai Clarke, of McDowell's command. A kinsman of Eslinger, Lieutenant John Eslinger (brother?), was killed at the battle of Eutaw Springs, South Carolina in September 1781 while serving under Captain Clarke. (*See Vol I, this work*)

Summary of Later Life:

George Eslinger lived for only a short while in Burke (then Lincoln County) after the war. He is listed on the 1790 census, but not thereafter. One source stated he may have "moved west". Census records of East Tennessee show family members of that name in Jefferson, Cocke and Greene counties. Lincoln County land records indicate that he was disposing of his property between 1787-1789.

Land Grant Data:

1. Burke County NC 400 acres on Lyle Creek, adjacent to land belonging to Barnet Sigmon, George Smith, and Conrad Brown. Entry states it contains his own improvements. Ent. #1236 December 116, 1778 Grant #577 Issued Oct 11, 1783 Book 50/205.

2. Burke County NC 150 acres on Lyle Creek including the place that widow Oliphant lived in, and adjacent to land of Palser (Sigmon). Ent #1343 Dec 30, 1778 Grant # 975 Iss Aug 7, 1787 Book 65/377.
3. Burke County NC 200 acres on a branch of Elk Shoal Creek and also called Snow Creek and including "improvements said Eslinger lives on ...." The land lay adjacent to that of John Summers. Grant states improvements were made by Michael Heafner. The land contained a portion of Perkin's Mill Path. Ent. #1345 Dec 30, 1778 Grant #1028 Issued Aug 7, 1787. Book 65/392.

Census Locations:

1790 Lincoln County, North Carolina

References:
Pruitt, Dr. R. B. "Abstracts of Deeds; Lincoln County NC. 1786-1793" (1988).
Huggins, Edith W. Miscellaneous Burke Records Vols. I-II-III.
Court martial records of Colonel Charles McDowell of Burke County NC 1782 (copy given to the author by the late Ms. Eunice Ervin of Morganton NC).
AIS Census Records 1790 NC 1820;1830 TN.
Land Grant Records in Burke County Library, Morganton NC.
Pope, C. David Jr. Article in Heritage of Catawba County NC .Vol. I (1986) p. 151.

Eslinger, John

Summary of Early Life:

At the beginning of the American Revolution, John Eslinger was residing in eastern Rowan, later Burke, Lincoln and now Catawba County. Captain George Smith stated he lived less than a mile away, near Lyle Creek. He was undoubtedly related to George Eslinger of the same region. George Eslinger had moved into the area ca 1770.

Summary of Partisan Activity:

John Eslinger was a lieutenant of militia in Colonel Charles McDowell's Burke Regiment. John Eslinger, during the Revolution, was of Loyalist sympathies. In the militia protocol, only patriots were subject to militia draft, divided into fifteen classes. Loyalists were not as a rule drafted. Many times certain loyalists would serve as substitutes for those who were subject to military duty – for money. Eslinger served on several occasions as a hired militiaman. His obedience to filling out the usual three-month tour of duty was not good. Colonel Charles McDowell, in his court martial trial, was criticized for his tolerance of Eslinger's conduct as well as that of his superior, Captain Mordecai Clarke.

Despite his bad record, Eslinger paid the ultimate price, being killed in action in South Carolina at the Battle of Eutaw Springs (Sept. 8, 1781). This may have been a tour he served in South Carolina for William Greenlee of Burke (mentioned in court martial minutes).

Summary of Later Events:

In 1792 Burke County court records show estate details relating to John Eslinger. James Greenlee was administrator. Members of the Eslinger name appear later in East Tennessee (Jefferson, Cocke, and Greene counties) and in Alabama.

Land Holdings and Transactions:

Burke County NC John Eslinger entered 200 acres on Falling Creek in eastern Burke County, now Catawba County. (Falling Creek empties into Lyle Creek.) No grant.

References:
Huggins, Edith W. Miscellaneous Burke County NC Records Vol. III p. 43. Vol II pp 30, 154. (includes court martial records of Colonel Charles McDowell).
AIS Census Records East Tennessee (1820-1830).
Pope, C. Daniel Jr. Articles in Heritage of Catawba County NC Vol. I. (1986) p. 151.
US National Archives. Revolutionary War Pension Declaration of Michael Houck. (#S32329 See Vol I this work, p. 132).

Estes, Pascal

Summary of Early Life:

It appears that members of the Estes family who settled or lived in Burke County (later Caldwell County) North Carolina were originally from the central counties of Virginia – Caroline, Lunenberg, Amelia, Halifax, etc. Reuben Estes was in Burke County by 1778 as indicated by land records. Pascal Estes, a brother of Reuben, came in at about the same time. Reuben and Pascal Estes were the sons of Charles and Mary (Thaxton) Estes of Virginia.

Summary of Partisan Activity:

Pascal Estes seems to have become a Loyalist during the Revolutionary War. British records indicate that he was a member of Nicholas Welch's Company of the North Carolina Royal Regiment. He was probably in the actions at Ramsour's Mill on June 20, 1780, though there is no direct confirmation. He was still on the British muster rolls in early 1781. Hillsborough North Carolina Revolutionary Army Accounts indicates payment for services, most likely militia services. Tories frequently were sent into Patriot units for duty, particularly late in the conflict. Pascal and Charles Estes are on the docket of late 1782 in Burke County relating to the Confiscation Acts ("Tory Docket").

Summary of Later Life:

Estes received his military compensation in 1784, indicating his presence in the area after the war. He may have returned to Virginia. Family data showed a visit of Pascal and Richard Estes to the home of Reuben Estes in later years. The data stated they came "from Virginia".

References:
Estes, Charles. "Estes Genealogies, 1097-1893" Salem, Mass. E. Putman, Publishers.
Clark, Murtie June. <u>Loyalists in the Southern Campaign of the Revolutionary</u>

<u>War</u>. Vol. I, p. 376. GPC 1981. Balti.

NC Revolutionary Army Accounts Vol. XII Book 7 Part XI folio 12 p. 2604. (from Haun, Wynette P. Durham NC, p. 1438 Vol. XII, 1999).

Triplette and Moore. <u>Moore and Estes Families</u> 1957. State Library RaleighNC.

<u>Heritage of Caldwell County NC</u>. Vol. I 1983 Article by Laxton, Mary E. p. 344 (Winston-Salem. Hunter Publ. Co.).

Lowder, Marvin Jr. Rutherford College NC   Recollections of Estes family in personal communications to author. 1980.

Estes, Reuben

Summary of Early Life:

Reuben Estes was born in the vicinity of Louisa County, Virginia. One source lists his date of birth as 1738, and the son of Richard Estes and Mary (Yancey) Estes. A second source gives his birth date as 1741, the son of Charles and Mary (Thaxton) Estes. Reuben Estes was married ca. 1760 to Delphia Adkins (or Atkins) b. 1741. After living in Virginia for a while, they moved to Caswell County, North Carolina and finally to the Johns River section of North Carolina, then Burke County, now Caldwell County. (*DAR records list a previous wife of Reuben Estes, Rhody _____*).

Summary of Partisan Activity:

Reuben Estes served as a militiaman in Morgan District ca 1782. His service is verified by extant pay vouchers. The National Society of DAR lists him as an American Patriot.

Summary of Later Life:

Reuben Estes was active in Burke County civic affairs during the late 1790's and early 1800's. He served often on various juries and other functions. Reuben and his wife Delphia had the following offspring:

> Laban 1716-1817 m. Elizabeth Webb
> Rhoda 1763-1833 m. Reuben Fletcher
> Leonard 1770-1842 m. Frances Brown
> Letta b. 1772 m. Thomas White
> Laura 1775-1847 m. John Loring
> Lott 1777-1857 m. Lara Gilbert
> Lance 1781-1851 m. Elizabeth Coffey
> Larkin 1784-1846 m. Clerice Gilbert
> Langston 1786-1851 m. Mary "Polly"

Reuben Estes died ca. 1811. His will was probated in July 1811. His wife and all nine children are mentioned in his will.

Delphia Estes died ca. 1817, as her will was probated in January 1818. They are buried in the Estes Cemetery on Johns River.

Land Holdings and Transactions:

1. Burke County NC 60 acres on Wilson's Fork of Johns River. Grant issued 26 Nov 1793. #1663 Bk. 81, p. 232.
2. Burke County NC 150 acres on right fork of Wilson's Fork of John's River. cc Reuben Estes and General Charles McDowell. Ent. 22 Dec 1778 #1173. Granted 26 Nov 1793 #1072 Bk. 81 p. 234.
3. Burke County NC 80 acres on Wilson's Fork of John's River. It lay adjacent to Husband's land. Ent. 20 May 1787 #67. Granted 26 Nov. 1793 #1674. Bk. 81, p. 235. cc Reuben Estes, John Loving.
4. Burke County NC 150 acres on Wilson's Fork of John's River. cc Reuben Estes; John Loving. Ent. 2 March 1778 #322. Granted 26 Nov 1793 #1676 Bk. 81, p. 236. Reuben Estes later was granted land in Burke County involving multiple transactions. See Land Grant Index Burke County Library, Morganton.
5. Burke County NC 100 acres on Wilson Fork John's River cc Reuben Estes and John Loving. Ent. 2 Feb 1778 #86. Granted 26 Nov 1793 #1679, Bk. 81, p. 237.

Between 1802-1810, Reuben Estes conveyed various land to Israel Pickens (400 acres), James Robertson (150 acres), Leonard Estes (100 and 125 acres), Lot Estes (100 acres), and William Penley (150 acres).

Census Locations:

1800 Burke County, North Carolina - Sons Lot, Laban, Leonard listed.
1810 Burke County, North Carolina

References:
Philbeck, Miles and Turner, Grace. "Burke County NC Surviving Will and Probate Abstracts 1777-1910", 1983 copy nos. 183, 185.
AIS Census Indices 1790, 1800, 1810. NC.

Vertical Files Caldwell County NC Public Library, Lenoir, NC, <u>Estes File</u>
        documents of Gerald Baarach, Minneapolis, MN, and La Velle Helton,
        Lenoir NC.
Internet Source: users. AP. Net/~Chenae/Estes 3 html.
Internet Source: <u>http://www.trevilans.com/others/estes.htm</u>.
DAR Patriot Index. Washington DC 1966 ed., p. 224.
Sullivan, Kathy G. Burke County NC Deeds Registered 1804 -1813 (1995 ed.).
Bentley, Elizabeth P. Index to 1810 Census of NC. GPC 1978 ed.

Fifinger, Frederick   (Fivenger, Fessinger)

Summary of Early Life:

  Frederick Fifinger was living in Burke County North Carolina during the Revolutionary War as indicated in war records relating to his capture at Charleston.

Summary of Partisan Activity:

  In 1780 Frederick Fifinger was drafted for a three month tour of duty and placed in a company commanded by Captain Jacob Collins. In late March 1780, they marched to Charleston, then being assaulted by the British. Frederick Fifinger took part in the military activities in the Charleston South Carolina area in May 1780. Upon the surrender of Charleston, Fifinger was made a prisoner of war, and later paroled. No additional military duties are listed.

Summary of Later Life:

  In late May 1780, Frederick Fifinger returned to Burke County upon release. His name appears in miscellaneous court records from 1781 through 1788. One of these was a lawsuit involving Fifinger and William Young.

  Fifinger died some time prior to April 1793, the date of his will probate. No family members are given.

References:
Wyche, K. Article in NC Genealogical Journal. Aug. 1978 issue.
Huggins, Edith. "Burke County NC Land Records and and More Important
   Miscellaneous Documents" Vol. III. pp 43, 80, 134, 136, 151.
McBride, R.. "Revolutionary War Papers". NC Genealogical Society Journal
   Aug 1977 ed. p. 175.

Ford, Joseph

Summary of Early Life:

Joseph Ford was born in 1757 in Frederick County Maryland. At the beginning of the American Revolution, he was residing on Avington's Creek, a tributary of Lower Creek in Burke County NC, now Caldwell County. His place of residence was close to the dividing line of Burke and Wilkes counties. What relation if any, to Captain Peter Fore or Ford, of the same area is not known.

Summary of Partisan Activities:

Joseph Ford first entered military service in the summer of 1776 (in his pension statements he says 1777, but the events he described were clearly in the year 1776). He served in a company of light horse headed by Captain Bartlett of Wilkes County, Colonel Francis Locke's Regiment. Ford then describes his participation in the Cherokee Expedition commanded by General Griffith Rutherford. They started at Crider's Fort near his home, marched to Davidson's Fort (now Old Fort, NC) and then across the Blue Ridge into the "near" towns of the Cherokees. After a "hot engagement", they advanced across the gap into the overhills towns, burning their houses and corn crops. Ford served six months on this tour of duty.

Ford next served a tour of duty in Charles McDowell's Burke Regiment under Captain Thomas Whitson and Lieutenant John Baldwin. They had a hard fight with the Indians in the North Cove of the Catawba (now McDowell County). In this engagement, Captain Reuben White was killed and Captain Whitson wounded. He also said a Private Zebulan Shelton was killed along with seven or eight others. The remainder of his tour was service in the western frontier forts, guarding against Indian incursions. Ford later served another tour of duty on the western frontier under a Lieutenant Carthy (Cathey?). He was discharged in 1779.

In July 1781, Joseph Ford received a lieutenant's commission issued by Governor Alexander Martin of North Carolina. He served under Captain James Roddy in Washington County, Tennessee, then part of North Carolina. Charles Ashe was ensign. His company was part of Colonel John Sevier's Regiment. From their area, they marched through North Carolina into lower South Carolina on the Santee River. There they joined forces with General Francis Marion of South Carolina. There was a short engagement at Moncks Corner, South Carolina in which ninety prisoners were taken. They later scoured the countryside for concealed Tories. His company then returned to the Wateree Settlement where he received his discharge on February 12, 1782.

Summary of Later Life:

Joseph Ford, during the Revolutionary War, sold his land on Avington's Creek. In his pension statements he says he remained in North Carolina until his move to Kentucky. There are tax records of one Joseph Ford in Carter County, Tennessee (1796, 1798). This suggests that he moved here during the war, then a part of North Carolina (Washington County).

In the early part of the nineteenth century, ca 1809, Joseph Ford moved to Floyd County, Kentucky, that portion which later became Pike County, Kentucky.

Joseph Ford applied for Revolutionary War pension in Pike County, Kentucky on February 25, 1834, age 77 years. He was awarded a pension of $79.23 per annum. A Mary Ford is listed on 1820 census Floyd County, Kentucky, relationship to Joseph Ford not definitely known.

Land Holdings and Transactions:

1. Burke County Land Entry #1245 Ent. 21 Dec 1778 "Beginning on a line or place he lives on" 150 acres right hand fork of Avington's Creek transferred to Henry Williams on 29 Dec 1782.
2. Burke County NC Land Entry #1444 Ent 22 Dec 1778 150

acres on Avington's Creek, a tributary of Lower Creek "including his own improvements" transferred to Henry Williams on 29 Dec 1782.

3. Burke County NC Land Entry #1445 ent 22 Dec 1778 150 acres on left hand fork of Avington's Creek, joining his own improvements transferred to Henry William 29 Dec 1782.

Census Locations:

1796, 1798 Carter County, Tennessee Tax Records
1820, ?   Floyd County, Kentucky – Mary Ford

References:
US National Archives Revolutionary War Pension Data #S15429.
Huggins, Edith W. Miscellaneous Burke County Records in 4 Vol., Vol. I pp. 116,134, 135. (land entry data).
Sistler, Byron and Barbara. EarlyTennesse Tax Lists Evanston, Ill.1977 ed. p. 68.
Index to 1820 Kentucky Census, compiled by Volkel, Lloyd. 1974 ed. Part I p. 35.
DAR Patriot Index 1966 ed.   Washington DC   National Society DAR   p. 244.
NC Revolutionary Army Accounts as given in Haun, Wynette P. In multiple soft back volumes or parts. Part II p. 177, Part IV, pp. 477,501.

Forgy, James (Forgey, Forgery)

Summary of Early Life:

During the Revolutionary period, James Forgy and his family were living on Crooked Creek in western Burke County, North Carolina, now McDowell County.

Summary of Partisan Activity:

James Forgy was an officer in the western Rowan Regiment with the rank of Lieutenant. He served under his superior officers, Colonel Charles McDowell and Captains Joseph McDowell and Jonathan Camp. His first tour of duty was the Cross Creek Expedition of early 1776. This was the follow up actions against the "Scotch Tories" of the Lower Cape Fear Valley.

In the summer and fall of 1776, Forgy took part in the Cherokee Expedition headed by General Griffith Rutherford. By this time, Forgy had been promoted to Captain. He and his company served on the western Catawba frontier, guarding against the incursions of the Cherokees, and conducting periodic raids. In his pension statements, Revolutionary War soldier Martin Coulter, Jr. states that he served under Captain Forgy in 1778. Captain Forgy commanded both Davidson's and Cathey's Forts.

Summary of Later Life:

From pension papers of Revolutionary soldier John Neill, it appears that Forgy's wife was named Rebecca, and their daughter Cynthia married John Neill. The Neills eventually moved to Logan County, Kentucky.

James Forgy's name appears on many court records between 1785-1790, as a juror on most occasions. In the early 1790's he seemed to be selling off his land. Several of his court appointed duties were taken over by other persons. Nothing in Burke records is seen after 1793, indicating his probable departure. The 1790 census figures indicate a rather large family, six males and four females. The Logan County, Kentucky connection as given above relative to his daughter Cynthia is of interest.

In Butler County, Kentucky, just at the border of Logan County, there is a historical marker labeled "James Forgy – Pioneer". It is on Kentucky Highway 106 near the Quality Church of Christ. The marker states that Forgy was born in 1752 and served in South Carolina and was one of the "first settlers in North Logan County, Kentucky". His death date was given as 1828.

Land Holdings and Transactions:

1. Burke County North Carolina 200 acres both sides of the main fork of Crooked Creek. The land included a ford of the Creek and both sides of a path that led from Thomas Brandon, where Lodwick Wray once lived. cc John Davidson; Benjamin Lockman.
2. Land Entries:
   #578 100 acres Crooked Creek, relating to grant above. 7 Aug 1778.
   #487 150 acres Crooked Creek 20 Jul 1778.

Census Locations:

1790 Burke County, North Carolina 4th Company

References:
www. Oriscus.com internet data.
US National Archives. Pension statement of George Cathey (S16699) John Grider (W358) John Neill (R7578) Martin Coulter, Jr. (R2363).
AIS 1790 NC Census.
Burke County Land Data. Burke County Library, Morganton, NC.
Huggins, Edith W. Miscellaneous Burke Records Vols. I-IV.
Swink, Dan. Minutes of the Court of Pleas and Quarter Sessions Burke County, NC 1791-1795. (1986)

Fulbright, Andrew (Vollbrecht)

Summary of Early Life:

Andrew Fulbright appears to have been living in Northampton County, Pennsylvania shortly before the American Revolution. Other Fulbrights were also there, including William, Jacob, and John. By the time of the Revolution, all had moved to what is now eastern Catawba County, near Lyle Creek, near its junction with the Catawba River.

Summary of Partisan Activity:

At the beginning of the Revolutionary War, the area around Lyle Creek was part of Rowan County, later Burke County. It was part of Burke County throughout most of the Revolutionary War. One of the first military actions in North Carolina was the Moore's Creek Bridge Battle of February 1776. The Rowan militia was called out and marched toward Cross Creek (Fayetteville). They assisted in mop up activities after the battle, sequestering supplies and arresting prominent Tories. During this campaign, Andrew Fulbright served as a sergeant in the 2nd Rowan Regiment, commanded by Colonel Christopher Beekman. The overall commander was Brigadier General Griffith Rutherford. The regiment later took part in the Cherokee Expedition of July and August 1776.

Summary of Later Life:

Very little is currently known about Fulbright's later life. He did enter land in eastern Burke County, North Carolina in 1778 and a warrant was authorized. Later the land data was marked through and William Fulbright's name was substituted.

Census Locations:

The name of Andrew Fulbright appears on the 1790 and subsequent censuses through 1840. This probably was Andrew Fulbright, son of Jacob Fulbright.

115

References:
Gephart, Laneil and Roger. "Fulbright Ancestors and Kinfolks". (1995 Derby, KS) softback ed in Catawba County NC Library.

Huggins, Edith W. Miscellaneous Burke County NC Records. In four softback ed. Vol. I, p. 32.

Land Grant records in Burke County NC Library.

AIS Census records 1790-1840

NC Revolutionary Army Accounts, Journal "A" as given in printed account by Haun, Wynette P. Part I, p. 4. (Durham, NC 1988 ed.).

Brown, Rachel Shook. Article in The Heritage of Catawba County NC Vol. I 1986 ed. pp. 166-167.

Fulbright, Jacob

Summary of Early Life:

Jacob Fulbright was born in Northhampton County, Pennsylvania on December 22, 1747. In 1769, he moved to the Catawba Valley of North Carolina. He settled in that portion that was part of Burke County during most of the Revolutionary War, later Lincoln, then Catawba County. He was a son of William Fulbright.

Summary of Partisan Activity:

Jacob Fulbright first entered military service in the summer of 1776 as a drafted militiaman. He was placed in a company commanded by Captain (Rudolph) Conrad of Colonel Christopher Beekman's 2nd Rowan Regiment. Lieutenant Colonel Charles McDowell was 2nd in command. His company took part in the Cherokee Expedition of 1776 commanded by Brigadier General Griffith Rutherford. Rutherford's troops crossed the Blue Ridge and took possession of the Cherokee Valley towns, destroying their crops and buildings. Fulbright stated that he was in no significant engagement.

Fulbright entered military service again in 1781 as a volunteer militiaman. He served in Colonel Charles McDowell's Burke Regiment, and Captain Daniel Smith's Company. Fulbright interestingly mentions the death of McDowell's 2nd in command of the regiment, Lieutenant Colonel Hugh Brevard. Fulbright stated, "Colonel Brevard got the small pocks and dyed." He was replaced by Major Daniel McKissick. This was in mid 1781. Fulbright, a blacksmith by trade, was relieved of his duties, but was to work as a blacksmith for the military mounted troops. He worked in this capacity until the end of the war two years later.

Summary of Later Life:

Following the close of the American Revolution, Jacob Fulbright remained active in Lincoln County civic affairs for several years. Court documents show him as a juryman on numerous occasions from 1789-1805. He is on the Lincoln County federal census from 1790-1820. In 1830, he appears on the Haywood County, North Carolina census. Jacob Fulbright applied for federal pension benefits in Haywood County NC in 1833. There were supporting statements by Jacob and Andrew Shook, both pensioned Revolutionary War soldiers that Jacob Fulbright had served in the Revolutionary War. Even though it is obvious that Jacob Fulbright did indeed serve, not all of the necessary prerequisites were met and his pension was rejected. His son Abraham Fulbright, in 1853, submitted a claim that his pension be approved and payment made to his heirs. Disposition not known.

Jacob Fulbright was married to Elizabeth Weisel. Jacob Fulbright died in Haywood County, North Carolina in 1835.

Land Holdings and Transactions:

Jacob Fulbright received a land grant in Lincoln County (now Catawba County NC) on water of Lyle's Creek – 100 acres.

Census Locations:

1790 Lincoln County, North Carolina
1800 Lincoln County, North Carolina
1810 Lincoln County, North Carolina
1820 Lincoln County, North Carolina
1830 Haywood County, North Carolina

References:
US National Archives Pension Data #R3826.
AIS Census Indices. NC 1790-1830.
McAllister, Anne W. and Sullivan, Kathy G. "Lincoln County NC Court of
        Pleas and Quarter Sessions. July 1796 Jan 1805". (1988 ed.), multiple
        listings.
Internet source: www.shookhistory.org. 2003 accession.

Giles, Samuel (Jiles)

Summary of Early Life:

Samuel Giles, as indicated in land records, appeared to have been residing in the Drowning Creek area of Burke County during the Revolutionary period.

Summary of Partisan Activity:

In 1796 Samuel Giles petitioned the county to exempt him from poll taxes because of disabling injuries sustained while on duty in the military. He stated, "I being a citizen now…appeal for relief (due to) a wound I received in the Armey". The request was approved.

Summary of Later Life:

Not much is known about Samuel Giles in Burke records. Other Giles' that appear in early Burke records include Crispen Giles (earlier in Randolph County, NC), James Giles, Richard Giles, John Giles, and Noble Giles. The exact relationship of these persons to the soldier Samuel Giles is unknown.

Land Holdings and Transactions:

1. Burke County NC 600 acres On Drowning Creek, a tributary of Catawba River (southside). The land adjacent to that of William Berry, widow Berry (of William?), and Jacob Settlemyre. The land included Giles' improvements. cc Joseph Simmons, Jason Murcer (Mercer) Ent. 23 Oct 1788 #134 Grant No. 1572 Iss. 27 Nov. 1792 Bk. 80 p. 46.
2. Burke County NC Deed to Benjamin Clarke 450 acres 7 Sept 1804 reg. 1811.

Census Locations:

1790 Burke County, North Carolina 2nd Company

1800 Burke County, North Carolina

References:

Huggins, Edith W. "Burke County NC Records 1755-1821". Vol. IV p. 143.

AIS Census Data.

Land Grant records in Burke County Library, Morganton, NC.

Sullivan, Kathy G. "Burke County NC Deeds Registered 1804-1813".(1995)
      p.41.

Grider, Valentine (Gryder)

Summary of Early Life:

Valentine Grider was born in Loudoun County, Virginia in the year 1762. He was living with his family in Burke County, North Carolina (now Caldwell County) when he first entered military service. A brother, Jacob Grider stated that the family moved from Virginia to North Carolina ca 1770.

Summary of Partisan Activity:

Valentine Grider first entered military service in 1779, serving in Colonel Charles McDowell's Burke Regiment of militia. Other officers included Major Joseph McDowell and Captain John Smith. Grider in his Revolutionary War pension statements, said that he served a three moth tour of duty as a substitute for his brother, Jacob Grider, and that he served a six month tour as a volunteer, and another six months tour as a substitute for his brother, Cornelius Grider. He was a drafted militiaman on his final tour of three months.

Grider was marched to South Carolina during one of his tours, but he did not list any specific duties or actions. He is more explicit about his final tour, occurring during the fall of 1781 (Wilmington Expedition). This expedition was headed up by recently released (as prisoner of war) Brigadier General Griffith Rutherford. The expedition, organized in September 1781 and concluded in December 1781, was designed to free Wilmington (and all of North Carolina) from British control. By the time they reached Wilmington, the British had already left (for Virginia and South Carolina), but there was a skirmish near Bluford's Bridge near the Northeast Cape Fear River. Grider mentioned all of these activities in his Revolutionary War pension statements. Other officers that he served under included Major Joseph White, Captain John Lucas, Colonel McGuire, and General John Butler.

121

Summary of Later Life:

Burke County records show that Valentine Grider remained in Burke County until the turn of the century. He is not listed in the 1790 census, but may have been in the household of another relative (Fred Grider, Sr.?). He is listed on the 1800 Burke census, but not on the 1810 census. Grider, in his pension declarations, states that he left Burke County, lived for a while in Powell's Valley, Virginia, and then later lived in Lee County, Virginia. He was living in Lee County at the time of his marriage to Mary Fugate, in 1816. Later records state that they "raised a large family". By 1820, he was living in Cumberland County, Kentucky.

While a resident of Cumberland County, Kentucky, Grider applied for Revolutionary War pension benefits on October 9, 1832. He was awarded an annual pension of $60.00.

The Revolutionary War soldier Valentine Grider died in Cumberland County, Kentucky on March 2, 1837. His widow, Mary Grider, continued to receive a pension following Grider's death (she was age 64 in 1853). Mary Grider applied for a Bounty Land Grant in 1855. She stated that her late husband "was a Captain in the War of the Revolution". There is nothing in the records to indicate this. The earliest pension records show him as a private.

Land Holdings and Transactions:

1. A pre-1800 Burke County NC tax list shows Valentine Grider with 50 acres land Captain Newland's Company (now Caldwell County NC)
2. 1795 Burke County NC tax list shows Valentine Grider with 100 acres land, Captain Connelly's District (near Caldwell County NC)

Census Locations:

1800 Burke County, North Carolina

1820 Cumberland County, Kentucky

References:
US National Archives Pension Data #W11082.
AIS Census Information NC 1800.
Volkel, Lowell. An Index to the 1820 Census of Kentucky (1974 ed.).
Huggins, Edith W. Miscellaneous Burke Records Vol. IV.
Grider, Jacob. Revolutionary War Pension Data #W3980.
Bounty Land Warrant. 19544-160-55.

Grindstaff, Isaac

Summary of Early Life:

Isaac Grindstaff was born ca 1754, or earlier. He was the son of Michael Grindstaff, Sr. The Grindstaffs resided on Clarks Little River (upper Little River) near the present day Caldwell County – Alexander County line. Isaac Grindstaff was a brother of Revolutionary War veteran Adam (d. 1781), Michael Jr., Jacob and Nicholas Grindstaff (see separate biographical sketches Vols. I and II).

The area in which the Grindstaffs lived was a part of Burke County during the Revolutionary War. The Grindstaffs, originally Grantzdorf or Crantzdorf, originated in the Rhine Valley of Southwest Germany.

Summary of Partisan Activity:

The North Carolina Revolutionary Army Accounts list Isaac Grindstaff as a militiaman. Being a resident of Burke County, he would have served in Charles McDowell's Burke Regiment.

Summary of Later Life:

Shortly after the Revolutionary War had ended, the Grindstaff boys all pulled up stakes and headed west. Brother Nicholas settled in Carter County, Tennessee. Brothers Michael and Jacob settled in Kentucky. Isaac Grindstaff settled in the Toe River Valley of North Carolina. There are comments that he may have originally lived in Carter County, Tennessee. One has to assume, however, that Nicholas' son Isaac was of age and probably lived in Carter County also. Isaac Grindstaff lived in present day Mitchell County, North Carolina near the Wing community. Isaac Grindstaff, Sr. died in 1825.

Isaac Grindstaff had the following children:

Isaac Grindstaff, Jr. b. 1779 m. Sally Hart; Prudence
Ledford
Sally m. George Hunsucker b. 1782
Mary m. Lawrence Effler b. 1785
Margaret m. Reuben Woody or Moody b. 1787
Henry b. 1789 m. Cynthia Penland
Arbella b. 179? m. Stephen Pitman

Land Holdings and Transactions:

One source states that Isaac Grindstaff lived on a 600 acre
tract in Mitchell County. Burke County NC 1815 tax listings show
an Isaac Grindstaff with two tracts of land on Mine Creek adjacent
to land of McKinney and Hunsucker. One was 144 acres, the
second 148 acres.

Census Locations:

1790 Burke County, North Carolina 8th Company
1800 Burke County, North Carolina
1810 Burke County, North Carolina
1820 Burke County, North Carolina

References:
Navey, William R. "Descendants of Dietrich Grantzdorf" copy in Burke County
        Library donated in 2001.
The Heritage of Toe River Valley. ed. by Lloyd Bailey Vol. I 1994 ed. pp. 258-
        259.
Roster of Soldiers from North Carolina in the American Revolution. NC DAR
        1967 reprint of 1932 ed. p. 381, R. W. Voucher #4964 Morgan District.
Pittman, Betsy. "Burke County NC 1815 Tax Lists" 1990 ed., p. 108.
AIS NC Census Indices. (1790-1820).
NC Revolutionary Army Accounts Vol. I. Bk 3 p. 42 #2159.

Grindstaff, Nicholas

Summary of Early Life:

From data of W. R. Navey, it appears that the Grindstaff family originated from the area of Zweibrucken, in Germany.

The progenitor was one Dietrich Grantzdorf, later changed to Grindstaff. One of the early settlers in Burke County was Michael Grindstaff, either a son or grandson of Dietrich. Michael Grindstaff settled on the Upper Little River; also know as Clark's Little River (near present day Caldwell-Alexander Counties, NC).

In 1767 Nicholas Grindstaff received a Crown Grant in Mecklenburg County, North Carolina (now Catawba County) on Pinch Gut Creek, near present town of Maiden. Michael Grindstaff may also have resided in this area as he was a joint deed owner of land set aside for a school, just southeast of Newton, also near Pinch Gut Creek (1773).

Nicholas Grindstaff was the son of Michael and brother to Adam, Isaac, Jacob and Michael, Jr. (all were Revolutionary War soldiers). Various birth dates are given for Nicholas Grindstaff – 1740, 1746, 1750, etc.

Summary of Partisan Activity:

Nicholas Grindstaff was a member of the 10th Regiment, North Carolina Continental Line. He enlisted in June 1781 and was discharged a year later on June 16, 1782. He was in Lytles' Company and served with brother Michael and Adam Grindstaff. They were engaged mainly in South Carolina under the overall command of General Nathaniel Greene. Their regiment took part in the battles of Ninety-Six (June 1781), and Eutaw Springs (8 Sept. 81), as well as several more skirmishes. Brother Adam died of wounds in a Camden Hospital in 1781.

Summary of Later Life:

Following the Revolutionary War, the Grindstaff brothers moved west. Isaac settled in Toe River Valley of North Carolina. Michael, Nicholas and Jacob went farther into what is now Carter County, Tennessee. Nicholas remained in Carter County. Jacob and Michael then moved westward into Kentucky. According to various sources, Nicholas Grindstaff was married to Mary (or Catherine?) Smith and they had the following children:

Nicholas b. ca 1766 m. Mary Stuart
John b. ca 1766 m. Elizabeth Brown
Isaac b. ca 1761
Henry b. ca 1775

A second marriage is given to Martha Wagner. Nicholas Grindstaff died ca 1789 in Carter County, Tennessee. Another source says he died 1794.

Land Holdings and Transactions:

1. North Carolina Crown Grant Mecklenburgh County, NC (now Catawba County) 400 acres on Pinch Gut Creek and Hagin's Fork adjacent to land of Lawrence Debury. #2159
2. Burke County, North Carolina 116 ac on both sides of Upper Little River (Clark's Little River) the land was adjacent to that of Martin Calor (Kaylor or Keller). The land included "his own improvements".
   cc Abraham Armatage, Michael Grindstaff Ent. 16 Oct 1778 #913 Grant #599 Issued Oct. 11, 1783. Bk. 50 p. 216.
   Burke County tax records indicate a delinquency in payments by Nicholas Grindstaff. This may be representative for his time of departure from the area.

References:
Navey, William R. "Descendants of Dietrich Grantzdorf" (from a copy donated to Burke County Library 2001) Holly Ridge NC.
Carter County Tennessee and Its People, 1796, 1993. pp. 345-353. Several individually written sketches on Grindstaff lineages. Elizabethton, Tennessee. 1995 printing.

The Heritage of the Toe River Valley ed. by Lloyd Bailey. Vol. I. 1994 ed. pp.
        258-259. Articles by Margaret Heinek, Ruby Grindstaff George, Lloyd
        Bailey and Evelyn Grindstaff.
Burke County Land Grant Records. Burke County Library Morganton, NC
Roster of Soldiers from North Carolina in the American Revolution. NC DAR
        1967 reprint of 1932 ed. p. 128
        *Note: Typo error Michs instead of Nichs Grindstaff is listed. Michael
        given as Mich'l CPL on same page.*
Hofmann, Margaret. Colony of North Carolina 1765-1775 Abstracts of Land
        Patents Vol. II 1984 ed. p. 448.
History of Catawba County. ed. by Charles Preslar 1954 ed. p. 124.

Haas, John (Horse, Hauss)

Summary of Early Life:

John Haas was the son of the pioneer Simon Haas and
Susannah Whittenburg Haas. The Haas family lived in what is
now Catawba County, near Newton. After the death of his father,
John Haas moved to Clarks Little River area of old Burke County
(Upper Little River).

Summary of Partisan Activity:

According to the historian, Charles J. Preslar, Jr. (ed. of
The History of Catawba County), John and Simon Haas
participated in the Kings Mountain Battle of October 7, 1780. The
North Carolina Revolutionary Accounts verify the service of Haas
as a militiaman from Morgan Military District. This would also
suggest service time later in the war, since Morgan District was
created in 1782.

Summary of Later Life:

John Haas was married to Hannah Rohr. They had the
following children:

Abraham	Hannah	John
Susannah	George	Henry
Peter m. Elizabeth Shell	Phillip	Simon

John Haas died in 1801. Thomas Scott and Phillip Haas
settled his estate. Probate Burke County Court 1802.

Land Holdings and Transactions:

1. Burke County North Carolina 100 acres. The land lay
    on the South side of Piney Mountain and included one
    head of the Roundabout branch and the head of the
    Cold Spring. Ent. 27 Oct 1792 Ent #200 Grant #1734
    Iss. 7 Jul 1794 Bk. 85 p. 73 cc Peter Haas, William

Thornton.

2. Burke County North Carolina 100 acres on a creek that empties into Steel's Mill Creek, lying between land of Samuel Steel and George Boglan (or Barlow?). Ent. #189 7 Mar 1793 Grant #1781 Iss. July 1794 Bk. 85 p. 89. cc Peter Haas, Alex West.

3. Burke County North Carolina 200 acres. The land lay on the South side of Chestnut Mountain, at the head of Gunpowder Creek, known as the Roundabout. Ent. 4 Jun 1791 #122 Grant #1886 Iss. 7 July 1794. Bk. 85 p. 129. cc Alex West, Thomas Scott.

4. Lincoln County North Carolina Deed of Sale John Horse to Simon and Joseph Horse May 20, 1791.

Census Locations:

1790 Burke County, North Carolina (8th Company)
1800 Burke County, North Carolina (John "House")

References:
Haynes, Mary Deal. Article in The Heritage of Catawba County North Carolina Vol. I. 1986 ed. p. 174.
North Carolina Revolutionary Army Accounts.
Roster of soldiers from North Carolina in the American Revolution NC DAR reprint of 1932 ed. (1967) p. 387.
A History of Catawba County. Ed. by Charles J. Preslar, Jr., Salisbury NC 1954 p. 77.
Land Grant Records Burke County Library Morganton, NC.
AIS Census Data 1790-1800.
McAllister, Anne W. and Sullivan, Kathy G. "Lincoln County NC Court of Pleas and Quarter Sessions Apr. 1789 through April 1796". p. 45.

Haas, Simon (Horse)(Hauss)

Summary of Early Life:

Simon Haas was the son of Simon Haas, Sr., the pioneer, and Susannah Whittenberg Haas. The Haas family lived on Clark's Creek in what is now Catawba County North Carolina. During the Revolutionary War, it was a part of Burke County. Simon Haas, Jr. was a brother of John Haas (also a Revolutionary War soldier), and George Haas.

Summary of Partisan Activity:

The North Carolina Revolutionary War Army Accounts verify the service of Simon Haas as a militiaman during the Revolutionary War. The Catawba County historian, Charles J. Preslar, Jr., in his A History of Catawba County, states that Haas took part in the Kings Mountain Battle of October 7, 1780.

Summary of Later Life:

Simon Haas, on the death of his father in 1779, inherited a portion of his estate on Clark's Creek. Later, when his brother John moved to Burke County, he received another portion by deed; as did his brother George.

Land Holdings and Transaction:

Burke County North Carolina land issued jointly to Simon, John and George Haas. 618 acres on Bollinger's Mill Creek and east of Clark's Creek. The land lay adjacent to property of Henry Bollinger, Joseph Steel, Nicholas Frye, Peter Icard (Eigert), Joseph Lutz and Rudolph Conrad including "improvements where on Simon Hoss, deceased, lived on." Ent April 26, 1780 (originally Jan 15, 1779) #780 Grant #627 Iss. 11 Oct. 1783. Bk. 50 p. 228. cc Peter Eigert, John Arndt.
This probably represents the property Simon Haas, St., had acquired on his arrival from Pennsylvania, most likely in mid 1760's. The original entry may have been made by Haas Sr., just prior to his demise the same year.

Census Locations:

1790 Lincoln County, North Carolina
1800 Lincoln County, North Carolina
1810 "widow Horse" Simon, Sr. or Simon, Jr.

References:
Preslar, Charles J., Jr. A History of Catawba County. Salisbury, NC 1954 p. 77.
Haynes, Mary Deal. Article on Haas Family in Catawba County Heritage Vol.
    I. p. 174. (1986 ed.).
NC DAR Roster of Soldiers from North Carolina in the Revolutionary War.
    (1967 reprint of orig. 1932 ed.). GPC Baltimore pp. 387, 411.
Haun, Wynette P. Durham NC Revolutionary Army Accounts. 4444. Part VII, p.
    895. Part XI, p. 1464.
AIS Census records NC 1790, 1800, 1810.
Land Grant Data   Burke County Library, Morganton, NC.

Harbison, William

Summary of Early Life:

William Harbison, during the Revolutionary War, was residing in what is today Southeast Catawba County, North Carolina. During most of the Revolutionary War it was a part of Burke County. His land was adjacent to Clark's Creek. He owned several tracts of land elsewhere in Burke County, also. His home place lay within the confines of Lincoln County from the close of the Revolutionary War until his death.

Summary of Partisan Activity:

The North Carolina Revolutionary Army Accounts show that William Harbison was a militiaman from Morgan Military District. The brigade commander was General Charles McDowell. The Burke County regimental commander was Colonel Joseph McDowell of Quaker Meadows.

Summary of Later Life:

William Harbison was married to Nancy Branch and together they ran an inn in their area. The 1790 census show a total of eighteen persons in the household – nine males and nine females in addition to three slaves. William Harbison died sometime before January 1794, the date of his will probate. His widow Nancy proved to be an able businesswoman and administrator, paying off all debt, and later purchasing several tracts of land.

Millie F. Harbison, in the Heritage series, mentions son Alexander who married Cynthia Scott. He was progenitor of many of the Burke County Harbisons. She also had a daughter, Lynchia who married James Kincaid. Three other sons, unnamed. Other Harbisons found in the literature, possibly his sons, include William Harbison, David Harbison, and Abraham Harbison.

Land Holdings and Transactions:

1. Burke County NC 150 acres on the Little Fork of Gunpowder Creek and which lay adjacent to land of John Barnhart, Joseph Simmons. It included possessions of James King. Ent. 27 Apr 1792 Ent #159 Grant #1856 Iss & Jul 1794 Bk. 85 p. 119. cc William Baldwin, Samuel Jiles.
2. Lincoln County NC Basil Dorsey to William Harbison 125 acres July 4, 1790.
3. Burke County NC David Witherspoon 200 acres on Falling Creek (a tributary of Lyle Creek) adjacent to Isaac Robinson and George Pitts. Ent 17 Sep 1779 transferred to William Harbison.

Census Locations:

1790 Lincoln County, North Carolina 3rd Company
1800 Lincoln County, North Carolina (Nancy Harbison)

References:
Roster of Soldiers from North Carolina in the Revolutionary War (NC DAR) reprint of original ed. 1932. GPC p. 354.
NC Revolutionary Army Accounts. Comptroller's office certificate #4489. (Vol. VIII Bk 8 pp. 148-9 folio 28).
Land Grant records in Burke County Library, Morganton NC.
AIS Census data 1790 NC.
Harbison, Millie Fox. Article in Burke County Heritage Vol. I, 1981 ed. p. 215.
McAllister, Anne W. and Sullivan, Kathy G. "Lincoln County NC Court of Pleas and Quarter Sessions" 1789-1796. (1987) p. 83.
Huggins, Edith W. Miscellaneous Burke Records Vol. II.

Hargrave, John

Summary of Early Life:

John Hargrave was born in South Carolina, near the North Carolina border, in November 1755. This was probably in lower South Carolina, as he served under Colonel Horry of that area.

Summary of Partisan Activity:

John Hargrave first entered military service in 1775 as a volunteer minuteman. He served in Captain Dennis Hankin's Company of Colonel Daniel Horry's Regiment. In the summer of 1776, they were ordered to march to Wilmington, North Carolina. En route to Wilmington they met and then joined the south bound army commanded by General Charles Lee. Their purpose was to prevent a planned British assault against Charleston, South Carolina. Hargrave was one of 500 soldiers stationed on Sullivan's Island to oppose any British invasion. The British were unsuccessful in their siege and returned to northern waters. After being discharged, Hargrave served as a substitute militiaman for six or seven weeks.

In 1780 he moved to the western frontier of North Carolina, Burke County in Captain Thomas Hemphill's district. Several Hargraves were residing on Crooked Creek and Newberry's Fork, now McDowell County, North Carolina.

In the spring of 1780, Hargrave entered service again as a volunteer militiaman in Captain Hemphill's Company. They marched to Ramsour's Mill, North Carolina on hearing of a Tory gathering (earlier they had captured Captain Ned Hampton and Lieutenant John Russell). They were now under the overall command of Colonel Francis Locke of Rowan County, North Carolina.

On June 20, 1780 Hargrave took part in the hard fought battle of Ramsour's Mill. He stated that many prisoners were taken.

135

In April of 1781, he entered service again in a South Carolina unit. He was a volunteer soldier in Captain Francis Boykin's Company of Colonel Charles S. Myddleton's Regiment. Under Colonel Myddleton they saw action on Congaree River of South Carolina with the siege and capture of Fort Granby and Fort Mahon. They also took a Fort on Edisto River. On September 8, 1781, under Colonel Myddleton, he fought in the Battle of Eutaw Springs, South Carolina. He described in his pension statements how they drove the British forward, and then were repulsed.

After the battle, he hired a substitute to serve out the remainder of his term. He then returned home and remained there until the end of the war.

Summary of Later Life:

After the war, Hargrave lived in western North Carolina until 1797. He moved to Logan County, Kentucky and lived there until 1809. He then moved to Union County, Illinois and remained there the remainder of his life.

John Hargrave applied for Revolutionary War pension benefits in Union County, Illinois on October 20, 1832, age 77 years. He was awarded an annual pension of $28.22. John Hargrave died October 30, 1834 leaving five children.

References:
US National Archives. Revolutionary War Pension Data # S32297.
Moss, Bobby G. Roster of South Carolina Patriots in the Revolutionary War GPC 1983 ed. p. 414
Huggins, Edith. Miscellaneous Burke County Records. Vol. I, pp 40, 42.

Harris, Gilliam (Gillum)

Summary of Early Life:

 During the American Revolution, Gilliam Harris was residing in southeast Burke County, North Carolina on Jacob's Fork, a tributary of the South Fork of the Catawba River. He was a neighbor of George Sealey.

Summary of Partisan Activity:

 In 1782 the name of Gilliam Harris appeared on a subpoena docket of Burke County, NC. He was to be indicted as a suspected Tory. The case was never resolved, as the Revolutionary War was to end only a few months later.

Summary of Later Life:

 Harris' name is not on the 1790 census, even though he had a land grant issued to him in 1788. A "Harris Gillum" appears on a tax list of 1799 in northwest Burke County adjacent to a John Harris (Capt. Kirkpatrick's Company). Buncombe County, North Carolina records of 1794 show "Gilliham" Harris purchasing two tracts of land on Little River. The name of Gilliam Harris also appears on later censuses of Mecklenburg County, North Carolina and Greene County, Georgia. The relationship to Gilliam Harris of Burke County, North Carolina is unknown.

Land Holdings and Transactions:

1. 100 ac Burke County NC on both sides of Jacob's Fork of South Fork Catawba River, adjacent (about a mile above) to land belonging to George Sealey. Harris had cut some timber on the property earlier. cc (Gilliam Harris, William Jones.) Ent. 28 Oct 1778 Grant No. 1128 Iss. 10 July 1788. Bk 66, p. 484.
2. Listed in Robert Kirkpatricks Company, Burke County, NC 1799. See Huggins IV – p. 124.
3. Buncombe County, NC July 7, 1794 100 acres, Little River

(NC Land Grant) #S1-2 233.
4. Buncombe County, NC July 7, 1794 100 acres, Little River (NC land grant) # 52-2, 233.

References:
Huggins, Edith W. Miscellaneous Burke County NC Records Vol. II; IV.
Land Grant Records in Burke County Library, Morganton, NC.
AIS Census Records 1790 NC 1810 NC 1810 GA.
Wooley, James E. Buncombe County NC Index to Deeds 1783-1850. SHP
      1983 ed. p. 212.

Hasselbarger, John

Summary of Early Life:

John Hasselbarger appears to have come to the Catawba Valley during the American Revolution. He first established his home on Pinch Gut Creek on land formerly owned by George Lutz (near present day Maiden, NC). Hasselbarger was married to a widow Lutz. The land lay within Burke County during the Revolutionary War, later Lincoln County and then Catawba County.

Summary of Partisan Activity:

By 1781, Hasselbarger had received a Captain's commission in Charles McDowell's militia regiment of Burke County. In September-December 1781, Hasselbarger led his company on the Wilmington expedition. This military expedition was headed up by the Salisbury Brigade, led by recently exchanged Brigadier General Griffith Rutherford. Their object was to free Wilmington from British control. This was accomplished in December 1781. Lieutenant Barnet Sigmon was one of Hasslebarger's subaltern officers. Hasslebarger's Revolutionary War service as a Captain was confirmed by Revolutionary Army Accounts – "John Hasselbarger, Captain". There were confirming statements by three Revolutionary War soldiers in his company (Casper Bolick, Adam Setzer, Jacob Typs).

Summary of Later Life:

John Hasselbarger had married the widow Lutz and lived on land previously owned by George Lutz. The 1790 census lists several children (some by widow Lutz from a previous marriage?). Later, Hasselbarger moved to South Fork (of Catawba River) where he built a mill. He was an early member of Grace Church (Lutheran and German Reformed). Catawba County records also give a second wife, Magdalena (Reip). John Hasselbarger's name appears on both Burke and Lincoln records in the late 1700's.

John Hasselbarger died ca 1806 – will probate1807. He was buried on old Andrew Yoder's farm. . Both wives were also buried there. Three daughters are listed -- _____ m. Paul Hartzoke, Susan m. George Lohr, Margaret m. George Aderholt.

Land Holdings and Transactions:

Burke County NC Land Entries #1167, p. 384. "George David and Daniel Lutes, 400 acres on Pinch Gut Creek and improvements formerly belonging to George Lutes, deceased, now occupied by John Hosillbarger, for complement. Ent. 11 Dec 1778 Warrant issued - from Huggins, Edith. Burke County Records Vol. I p108.

Census Locations:

1790 Lincoln County, North Carolina 4th Company
1800 Lincoln County, North Carolina

References:
US National Archives. Revolutionary War Pension Statements of Casper Bolick (W18566), Beal Baker (W5212), Elias Baker (W5773), Jacob Typs (R10616), and Adam Setzer (R9389).
NC Revolutionary Army Accounts. (1) Book "A", p. 228, #54. (2) Vol XII, Bk. 6, Part XI, p. 1935. (3) Vol. XII, Bk 7,   part XI, p. 3252. (4) Vol. I, Bk w, Folio 8, #135. (5) Vol. I, Bk 5, folio 38, #1934.
Huggins, Edith. Burke County Miscellaneous Data in 4 volumes.
 McAllister, Anne W. and Sullivan, Kathy G. "Lincoln County NC Court of Pleas and Quarter Sessions. 1789-1796. 1987 copy, p. 54.
AIS Census data. 1700-1800. NC
Yoder, Colonel George M. "A Condensed History of the Early Settlers of the Catawba Valley". C. 1890. Copy in Catawba County Library, Newton NC.

Hennessee, Patrick

Summary of Early Life:

Patrick Hennessee was of Irish descent and came into western North Carolina in the 1760's. He was closely associated in land affairs with Colonel Charles McDowell. There is record of a Crown grant issued to Hennessee in 1775 (Feb.) in Tryon County, North Carolina, on a tributary of Green River.

Summary of Partisan Activity:

After the conclusion of the Revolutionary War, Patrick Hennessee received monetary compensation for services rendered during the war. This is verified by the North Carolina Revolutionary Army Accounts, Vol. VII. The compensations were in form of certificates. In explanation, it states that the compensation was for "militia pay and for supplies furnished to the militia and continental troops".

In a 1783 land entry by Colonel Charles McDowell on behalf of General Rutherford, located on Ream's Creek in Buncombe County, mention is made of "Patrick Hennessee's Camp". Other references to camps in this time period refers to encampments made by militia Captains on various Indian campaigns. No further proof at this time.

Summary of Later Life:

Patrick Hennessee was active in Burke County affairs until his death, which occurred prior to October 1796, the date of his will probate. Between 1783 and 1789, he served on various juries and was involved in several minor court cases.

According to family historian Allen R. Hennessee, he had two sons, James and John Hennessee. James (1766-1851) married.. Sally Welcher. They migrated to Warren County, Tennessee ca 1810. John (d. 1844) m. Elizabeth Sumter. John Hennessee's son Patrick Hennessee (1793-1845) married Nancy

Sudderth (1799-1889). They had eleven children. Most of the Burke County Hennessees stem from this union.

Land Holdings and Transactions:

1. Burke County NC 300 acres south side Catawba River adjacent to land belonging to John Deal, John Carswell, John Ballew. The property included bottom land known as "Allen's Bottom". Ent. Jan 28, 1778 No. 185 Grant #226 iss. Nov. 14, 1780 Bk. 28, p. 225. cc John Ballew; Joseph Ballew. The above tract was just below mouth of Hunting Creek "whair on said Hensey lives".
2. Burke County NC 150 acres south side Catawba River including Lockhart's improvements and which lay adjacent to land belonging to John Ballew, Abraham Harshaw and to his own lines. Ent. 2 Oct 1778 #292 Grant #267 Iss. Mar. 14, 1780 Bk. 28, p. 266. cc John Ballew, Allen Leavander.
3. Burke County NC 274 acres north side Catawba River including mouth of Lower Creek. It included improvements made by Dimion Baker and was known as Allen's Place. The land lay adjacent to that of Thomas Welcher, John Franklin; Ent. 11 Dec 1778 #1015 Grant no. 320 Iss. 28 Oct. 1782 Bk. 44 p. 114 cc Joseph Rogers; John Hennessee.
4. Crown Grant Tryon County NC 28 Feb 1775 200 acres on South Fork of White Creek, a tributary of Green River. Patent Book 26 #9053, p. 209.

Census Locations:

1790 Burke County, North Carolina

References:
Hennessee, Allen R. Article in Heritage of Burke County NC Vol. I (1981 ed. pp. 225-226).
Land Grant Data. Burke County Library, Morganton, NC.
AIS 1790 Census NC.
NC Revolutionary Army Accounts as presented by Haun, Wynette P. Durham, NC (1994) Part V, p. 627. (from Vol. VII Book G-16, p. 65, Revolutionary Army Accounts).

Huggins, Edith W. Burke County NC Records Vol. I-IV. Multiple Listings.
Hofmann, Margaret M. <u>Colony of NC 1765-1775 Abstracts of Land Patents</u>.
     Vol. II, 1984 ed.

Hewey, John (Hughey)

Summary of Early Life:

The North Carolina Revolutionary Army accounts state that continental soldier John Hewey was from "Burke County". He may have been related to Samuel and Elizabeth Hewey of the John's River area of Burke County.

Summary of Partisan Activity:

Revolutionary Army Accounts confirm John Hewey as a continental soldier. Another Revolutionary Army account states that he was an express rider.

References:
Roster of Soldiers from North Carolina in the American Revolution. (NC
    DAR) Reprint of orig. 1932 ed. GPC, p. 345.
NC Revolutionary Army Accounts. Vol. X, Part VIII, p. 99, folio 4, #4392.

Hinds, John

Summary of Early Life:

John Hinds and family were living on Blair's Fork in Burke County, North Carolina during the American Revolution (now Caldwell County). DAR data gives an earlier residence in Randolph County, North Carolina. (A Joseph Hinds of Guilford County, NC died 1812 in Knox County, Tennessee, may have been related ... father?).

Summary of Partisan Activity:

The North Carolina Revolutionary Army Accounts definitely confirm John Hinds as being a Captain of militia in Morgan District. He most likely served in the Burke militia, as he is grouped with other Burke County Captains (Captains Thomas Kennedy, Henry Highland, Alex Erwin, George Penland, et al).

Earlier Revolutionary Army accounts also show him as a member of the North Carolina Continental Line, residing in Burke County (? earlier service in Randolph County?).

Summary of Later Life:

Following the end of the Revolutionary War, John Hinds was active in Burke County affairs. He served on several juries and was elected a constable on at least two occasions. About 1800-1807, John Hinds began to sell his land and make other legal changes. This, in most likelihood, represents the time of his move to East Tennessee, Knox County. His son, Silvenus and other family members, had earlier received a large grant of land in Knox County and were residing there.

John Hinds, after moving to Knox County, died in late 1810. (His Last Will and Testament was in August 1810, proved in Knox County court in Jan. session 1811).

John Hinds was married to (?) Mary (?) Nancy, and they

had the following children:

Silvenus	Levi
Hannah m. Newport	Susannah m. Newport
John	Simeon
Abigail	Asa
Joseph	

Land Holdings and Transactions:

1. Burke County NC 100 acres on Blair's Fork of Lower Creek beginning at Tinker's Path. cc William Bowman, John Bowman. Ent. 16 Jan 1779 #865 Grant # 1425 Iss. 4 Jan 1792 Bk. 75 p. 422.
2. Burke County NC 100 acres on Warrior Gap of Blair's Fork. The land was near the head of North Fork of Blair's Creek. cc Josiah Mason; Silvenus Hinds. Ent. 23 Jul 1780 #80 Grant No. 1591 Iss. 27 Nov 1792. Bk. 80 p. 52.
3. Burke County NC 100 acres on Blair's Fork adjacent to his own survey. cc Josiah Mason; Silvaneus Hinds. Ent. 16 Jan 1779 #865 Grant # 1599 Iss. 27 Nov. 1792. Bk. 80 p. 55.
4. Knox County TN. In his will, John Hinds describes land holdings on East Fork of Whit's Creek (200 acres, formerly belonging to his son, Levi). He also describes property on Wolf River. These tracts were all in the Tennessee River Valley (now Roane County, TN).
5. Burke County NC court records show John Hinds as selling the following:
    a. 200 acres to John Pacely (Nov. 1799)
    b. 450 acres to Abraham Suddreth (1801)
   On 7 Nov 1800, he gave power of attorney to Jacob Baldins (Baldwin).

Census Locations:

1790 Burke County, North Carolina 9th Company

References:

North Carolina Revolutionary Army Accounts. Dept. Archives And History.
    Raleigh NC. Book "A" Accounts paid in Salisbury District Nov. 1781,
    p. 224 #6957, Book "A" p. 224, #36, Cast 1782 (for himself and
    payrolls).
NC DAR. Roster of Soldiers from North Carolina in the American Revolution.
    GPC 1967 ed., p. 345.
Johnson, William Hinds. Castle Dr. Chattanooga, Tennessee. Conversations
    with author 1959-1960.
Knox County Tennessee Records. Last Will and Testament of John Hinds, with
    codicil. Aug. 25, 1810. Proved Knox County Court. Jan. session
    1811.
AIS Census Data North Carolina 1790.
Huggins, Edith W. Burke Records (SHP) Vol. II, p. 138. Vol. IV, pp. 30, 34,
    138.
Burke County Land Grant Data. Burke County Library, Morganton, NC.
Marsh, Helen C. Roster of Soldiers and Patriots of the American Revolution
    Buried in Tennessee. 1974 TN DAR. p. 84.
Burke County NC "Minutes of Court of Pleas and Quarter Sessions".
    1791-95, 1795-98, 1799-1803. ed. by Dan Swink, multiple entries.

Holmes, Robert

Summary of Early Life:

During the Revolutionary War, Robert Holmes was living in what is now Alexander County, North Carolina, then a part of Burke County. His borderline home location brought his into contact with Surry, Wilkes and Rowan militia units, as well as Burke.

Summary of Partisan Activity:

Robert Holmes was appointed as a member of the Rowan County, North Carolina Committee of Safety 20 Aug 1775. Robert Holmes was commissioned a Captain early in the war and served with Colonel Hambright during the 1776 unsuccessful siege of Charleston, South Carolina by the British. In 1780, his company fought against the Tory Partisan Colonel Samuel Bryan at Hanging Rock (Aug 6, 1780). This was probably with the Surry and Rowan militia. In 1780 and 1781, troops under his command fought at Kings Mountain (7 Oct 1780) and Cowpens (17 Jan 1781), and Cornwallis' crossing of the Catawba (Feb 1781).

In 1781, Holmes became a field officer of Burke militia with the rank of Lieutenant Colonel, most likely succeeding Lieutenant Colonel High Brevard, who had died of smallpox. He remained active for the remainder of the war, being engaged against local Tories.

Summary of Later Life:

At this time, the author is not certain of the details of Colonel Holmes later life.
A Robert Holmes, Sr. died in Oglethorpe County, Georgia, his will probated 1816. Mentioned are a daughter, Jane Walder and additional heirs: John Holmes, Joseph Walker, Robert Holmes, Jr., Samuel Patton and William Holmes. Mentioned also is 5000 acres of granted land in Tennessee. Interestingly, there were neighbors of Colonel Holmes from Wilkes County, North

Carolina in Oglethorpe County (Combs family).

Land Holdings and Transactions:

1. Burke County NC 100 acres on Walker branch lower Little River (now Alexander County) adjacent to land of Isaac Elledge, Patrick Sloan. cc Adam Holt, Patrick Sloan. Ent. 28 Feb 1778 #310 Grant n. 1003. Iss. 7 Aug 1787. Book. 65, p. 385.
2. Burke County NC 365 acres on Lambert's Fork and John's Fork of Lower Little River. Entry states "being the place wherein he now lives". The land lay adjacent to that of Patrick Sloan, George Brown, Simon Walker and to his own land. cc Adam Holt, Patrick Sloan. Ent. 10 Sep 1778 #69 Grant no. 508 Iss. 28 Dec 1782, Book 44, p. 233.

References:
US National Archives Revolutionary War Pension statements:
  Lytle, Thomas S3873 (Charleston)
  Boyd, Thomas (Hanging Rock)
  Forbis, John W25591 (Kings Mountain, Cowpens)
  Rainbolt, Adam S32446 (Cowpens)
  Smith, William S7536 (Lincoln Co Tories)
  Smith, John S1931 (Tories)
  Chapman, John W18895 (Rowan militia)
  Reed, Robert W22054 (Charleston)
  Steele, Samuel S17123 (Charleston)
  Ford, Peter See Bowman, S. (Charleston) S6678.
Land Grant data Burke County Library, Morganton, NC.
Smith, Sarah. "Abstracts of Oglethorpe County, Georgia Wills". Washington, Georgia. 1962. p. 30.
Wheeler, John H. Historical Sketches of North Carolina. Regional Publishing Co., Baltimore 1964 reprint of 1851 ed., p. 368.

Holt, Peter

Summary of Early Life:

Peter Holt, a well known established land owner, resided in the Zack's Fork area, now Caldwell County. His land lay mainly within Burke County during the American Revolution. Peter Holt may well have been related to the Holts of Alamance County. It is quite possible that he may have had connections to the Regulator movement of central North Carolina (1765-1771). Many former regulators moved into the Lower Creek area just prior to the Revolution. Regulator names include Husbands, (Von) Cannon, Clarke, Murray, Baldwin and others.

Summary of Partisan Activity:

Peter Holt was a Loyalist during the Revolutionary period. In Lieutenant Anthony Allaire's (a captured British officer) diary, telling of the route taken by the Kings Mountain soldiers after the battle of October 7, 1780, he states on Oct. 17, 1780, "moved at eight o'clock in the morning – marched fifteen miles; halted at Captain Hatt's plantation…" The historian Draper, in his book Kings Mountain and Its Heroes, says that the "Hatt" in Allaire's diary was either "Holt or Hall". It appears to have been Holt, since the error in handwriting interpretations is repeated in the 1790 census. In the 1790 census, there is a question - it refers to Peter Holt, but is spelled "Hott" – in other words the interpreter had crossed the "l" and the "t" in both instances.

During the course of the conflict, Holt was captured by soldiers of the Wilkes militia, commanded by Captain William Lenoir. Details of his capture were given by Patriot soldier George Parks in his pension application. During late 1782, Peter Holt was subpoenaed to appear in Burke County Court to show cause as to why his property should not be confiscated, for being disloyal to the American cause. Witnesses in the case included Major Joseph White, John Mackey and James Blair.

The court actions were never completed, due to the

conclusion of the Revolutionary War a few months later, and eventual amnesty.

Summary of Later Life:

In the 1790 census, Holt is listed as having in his household – five females and four males. A Jacob Holt also listed. Chain carriers John and Joel Holt listed on grant records.

Peter Holt was very active in Burke County civic affairs after the Revolutionary War and extending into the early 1800's. He appeared often as a juryman and served in several civil capacities.

Peter Holt died ca 1816, the date of his will probate.

Land Holdings and Transactions:

1. 300 acres Burke County NC on Lower Creek, Zack's Fork – entry states"…including ye improvements sd. Holted now libes on…", adjacent to "step's line". cc (Peter Ford, John Cothran). Ent. 5 June 1778, #265, Grant No. 35, Iss. Dec. 10, 1778. Book 28, p. 35.
2. 300 acres Burke County NC on Warriors Gap Branch adjacent to land belonging to Reuben Coffey, Jr. and Soloman Smith, and also adjacent to his own line. Ent 29 Sep 1798, #3444, Grant No. 2670, Iss. 6 Dec 1799. Book 107, p. 50. cc (Joel Holt, John Holt).

Census Locations:

1790 Burke County, North Carolina 9th Company

References:
Huggins, Edith W. Miscellaneous Burke County NC Records in 4 soft back volumes (SHP) Vol. II.
Draper, Lyman E. Kings Mountain and Its Heroes. GPC reprint of original 1881 ed. p, 350. (1997).
AIS Census data NC. 1790, 1800, 1810.
Land Grant Data Burke County NC Library, Morganton, NC.

Diary of Lieutenant Anthony Allaire of Ferguson's Corps is given in Draper, above, p. 511.

Parks, George. US National Archives Pension Statements. #W27457. (also see Vol. II, this work, p. 241).

Hood, Morgan

Summary of Early Life:

Morgan Hood was born in Prince William County, Virginia ca 1764. At the time of the American Revolution, he was residing in Burke County, North Carolina.

Summary of Partisan Activity:

Morgan Hood first entered military service in Burke County, North Carolina as a substitute militiaman in the place of Dick Bell. He served a two-month tour of duty on the Catawba frontier in Captain William Johnson's Company of Lieutenant Colonel William Wofford's command. He was stationed at Wofford's Fort on the North Catawba River. In view of his age, this was probably in the early 1780's, though a date is not given.

He served another two-month term as a drafted militiaman and was again stationed on the Catawba frontier – at Rutherford's Station.

His third and last tour of duty was again as a substitute militiaman (for Samuel Wells). He served for three months under Captain Daugherty and Major Joseph McDowell. This was a punitive Indian raid, most likely the spring of 1782 action headed by Major McDowell.

Summary of Later Life:

After the Revolution, Morgan Hood moved to Ninety-Six District South Carolina, Pendleton County. 1790 South Carolina census records show him with one male and three females – presumably his wife and three children. He remained nine years in Pendleton County and then moved to Laurens County, South Carolina where he lived for about seven years. Hood and his family then moved to Dickson County, Tennessee.

Morgan Hood applied for Revolutionary War pension on

Jan 9, 1833 and was then 69 years of age. He was awarded a pension in the amount of $23.33 per annum.

Census Locations:

1790 Ninety-Six District, Pendleton County, South Carolina
1800 Pendleton District, South Carolina
1820 Dickson County, Tennessee

References:
US National Archives, Pension Data, #S4389.
AIS Census Records (SC,TN).

Hood, Thomas

Thomas Hood was born in Halifax County, Virginia in 1762. He was the son of John Hood and a nephew of John Chapman. The family moved to Burke County, North Carolina ca 1764 when Hood was two years old. The Hoods lived in the Little River section of Burke County, later Alexander County.

Summary of Partisan Activity:

Thomas Hood first entered military service in Burke County, North Carolina as a volunteer militiaman for a tour of four months. He served in Captain William Reed's company in a regiment commanded by Lieutenant Colonel Robert Holmes. Other officers were Lieutenant James McKnight and Ensign Joshua Freeman. He was marched to a fort near Johns River. Hood, in his pension statements, described an encounter with the Indians in which he was shot through the foot. He killed one Indian and than made his way back to the fort. His next tour was in September 1781. He served as a substitute for his father, John Hood. He was placed in a company commanded by Captain Charles Forrester of Holmes' regiment and marched to the fort at head of Johns River (probably White's Fort). Lieutenant Colonel Holmes left to take part in Rutherford's Wilmington Expedition. Major (Leroy) Taylor was left in command. The tour lasted three months.

His last tour of duty was in a company commanded by Captain William Morrison, along with Lieutenant Richard Brown and Ensign George Brown. The company served in the same area, under Major Taylor. There were several skirmishes with the Indians. This tour of duty began in February 1782 and lasted three months.

Summary of Later Life:

After the Revolution, Thomas Hood moved to Pendleton District, South Carolina and still later to Greenville District, South Carolina. He moved from South Carolina to Tennessee, Roane

County. From Roane County he moved to Jackson County, Tenn.

Hood had been living in Jackson County for about 14 years when he applied for Revolutionary pension on November 12, 1834. He was awarded a pension in the amount of $30.00 per anum.

Census Locations:

1790 Ninety Six District; Pendleton County SC
1800 Pendleton District, SC (another Thomas Hood in Laurens
     District)
1830 White Company, TN (?) adjacent to Jackson County

References:
US National Archives, Pension Data, #S21289.
AIS Census Records (SC,TN) 1790 & 1800.
Sistler, Byron. Evansville, IN 1971, 1830 TN census.

Hudson, Daniel

Summary of Early Life:

According to family records, Daniel Hudson was born in Virginia ca 1750 (possibly a little earlier). In 1767 he received a Crown Grant for 200 acres of land on Indian Creek in Tryon, later Lincoln County, North Carolina. Sometime at the beginning of the Revolutionary War, he had settled on Camp's Fork of Jacob's Fork in Burke County, later Lincoln and then Catawba County, North Carolina.

Summary of Partisan Activity:

In late 1782, Daniel Hudson was cited to Burke County, North Carolina Court on grounds of being a suspected Tory and subject to property confiscation. The case was never resolved as peace was declared a few months later in April 1783. Amnesty was also administered the same month. Sworn witnesses included Major Daniel McKissick, Captain Henry Whitener and others.

Summary of Later Life:

Daniel Hudson was married and had at least five children – Daniel Hudson, Jr., John Hudson, Alexander Hudson, Ruth and Jane Hudson. Daniel Hudson died in 1811. Daniel Hudson, Jr. (1775-1847) married Catherine Gross. They were the progenitors of many of the Hudson kin in Lincoln, Catawba, and Burke Counties in North Carolina.

Land Holdings and Transactions:

1. 250 acres Burke County, NC on Camp's Fork, a tributary of Jacob's Fork of South Fork on Catawba River. The plot includes the mouth of Camp Creek as it enters Jacob's Fork (on North side). Entry data states, "including the improvements said Hutson now lives on…" Ent. 29 Jan 1779 #1371 Grant No. 638 Iss. Oct 11, 1783, Book 50, p. 235.

2. Tryon County, North Carolina (William Tryon, Governor). Crown Grant #7122 (Bk. 23) in Tryon County, North Carolina 200 acres on both sides of Indian Creek, above the "scout camps", adjacent to land of Peter Johnston. 22 Dec 1768. This land later appears in Lincoln County Land Records.

Census Locations:

1790 Lincoln County, NC 4th Company (4 females, 5 males)
1800 Lincoln County, North Carolina
1810 Lincoln County, North Carolina (Daniel Hudson, Jr.)

References:
AIS Census (NC) 1790, 1800, 1810.
Burke County, NC Heritage Vol. I. Morganton, NC 1981, Articles by Mavis Hudson Fortenberry and Myrtle Hudson Hoyle. pp. 244-246.
Burke County NC Land Grant Data. Burke County Public Library, Morganton, NC.
Hofmann, Margaret M. Colony of North Carolina 1765-1775 Abstracts of Land Patents. Weldon, North Carolina 1984, p. 535.
Morgan, Zelma. Swannanoa, NC. Data on Hudson Family Vertical Files, Burke County Library, Morganton, NC, 1984.

Hulse, Jesse

Summary of Early Life:

The pre-Revolutionary domicile of Jesse Hulse is not definitely known. There was a supporting statement in a petition declaration from one Exum Franklin, a former resident of Anson County, North Carolina. He stated that he had known Hulse "since infancy".

Summary of Partisan Activity:

In 1781, Jesse Hulse was serving a tour of duty on the Western Carolina frontier at Wofford's Fort (then Burke County, now McDowell). He was in a militia company commanded by Captain William Johnson of Colonel Charles McDowell's Burke Regiment. During an Indian attack, Hulse received a severe disabling wound of the left arm. He stated that the "bone between the shoulder and elbow is gone".

Summary of Later Life:

After the Revolution, Hulse moved to Hall County, Georgia. A kinsman, Charles Hulse also moved there. On petitioning the North Carolina Legislature (1824) for financial relief, Hulse stated he had a wife and seven children, and that he was old and poor. Captain William Johnson had certified in 1795 that Hulse was a soldier under his command in 1781. There were supporting statements by former Revolutionary War soldiers, Jesse Moore of Burke County, North Carolina, Charles Hulse and Exum D. Franklin.

It was recommended that Hulse be awarded an annual sum of $50.00 per life.

Census Locations:

1820 Hall County, Georgia
1830 Hall County, Georgia

References:

Linn, Jo White. Abstracts from Delamar Transcripts. Revolutionary War
    Claims. NC Genealogical Journal Vol. III. No. 4, Nov 1977, p. 225.
AIS Census Indices. NC 1790; Georgia 1820, 1830.

Hyatt, Hezekiah

Summary of Early Life:

Hezekiah Hyatt was the son of Seth Hyatt, Sr. and Priscilla Hyatt and a brother of Seth Hyatt, Jr. They originally were in Ann Arundel County, Maryland and later settled in western Burke County near Shadrick's Creek, a tributary of the Catawba River.

Summary of Partisan Activity:

Hezekiah Hyatt was a Loyalist, as well as numerous members of several associated families in the same area. (Hodge, Inman, Wilson, McPeters, Young)

In November 1782 his name appears on the Burke County court docket as a suspected Tory. His land was subject to confiscation if convicted. No disposition of case, as hostilities with Great Britain ceased a few months later in April 1783, and amnesty declared.

Summary of Later Life:

Hezekiah Hyatt continued to live in Burke County, North Carolina following the Revolutionary War. In the 1790 census he is listed along with six females and three males, presumably wife and children. His name appears in public records numerous times on past the turn of the century – road juries, court juries, inspection teams and the like. His name appears on census schedules through 1810. Numerous persons named Hyatt settled after the turn of the century in Buncombe and Haywood Counties, most likely his progeny. Hezekiah Hyatt died prior to April 1820, the date of his estate probate. Thomas Young, executor.

Land Holdings and Transactions:

1. 202 acres Burke County, NC on both sides of main Catawba River bounded by John Doty on the West side, by Thomas Young on the South side. The property lay about

161

25 poles above tract owned by Captain William Moore. cc (Thomas Young, Seth Hyatt). Ent. 9 Oct 1778 #342 Grant No. 60 Issued 20 Sep 1779. Book 28, p. 60.

2. 100 acres Burke County, NC on Shadrick's Creek, a tributary of Catawba River on South side. The land lay just above that of Thomas Young. cc (Thomas Young, Boyce----.). Ent. 9 Oct. 1778 #45 Grant No. 762 Iss. Oct 1783. Book 50, p. 268 (?).

Census Locations:

1790 Burke County, North Carolina 6th Company
1800 Burke County, North Carolina
1810 Burke County, North Carolina

References:
AIS Census and Census Indices (1790, 1800, 1810).
Swink, Dan D. "Burke County NC Minutes of the Court of Pleas And Quarter Sessions". (1791-1795) and (1795-1798) Lawndale, NC. 1986,1987.
Huggins, Edith W. Burke County Records. Vol. I-IV.
Land Grant Data; Burke County Public Library, Morganton, NC.
Young, Penny: "The Hyatt Family". Vertical Files, Burke County Library, Morganton, NC.
"Burke County NC Surviving Will and Probate Abstracts 1777-1910". M. S. Philbeck, G. Turner. 1983, p, 278.

Hyatt, Seth

Summary of Early Life:

From family data, it appears that Seth Hyatt was the son of Seth Hyatt, Sr. and Priscilla Hyatt, and a brother of Hezekiah Hyatt. They Hyatt's were earlier from Ann Arundel County, Maryland, and were closely related to the Inman and Birchfield families of Burke County. They resided in western Burke County on the Catawba River near Shadrick's Creek.

Summary of Partisan Activity:

Seth Hyatt was an active Loyalist during the Revolutionary War. Later in the war he was captured and his gun taken from him. Colonel Charles McDowell then "sentenced" Hyatt to the duty on the Western Burke Frontier, guarding against the incursions of the Cherokee Indians. This data was brought out in the court martial proceedings against Colonel McDowell in early 1782. In late 1782, Hyatt's name was placed on the Tory docket. This related to the Confiscation Acts of the North Carolina Legislature.

Summary of Later Events:

By the time the Tory docket was brought out, Seth Hyatt was dead. The nature of his demise is unknown. Administrative court proceedings were started on October 24, 1782. Ruth Hyatt, administrator with Greenberry Wilson, who was later to move to Tennessee. A child, Jemima Hyatt was listed. The estate settlement was still in progress as of April 1795.

References:
Young, Penny. "The Hyatt Family". Vertical files, Burke County Library, Morganton, NC.
Huggins, Edith W. Burke County records Vol. II, pp.154c: 166.
Swink, Dan D. Burke County Minutes of the Court of Pleas and Quarter Sessions (1791-1795). (Lawndale 1986) p. 43.

Icard, George

Summary of Early Life:

George Icard was born ca 1759, the son of Peter Icard, Sr. and Susannah Icard. Peter Icard lived on a large tract of land between Pinch Gut Creek and Bill's Creek, now Catawba County, North Carolina. His son George inherited a portion of the land on the death of his father ca 1784. George Icard was a brother of Peter Icard, Jr., Lawerence, Henry, Susanna, and Philip Icard. During the Revolutionary War, their property lay within Burke County, later Lincoln County, North Carolina.

Summary of Partisan Activity:

In late 1782, George Icard's name appeared on a subpoena docket of suspected Tories. They were to appear in court and show cause as to why their property should not be confiscated, for being disloyal to the America Cause.

The outcomes of these actions were mainly undetermined, as the American Revolution came to an end only a few months later. Amnesty was granted by the North Carolina Legislature simultaneously.

George Icard, undoubtedly performed patriotic services, also as he was to receive some reimbursement for Revolutionary War services later.

Summary of Later Life:

George Icard was married to Barbara Fry. They had land on HopCreek (now Catawba County NC) willed to them by Nicholas Fry, Sr.

Land Holdings and Transactions:

1. Lincoln County NC, Feb. 11, 1786. Philip and Elizabeth Fry, executors of Nicholas Fry, dec. to George Icard 240

164

acres in Lincoln County on both sides Hop Creek, formerly part of a Crown Grant to Nicholas Fry, Sr. Bk 3, p. 24. Bk. 14, p. 6.

Ceusus Locations:

1790 Lincoln County, North Carolina 4th Company

References:
Huggins, Edith W. Burke County Records Vol. II (Tory Docket).
AIS Census Data. NC 1790.
Haun, Weynette P. Revolutionary Army Accounts Part XI, 1999, p. 1439.
Robinson, Ward. Articles in Catawba County Heritage Vol. I, 1986, p. 241, and
        in special supplement in Hickory Daily Record, Apr 28, 1993.
Ricketts, Mae Sherman. Article in Catawba County Heritage, 1986, pp. 146-7.

Icard, Henry

Summary of Early Life:

Henry Icard was born ca 1761 (another source says 1756), the son of Peter and Susannah Icard. He was a brother of Peter Icard, Jr., George, Philip, and Lawerence Icard. The Icards were early settlers of the Catawba Valley. The area in which they lived was part of Burke County during the Revolutionary War, later Lincoln County and now Catawba County, North Carolina.

Summary of Partisan Activity:

The North Carolina Revolutionary Army Accounts verify the service of Henry Icard as a militiaman in Morgan District. The area in which he lived was in Burke County during most of the Revolutionary War. The regimental Commander was Colonel Charles McDowell of Burke County. Morgan District was created in 1782, near the end of the Revolutionary period.

Land Holdings and Transactions:

1. Lincoln County, NC. Apr 9, 1788. Received from Peter Iker (Jr.) 175 acres on waters of Clark's Creek, previously owned by Peter Iker, Sr. Bk. 3, p. 406. Bk. 15, p. 87. (This was part of a 508 acre tract, willed to Henry Icard by his father, Peter Icard, Sr.) The land was acquired by Peter Icard, Sr. in 1762,

Census Locations:

1790 Lincoln County, North Carolina 3rd Company
1800 Lincoln County, North Carolina

References:
NC Revolutionary Army Accounts. #4442 as quoted in Roster of North Carolina Soldiers in the American Revolution. NC DAR reprint of 1932 ed. (GPC), p. 393.
Hickory Daily Record. April 28, 1993 ed. article by Rena Ikard Robinson and Mr. and Mrs. Ward Robinson.

Heritage of Catawba County North Carolina. 1986 ed. Article by Ward
Robinson, p. 241.
AIS Census Data 1790 NC.
Pruitt, Dr. R. B. "Abstracts of Deeds. Lincoln County, NC. 1786-1793".
(1988), p. 43.
Patriot Index. National Society DAR. Washington, DC. 1966 ed., p. 360.

Icard, Peter (Ikerd, Ikard, Eiger (t), etc.)

Summary of Early Life:

Peter Icard was born ca 1750, in Pennsylvania. His family had immigrated earlier to America from the Rhenish Palatinate region of Germany. The Icards, along with the Haas family, were early settlers of the trans-Catawba area, now Catawba County. During most of the American Revolution, it lay within Rowan County, and Burke County, later Lincoln County. Peter Icard was the son of Peter and Susannah Icard and a brother of George, Lawerence, Henry, Phillip, and Susanna Icard.

Summary of Partisan Activity:

During the early phases of the American Revolution, Peter Icard served in the 2nd Rowan Regiment of militia, Colonel Christopher Beekman and Lieutenant Colonel Charles McDowell commanding.

In March of 1776, he took part in the Cross Creek Expedition. This was the later phase of the Moore's Creek Bridge battle. Their duties mainly were to mop-up activities following the battle (confiscating property, conveying prisoners, etc.). The Revolutionary Army accounts verify this participation by Icard as well as some later patriotic activity.

Summary of Later Life:

Peter Icard married Mary Shuford. There were the following children:

John 1771-1855 m. Margaret Smith
Barbara b. 1773 m. William Oxford
Chastity b. 1773 m. Moses Bumgarner
George 1779-1849 m. Polly Boovey
Mary M. 1775-1841 m. Elias Bost
Catherine 1783-1857 m. William Bost, Jr.
Jacob b. 1786 m. Catherine Cressnore

Peter Icard took part in Lincoln County civic affairs during the 1790's. He served on various juries and was involved in several civil suits.

His son John moved to Lawerence County, Indiana ca 1816. Peter Icard, according the one source, moved also to Lawrence County, Indiana and died there ca 1820-1830. He is said to be buried in the Ikerd cemetery near Bedford, Indiana.

Land Holdings and Transactions:

Peter Icards father, Peter Icard, Sr. had acquired a rather large tract of land near Pinch Gut Creek, now Catawba County, North Carolina in 1762 (Rowan deed).

Some of this land was conveyed to Peter Icard, Jr. via will on the death of his father ca 1784. During the late 1780's, Peter Icard, Jr. began to sell some of his property.

1. Lincoln County NC. Peter Iker to Lawerence Iker 175 acres, part of a large tract that belonged to their father, Peter Iker, Sr. Apr. 7, 1788 on Clark's Creek. Bk. 3, p. 385; 15, p. 63.
2. Lincoln County, NC. Peter Iker to Henry Iker. 175 acres, part of a large tract that belonged to his father, Peter Iker, Sr. on waters of Clark's Creek. Apr 9, 1788. Bk. 3, p. 406; Bk. 15, p. 87.

Census Locations:

1790 Lincoln County, North Carolina
1800 Lincoln County, North Carolina

References:
Ricketts, Mae Sherman. Article in Catawba County NC Heritage Vol. I, 1986 ed. pp. 146-147.
Robinson, Ward R. Article in Catawba County NC Heritage Vol. I, 1986 ed. p. 241.
Pruett, Dr. R. B. "Abstracts of Deeds Lincoln County NC, 1786-1793, 1988. #323 and #308.

AIS Census data NC 1790, 1800.

McAllister, Anne W. and Sullivan, Kathy G. "Civil Action Pages 1771-1806". Lincoln County NC, 1989 ed.

McAllister, Anne W. and Sullivan, Kathy G. Lincoln County NC Court of Pleas and Quarter Sessions. 1789-1796. 1987 ed.

Bourgeois, Mildred Ikard. "For A Better Life". 1995. pp. 19-20.

Hickory Daily Record Scrapbook Edition. April 28, 1993 on Icard Family (Rena Icard Robinson, Mr. And Mrs. Ward Robinson). Copy in Beaver Library, Hickory, NC.

Haun, Weynette Parks. NC Revolutionary Army Accounts, Part I, p. 5. (Cross Creek Exp.) Part XI, p. 1439. Durham, NC. 1989 and 1999 eds.

Linn, Jo White. <u>Abstracts of the Deeds of Rowan County NC</u>, (1983) p. 46.

Inman, Abednigo

Summary of Early Life:

Abednigo Inman was the son of Ezekial and Hannah Hardee Inman. The family settled in western Burke County (now McDowell County NC) during the Revolutionary period. They had lived earlier in Virginia. Abednigo Inman, according to DAR records was born (in England?) on July 1, 1752. A brother, Shadrach Inman, was a Burke County Loyalist (see Vol. II).

Summary of Partisan Activity:

Abednigo Inman served as a militiman in North Carolina, Watauga and Georgia. Under the command of Colonel John Sevier, Inman participated in the Kings Mountain Campaign and battle (Oct. 7, 1780). During this battle, Inman was wounded. Inman also took part in activities against the Cherokee Indians, then allies of the British.

Summary of Later Life;

Abednigo Inman was married to Mary Ritchie (1757-1836) daughter of Alexander Ritchie. Children were:

William b. 1779 m. Eleanor Wilson
Hannah b. 1782 m. (1) Daniel Wilson (2) Jacob Seahorn
Jean b. 1784 m. LeRoy Taylot
Ezekial b. 1786 m. Matilda Taylor
John b. 1788 m. Jane Walker
Benjamin b. 1790 m. Dorcas Dougherty
Shadrack b. 1793 m. Sarah Henderson
Mary b. 1795 m. John Baer
Annis W. b. 1797 m. Joel Cowan
Savannah b. 1800
Margaret b. 1805 m. Jonathan Wood

Sometime near the end of the Revolutionary War Abednigo Inman moved to Jefferson County, Tennessee, where he had received a land grant. He continued to live in Jefferson County until his death on February 2, 1831, age 79. His wife died in 1836.

Abednigo Inman is buried in an old graveyard near the court house in Danbridge, Tennessee, marked by the DAR.

Land Holdings and Transactions:

1. Burke County NC 100 acres on Catawba River above mouth of Hodges' Mill Creek. The property included his improvements. The land lay adjacent to that of Michael Montgomery, Daniel Russell, Charles McPeters, John Montgomery. Most of the land was on North side Catawba, some on South side. cc John Montgomery, Sr. and Jr. Ent. 9 Oct 1778 #436 Grant no. 89 Iss. 20 Sept. 1779 Bk. 28 p. 89.
   (There were also several entries made by Abednigo Inman in Burke County (North Cove area – no grants).

Census Locations:

1800 Jefferson County, Tennessee (tax list)
1822 Jefferson County, Tennessee (tax list)
1830 Jefferson County, Tennessee

References:
Bates, Lucy and Marsh, Helen. "Roster of Soldiers and Patriots of The American Revolution Buried in Tennessee". TN DAR, 1979 ed. p. 90.
Huggins, Edith W. Miscellaneous Burke Records in four soft back volumes. SHP
Burke County Land Grant Data. Burke County Library, Morganton NC.
AIS Census Data. 1790 NC.
NC Revolutionary Army Accounts. Vol. I, Bk. 3, p. 28, as given in Haun, Wynette P. NC Revolutionary Army Accounts. Secretary of State Part II, Durham, NC 1990. p. 213.
White, Katherine Keogh. The Kings Mountain Men. GPC 1970. ed. pp/ 191-192.
Sistler, Byron and Barbara. Early Tennessee Tax Lists. 1977 ed., p. 103.
Sistler, Byron and Associates. 1830 Census East Tennessee. 1969, ed., p. 98.

Isom, Christian

Summary of Early Life:

Christian Isom and his family, at the time of the American Revolution, were living on John's River in Burke County, North Carolina. They were close neighbors of Colonel Joseph McDowell of Quaker Meadows.

Summary of Partisan Activity:

In December 1782, the name of Christian Isom appeared on a subpoena list of suspected Tories. He was to show cause as to why his property should not be confiscated, for being opposed to the American cause. These cases never were concluded, as the Revolutionary War was to end in about four months, along with amnesty. Christian Isom also rendered patriotic services, being later reimbursed as shown in extracts North Carolina Revolutionary Army Accounts.

Summary of Later Life:

Christian Isom was very active in Burke County civil affairs until near the turn of the century. He served on numerous juries from 1783 until 1797. The 1790 census lists him along with four males and three females. He is not listed on the 1800 census.

In 1793, he sold his John's River property to his neighbor, Colonel McDowell (150 acres). Earlier, he had purchased a plantation from Greenberry Wilson. The 1797 tax lists show him with 250 acres of land.

Persons of this name shown later on Tennessee records, Maury County. The names include an Elizabeth Isom (widow?). She died ca 1844 in neighboring Lewis County, Tennessee.

Land Holdings and Transactions:

1. 150 acres Burke County NC on the East side of Johns River

adjacent to land belonging to Joseph McDowell and David Baker. cc (James McKinney, Joseph McKinney). Ent. 17 March 1778 #365 Grant No. 1423 Iss. 4 Jan 1792. Book 75, p. 422.

2. Burke County NC Court Records as given in Huggins, E. W. Vol. II, p. 179. "Deposition of Philip Stephens. Christian Isom stated he was going to purchase a plantation from Greensberry Wilson, the property lay in on James Russell…" 1789 file.

Census Locations:

1790 Burke County, NC 7th Company
1797 Burke County, NC (tax list – Captain Joseph Dobson's Co.)

References:
Huggins, Edith W. Miscellaneous Burke Records in four soft back Volumes. SHP
Swink, Daniel. Minutes of Burke County NC Court of Pleas and Quarter Sessions 1791-1803. 3 soft back volumes. (multiple references)
AIS Census Data NC 1790.
Sistler, Byron and Barbara. Early Tennessee Tax Records.
Land Grant Data. Burke County NC Library, Morganton, NC.
Sistler, Byron and Barbara. Index to Tennessee Wills and Administrations 1779-1861. p. 188, 1990 ed.
Haun, Wynette P. NC Revolutionary Army Account. Part II, p. 198 (1990).

Jeffrey, Drewry   (Jefferies, Jeffries)

Summary of Early Life:

During the American Revoluton, Drewry Jeffrey was a resident of Burke Co. NC. He was born ca 1760. (age 78 in 1838).

Summary of Partisan Activity:

Drewry Jeffrey enlisted in the North Carolina Continental Line in July 1781. He served in the 10th Regiment under Col. Charles Dixon. Other officers included Captain (Griffith) McRee, Capain (Archibald) Lytle, Captain William Walton, and Lieutinant (Wynn) Dixon. His regiment participated in the battle of Eutaw Springs, SC in Sep 1781. In this engagement, Jeffrey served as a wagon guard and was not directly involved in the fighting. Later, he served in activities directed against the hostile Cherokee Indians. Jeffrey served a total of 12 months on active duty and was discharged in 1782.

Summary of Later Life:

After the conclusion of the Revolutionary War, Jeffrey moved from Burke County, North Carolina to Paulding County, Georgia. He applied for Revolutionary War pension benefits while a resident of Paulding County in 1838, age 78 yrs. He was awarded an annual pension of $ 40.00.   Later Jeffrey was a resident of Cobb County, Georgia, where he died.

Census Locations:

1830 Habersham County, Georgia

References:
U.S. Nat. Archives,   RW pension data,   # S 7067.
Roster of Soldiers from North Carolina in the American Revolution. Reprint of orig. 1932 ed., GPC p.137
      NCDAR

175

Jeffries, John   (Jeffers, Jefferies)

Summary of Early Life:

John Jeffries, during the Revolutionary War, lived in Burke County, NC on the south side of Catawba near Ward's Branch.

Summary of Partisan Activity:

In late 1782, John Jeffries name appeared on a subpoena docket of suspected Tories. He was to show cause as to why his property should not be confiscated, pursuant to laws passed by the North Carolina General Assembly (Confiscation Acts). The cases never resolved due to the end of the Revolutionary War, occurring four months later along with general amnesty.

Summary of Later Life:

John Jeffries was involved in several court actions from 1779-1778. His family is listed on 1790 census, though head of household is not listed. John Jeffries died in Burke County North Carolina ca 1818 (estate matters in Oct. session Burke County Court 1818).

Land Holdings and Transactions:

1. 100 acres Burke County NC on south side Catawba River adjacent to land belonging to Josiah Bradshaw, Humphrey Montgomery and to his own land. Land was on Ward's Branch and on river. Ent. 31 Aug 1778, No. ?, Grant No. 1624. Iss. 27 Nov 1792, Book 80, p. 65. c.c. Thomas Jeffers, William James.

References:
Huggins, Edith W. Miscellaneous Burke Records in four soft back vols. SHP, Vol. II p. 154, Vol. III, pp. 144, 148.
AIS Census Data NC 1790, 1800.
Land Grant Data in Burke County Library, Morganton, NC
Phifer, Edward W. Jr. Burke. 1977.
1818 Burke County Court Records, June microfilm copy.

Jones, William

Summary of Early Life:

Prior to the Revolutionary War, William Jones was a resident of Orange County, North Carolina.

Summary of Partisan Activity:

William Jones was a captain of militia in Orange County, North Carolina. His service is documented by the North Carolina Revolutionary Army accounts.

Summary of Later Life:

Captain William Jones was married to Susannah Bush in 1782 (Susannah Bush was age 80 in 1844). Sometime prior to 1798, Jones left Orange County, probably going to Burke County, North Carolina (now Caldwell County). Captain William Jones died April 27, 1798. Later, Susannah Bush Jones was married to Bennett Bradford, also a Revolutionary War soldier. Bradford died November 27, 1828. Susannah Bradford applied for revolutionary war pension in 1844. She was awarded an annual pension of $480.00.

References:
US National Archives Pension Data #W5935.
Caldwell County Library, Lenoir NC. Misc. records.

Kelton, William

Summary of Early Life:

William Kelton was born 26 September 1753, in Chester County, Pennsylvania. During the American Revolution, he was living in western Burke County, NC, near McDowell County, in the vicinity of the Pleasant Garden area near Nick's Creek (western Catawba River Valley).

Summary of Partisan Activity:

North Carolina Revolutionary Accounts show payment to William Kelton for patriotic service, most likely militia duties. He was living in the vicinity of the frontier outposts at Davidson's and Cathey's Forts. There were many skirmishes and confrontations with the Cherokee Indians, allies of the British. DAR records also denote him as a Revolutionary Patriot.

Summary of Later Life:

William Kelton was married to Elizabeth Ramsey (b. Chester County, PA 8 Mar 1753). By the time of the 1790 census, they had a large family and several slaves. Their children were as follows: (all born in Burke County)

Mary b. 1774 m. John Sloan
Robert b. 1776 m. Rachel Jetton
Agnes b. 1777 m. Archibald Sloan
William b. 1778 m. Minerva
Margaret b. 1780 m. Alexander Lackey
David b. 1780 not married
Elizabeth b. 1785 m. James Wilson
James b. 1788 m. Elizabeth White
Samuel b. 1791 m. Elizabeth Manley

William Kelton was active in Burke County Court affairs from the close of the Revolution until the turn of the century. On a court document of 1799, the name "Cumberland" was entered

adjacent to his name. This was probably in reference to his removal to Tennessee ca 1799-1800.
Summary of Later Life:

The Keltons moved to Rutherford County, Tennessee and remained there until their deaths. William Kelton died in Murfreesboro, Rutherford County, Tennessee on May 18, 1813. Elizabeth Kelton died July 30, 1830 in Rutherford County Tennessee. Both are buried on Black Fox Plantation at Murfreesboro.

Land Holdings and Transactions:

1. Burke County NC 100 acres south side of Catawba River opposite the mouth of Buck Creek, and including an island in the river. The land lay adjacent to that of Elijah Patton. cc William Kelton, George Davidson. Ent. 9 Oct 1778 #134 Grant issued 14 March 1780 # 180 Bk. 78 p. 179.
2. Burke County NC 100 acres on both sides of Nick's Creek, below the mouth of Buck Creek. cc William Kelton; George Davidson. Ent. 5 Jan 1779 #828 Granted 15 March 1780 #298 Bk. 28 p. 297.
3. Burke County NC 100 acres on south side of Catawba River and on both sides of Nick's Creek. cc William Loyd, John Loyd. Ent. 9 Oct 1778 #135 Granted 11 Oct 1783 #565 Bk. 50 p. 200.
4. Burke County NC 150 acres on Nick's Creek and including a fork, and lying on path that leads from Lizah Patton's to William Pattons. The land lay adjacent to his own land. * cc James Monker, Robert Kelton. Ent. 30 July 1794 #654 Granted 17 Oct. 1796 #2152 Bk. 91 p. 75.
   *The land lay near a new "wagon road".
5. Burke County NC 350 acres located adjacent to his own land and to that of Jesse Stroud and John McCanless. It included some of the headwater of both Nick's Creek and Muddy Creek. Ent. 30 April 1794 #636 Granted 17 Oct 1796 #2153 Bk 91 p. 75. cc James Marler, William Kelton.
6. Burke County NC 640 acres including land on both sides of Catawba River and Nick's Creek. The land lay adjacent to

his own land and to that of Joseph McDowell (entry), John Jones, Elijah Patton, Davidson and Cox. Ent. 30 Oct 1793 #545 Granted 17 Oct 1796 #2154 Bk. 91 p. 75 cc Robert Kelton, Dan Alexander.

7. Rutherford County TN 20 acres from Richard W. Cummins, John Edwards, U. S. Cummins, etal to William Kelton Jan 1811 court minutes.

Census Locations:

1790 Burke County, North Carolina 1st Company

References:
"Roster of Soldiers and Patriots of the American Revolution Buried in Tennessee"; ed. by Helen C. Marsh Tennessee Society DAR, Brentwood, TN, 1979. p. 98.
AIS 1790 Census North Carolina.
Huggins, Edith. Miscellaneous Burke County NC Records Vols. I-IV, multiple listings.
Burke County NC Court Minutes on microfilm. Burke County Library, Morganton, NC.
Land Grant Data. Burke County Library, Morganton, NC.
NC Revolutionary Army Accounts. Vol. I, Book 4, Folio 45, #1830, and Vol. I, Book 5, Folio 20, #1750. (as given in Haun, Wynette P. 1990 Durham, NC, pp. 236, 234.
DAR Patriot Index. Washington, DC. 1966 ed., p. 381.
Wells, Carol. "Rutherford County TN Court Minutes 1811-1815", p. 4.

Killian, Adam

Summary of Early Life:

Adam Killian was the son of Leonard and Mary Margaret Killian and the grandson of the pioneer settler, Andrew Killian, Sr. The Killian's first settled in eastern Lincoln County near Killians Creek, but many then migrated north into present day Catawba County near Clark's Creek. Leonard Killian continued to live on Killian's Creek, but son Adam moved into the Maiden Creek area of Catawba County (a part of Burke County during the American Revolution), later becoming part of Lincoln County, then Catawba.

Summary of Partisan Activity:

A duty roster of Major Nicholas Welch's Lincoln Loyalist Regiment lists Adam Killian as a private soldier. He later deserted.

In 1782, as part of the North Carolina Confiscation Acts, a subpoena list of suspected Tories was issued. Both Adams and Leonard Killian are listed.

Summary of Later Life:

After the conclusion of the American Revolution, Adam Killian had moved into the Maiden Creek area of present day Catawba County. Lincoln County court records show him serving in various civic capacities. He continued acquiring land in the Maiden Creek area until after the turn of the century. He was listed on both the 1790 and 1800 federal census in Lincoln County. J. Yates Killian, in his book on the Killian family indicated that by 1808 several of Leonard's children were contemplating a move to Indiana in Davies County. The fact that Adam's name was on the 1810 census of North Carolina for Haywood County may well have been a part of that migration. Yates Killian further stated that Adam Killian died ca 1821-1822. Heirs listed included Aaron, David, Matthias, Eli, and Moses. Administrators were Charles Joler and Gabriel Killian.

Land Holdings and Transactions:

1. Lincoln County NC Grant #905 Ent. May 24, 1798 100 acres on Maiden Creek.
2. Lincoln County NC Grant #1485 Entered Feb 24, 1801 40 acres on Maiden Creek adjacent to Lawrence Eigert and Jacob Lutz.
3. Lincoln County NC Grant #1486 Ent 24 Feb 01 100 acres on Maiden Creek adjacent to James Martin and David Killian.
4. Lincoln County NC Grant #1643 (with Elias Platt) ent Feb 8, 1802 200 acres on Maiden Creek.
5. Davies County IN 480 acres Section 6 Vincennes District 1819, relinquished and later re-purchased.

Census Locations:

1790 Burke County, North Carolina
1800 Lincoln County, North Carolina
1810 Haywood County, North Carolina
1820 Harrison County, IN

References:
Killian, J. Yates. The History of the Killian Family in North Carolina. (copy) 1935, pp. 4-5.
Pruitt, Dr. R. B. "Abstracts and Land Entrys Lincoln County NC. 1798-1825". 1987 ed.
Clark, Murtie June. Loyalists of the Southern Campaign of the Revolutionary War. GPC 1981 ed., Vol. I, p. 378.
AIS Census Indices. 1790, 1800, 1810, NC.
1782 Lincoln County NC Subpoena Docket of Suspected Tories as abstracted from court records.
1820 Federal Census for Indiana, compiled by W. Hess, Indianapolis, IN 1966 rep. 1975, p. 0266.

Killian, Samuel

Summary of Early Life:

Samuel Killian was born ca 1760-65, the son of Andraes Killian, a pioneer settler of the Catawba Valley. Samuel Killian lived on Clark's Creek, that portion that is now in Catawba County, but within Burke County during much of the Revolutionary War.

Summary of Partisan Activity:

The North Carolina Revolutionary Army Accounts verify the military service of Samuel Killian in Morgan District. In 1782, Killian served as a militia captain in Joseph McDowell's mounted battalion. The main action in 1782 was the primitive raid against the Cherokee Indians in the summer and fall. Samuel Killian is listed as an American patriot by the National Society of the DAR.

Summary of Later Life:

Samuel Killian was married ca.1784 to Barbara Hager. They had the following offspring:

Elizabeth m. William Herman
Sallie m. John Gross
David m. (1) Catherine Cline (2) Christine Deitz
William m. (1) Elizabeth Bost (2) Nancy Cesamore
Frederick b. 1793 m. (1) Anne Gross (2) Catherine Lutz
Barbara m. David Bost
Polly m. Daniel Herman
Samuel, Jr. m. _____ Barnes
Joseph b. 1800 m. Regina Bolick
Andrew b. 1804 m. Sophia Reece

Samuel Killian died ca. 1807, as his will was probated in January 1808. Other sources give his death in 1813.

Land Holdings and Transactions:

1. Lincoln County NC land grant 50 acres Clark's Creek ent. Dec 6, 1792.
2. Lincoln County NC land grant 100 acres Clark's Creek ent. Jan 2, 1797.

Census Locations:

1790 Lincoln County, North Carolina 3rd Co.
1800 Lincoln County, North Carolina

References:

Killian, J. Yates. The History of the Killian Family in North Carolina. (1935), pp. 20-23 of a reprint copy.

NC Revolutionary Army Accounts as given in soft back edition By Haun, Wynette P., Part IV and Part XII, (Durham NC, 1992, 1999).

Pension Statements of Revolutionary War soldier Andrew Shook. (Pens. No. S7485), See Vol. I, this work, p. 252.

AIS Census Indices NC 1790, 1800.

McAllister, Anne and Sullivan, Kathy G. "Lincoln County NC Court of Pleas and Quarter Sessions April 1805-October 1808". (1988 ed.), p. 125.

National Society DAR, Washington DC. Patriot Index. Part II, 1990 ed., p. 1675.

Pruitt, A. B. Abstracts of Lincoln County NC Land Entries 1780; 1795-1797…1988 ed. Nos. S27, S45.

Pruitt, A. B. Abstracts of Deeds Lincoln County NC (1786-1793) 1988 ed., no. 813.

Kilpatrick, Hugh (often written as Kirkpatrick)

Summary of Early Life:

Hugh Kilpatrick was age nineteen in late 1782. He possibly was related to the Hugh Kilpatrick who lived on a 300 acre tract on the south Muddy Creek area adjacent to Burke County.

Summary of Partisan Activity:

In 1782, Hugh Kilpatrick was recruited into the NC Continental Line for a tour of eighteen months. On entering military service, he was described as being 6'7" tall, light hair and fair complexion. He was a farmer by occupation. He was initially placed in a company commanded by Captain (Henry) Highland of McDowell's Burke militia. After being transferred to the Line establishment, he served in Lytle's Company of the 10th Regiment. One source says he had also served earlier in North Carolina Continental Line (1780).

Summary of Later Life:

As payment for his service in the North Carolina Continental Line, Hugh Kilpatrick received a military land grant of 274 acres. Members of the Kilpatrick and Kirkpatrick families appear later in Burke (Captain Robert Kirkpatrick) and Rutherford Counties North Carolina (Hugh Kilpatrick). The Rutherford County family lived on upper Broad River. Hugh Kilpatrick may have lived in East Tennessee. Still later he appears as a resident of Garrard County, Kentucky.

Census Locations:

1790 Rutherford County Hugh Kilpatrick 1st Co.
1790 Burke County Robert Kilpatrick 5th Co.

References:

Huggins, Edith W. Miscellaneous Burke County Records in 4 soft back
        editions. (SHP). Vol. I, p. 126, 156. Vol. II, p. 157.

Roster of Soldiers from NC in the Revolutionary War. NC DAR reprint of 1932
        ed. (GPC) p. 140.

AIS Census Data. 1790 NC.

Land Grand records in Burke County Library, Morganton, NC.

Haun, Wynette P. NC Revolutionary Army Accounts in multiple soft back
        volumes or parts. (Durham, NC). Part XV. p. 21, 2114 (1999).

Calico, Forrest. History of Garrard County Kentucky and its Churches. (New
        York 1947) p. 111.

186

Little, Abraham

Summary of Early Life:

Abraham Little and family were living on Little's Branch, a tributary of Lower Creek in Burke County, North Carolina, later Caldwell County.

Summary of Partisan Activity:

Abraham Little was summoned to Burke County court in late 1782 on charges of being a suspected Tory. He would have to show cause as to why his land should not be confiscated, for being disloyal. The court actions were pursuant to earlier Confiscation Acts, passed by the North Carolina General Assembly. Witnesses called in the case included William White, James Davenport, and Charles Wakefield. No action, as the Revolutionary War would end a few months later along with a general amnesty.

Summary of Later Life:

Abraham Little's name appeared sporadically in Burke County court minutes into 1786. A 1778 entry gives his wife's name as Mary Little. He is not listed on subsequent Burke records or censuses.

Land Holdings and Transactions:

1. 150 acres Burke County NC on Little's Creek, a tributary of Lower Creek (includes fork and mouth of Little's Creek). The land lay adjacent to that of Conrad Kerns. Ent. 3 Sep 1778 #414 Grant no. 157 Iss. 15 Mar 1780 Book 28, p. 156. cc Thomas Pearson, Joseph Dorighty.

References:
Huggins, Edith W. Miscellaneous Burke County Records in 4 soft back volumes (SHP). Vol. II, pp. 149, 154. Vol. II, pp. 55, 60, 58, 110, 117.
Land Grant Data in Burke County NC Library, Morganton, NC.

Lockman, Isaac

Summary of Early Life:

During the Revolutionary period, Isaac Lockman was residing in eastern Burke County, North Carolina, later Lincoln County.

Summary of Partisan Activity:

In the court marital proceedings involving Colonel Charles McDowell of Burke County (early 1782), mention was made of preferential treatment given to Isaac Lockman. He was assigned as "sentenced" to serve in the western Catawba River region, guarding against the incursion of the Cherokee Indians, then allied with the British.

In late 1782, Lockman's name appeared on a subpoena docket as a suspected Tory. This was in relationship to possible land confiscation.

Summary of Later Life:

Isaac Lockman's name appears on later Lincoln County records and censuses. Other Lockman's listed include a Sarah Lockman and John Lockman.

References:
Huggins, Edith W. Miscellaneous Burke County NC Records in 4 soft back volumes. (SHP). Vol. II, p. 154. ca 1987.
AIS Census Data.
Minutes of Charles McDowell Court Martial. Copy of transcript in possession of author.

Lowdermilk, Jacob

Summary of Early Life:

Jacob Lowdermilk was born 1751, probably in Pennsylvania, the son of Jacob Lowdermilk, Sr. and Mary Rebecca Meyers Lowdermilk.

Summary of Partisan Activity:

Jacob Lowdermilk served in the Revolutionary War as an ensign in the German Battalion of Continental Troops, Captain John Woelpper's Company. The battalion was commanded successively by Colonel Arendt, Stricker, Weltner, and Howegger. He was appointed a sergeant in July 1776, and commissioned an ensign in November 1776. He resigned in April 1778.

The above is the military record as attributed to Jacob Lowdermilk, Sr. as "he is the only Lowdermilk in Randolph County". Of course this is not the case since Jacob Lowdermilk, Jr. was also living in Randolph County. His age would fit much better as a sergeant and then ensign (age 25 years as opposed to 50 years for Jacob Lowdermilk, Sr. – six years older than George Washington).

Summary of Later Life:

Jacob Lowdermilk moved, after the Revolutionary War, from Randolph County, North Carolina to Burke County, North Carolina. He is listed on the 1800 Burke County census. He and his wife had the following children:

> Jacob (1773-1843)
> Henry (1781-1840) m. (1) ? m. (2) Margaret Taylor
> Solomon (1783-1838) m. (1) Sally Starnes (2) Melinda Pence

Joseph Lowdermilk died in Burke County North Carolina ca 1804 or 1805. His will probated in July 1805 with Elizabeth

Lowdermilk serving as executor.

Land Holdings and Transactions:

1. NC state grant to Jacob Lowdermilk 100 acres on Crooked Creek "adjacent to his father", 28 Nov 1792.
2. James Garner to Jacob Lowdermilk, both of Randolph County, 100 acres on Deep River and Crooked Creek 20 Feb. 1794.

Census Locations:

1790 Randolph County, North Carolina*
1800 Burke County, North Carolina
*The 1790 Randolph County NC census data indicates a young person (with 4 males under age 16 in the household). This fits more with Jacob, Jr., rather than Jacob, Sr. (now age 64 or so).

References:
"Randolph County NC Deed Abstracts". Books 1-5, 1779-1794, Vol. I, pp. 91-94, Abstracts by Grigg, Barbara W., Asheboro, NC.
Internet Source: http://elowdermilk.com/lowdermilk.htm.
AIS Census Indices. NC 1790, 1800.
Philbeck, Miles and Turner, Grace. "Burke County, NC Surviving Will and Probate Records 1777-1910". 1983 ed., #312.

Lyons, John

Summary of Early Life:

John Lyons was a resident of Burke County North Carolina at the time of the Revolutionary War. The 1790 census shows that he resided in Eastern Burke County (later Lincoln County and then Catawba County, NC).

Summary of Partisan Activity:

In late 1778, John Lyons entered military service as a member of the 4th Battalion of the North Carolina Continental Line commanded by Major John Armstrong (of Surry County, NC). They marched to South Carolina and on June 20, 1779 participated in the Battle of Stono Ferry, near Charleston. Lyons served for a period of nine months.

Summary of Later Life:

In 1792 Lyons, through power of attorney to William T. Lewis, applied for service benefits. There was testimony stating verification of his military service by Captain James Mackey of Burke County.

Later domicile of John Lyons not definitely known. There was a John Lyons who obtained land in Kentucky, south of Green River (Barren County), and another whose estate papers were listed in Knox County, Tennessee. Relationship, if any, to Revolutionary War soldier John Lyons, not known. 1790 North Carolina census show Lyons with one female and six males in household.

Census Locations:

1790 Lincoln County, North Carolina 1st Co.

References:

Huggins, Edith W. Miscellaneous Burke County Records in 4 soft back
    volumes. (ca 1987). SHP Vol. II, p. 159.

NC Revolutionary Army Accounts as given in Haun, Wynette P. Durham NC in
    multiple soft back volumes (parts). Part III, p. 406, Part IV, pp. 436,
    480, Part VI, p. 833, Part VIII, pp. 1074, 1086.

Roster of Soldiers from NC in the American Revolution. 1967 reprint of orig.
    1932 ed. pp. 197, 218, 228.

The Kentucky Land Grants. Jillson, W. R. GPC Balti. 1971 ed., Vol. I, pp. 357,
    631.

Tennessee Wills and Administrations. Byron and Barbara Sistler, Nashville,
    1990 ed., p. 225.

AIS Census data NC 1790, KY 1810.

McClure, Andrew

Summary of Early Life:

Andrew McClure and his family were living on Tom's Creek in the Upper Catawba River Valley during the Revolutionary War. Today, this area is on McDowell County, North Carolina, northwest of Marion. It lay within Burke County during most of the Revolutionary War. There were many persons of this name serving in South Carolina troops.

Summary of Partisan Activity:

In 1782, Andrew McClure was suspected of being a Tory. He was subpoenaed to appear in Burke County Court to show cause as to why his land should not be confiscated, for being disloyal to the American Cause. Most of these cases were never brought to trial, as the Revolutionary War was to end only a few months later, along with a general amnesty.

Summary of Later Life:

Andrew McClure continued to live in Burke County until the turn of the century. During this time, he was active in civic affairs. He served as a Burke County constable on at least two occasions, and also served on various juries. He lived in Captain Cashion's district, which was the 1st Company on the 1790 census listing. He had a large household. The 1790 census lists him along with five females and seven males.

Ca 1804, Andrew McClure moved further west into the Pigeon River Valley, now Haywood County and Macon County, North Carolina. Other McClure's, most likely relations, who also moved to the same area, included William, James, John, and Joseph McClure.

Land Holdings and Transactions:

1. Burke County NC 150 acres on both sides of Tom's Creek

and "including the improvements that said McClure now lives on". The land included a part of the road that extended from the "Limestone Hills to Sherrill's Ford". The land was adjacent to that of David McCracken. c. c. David McCracken; John Wilson. Ent. # 1098 2 Dec 1780 Bk # 381 Iss. 28 Oct 1782 Bk 44 p. 149 (apparently entered earlier in 1778 also).

2. Burke County NC 200 acres on both sides of Sugartree Creek; a tributary of Tom's Creek. cc David McCracken; John Wilson Ent. 2 Dec 1778 # 10041 Gr. # 440 Iss. 28 Oct 1782 Bk. 44 p. 186.
3. Buncombe County NC Land on Crabtree Creek 16 Nov 1804 Bk. 10 p. 59.

Census Locations:

1790 Burke County, North Carolina 1st Company
1800 Burke County, North Carolina
1810 Haywood County, North Carolina
1820 Haywood County, North Carolina
1830 Macon County, North Carolina

References:
Huggins, Edith W. Miscellaneous Burke County NC records in soft-back volumes. Multiple references.
AIS Census Data.
Swink, Daniel D. Minutes of the Court of Pleas and Quarter Sessions. Burke County NC 1791-1803 in 3 soft back volumes.
Land Grant Data in Burke County Library, Morganton, NC.
Moss, Bobby G. South Carolina Patriots in the AmericanRevolution. GPC 1983 ed., pp. 604-605.
Wooley, James E. Buncombe County NC Index to Deeds 1783-1850. SHP 1983 ed., pp. 311-312.

McCorkle, Francis

Summary of Early Life:

Frances McCorkle, son of Matthew McCorkle, was born ca 1741 of Scotch Irish descent. He was an early settler of the Catawba Valley, appearing first in 1765. In 1769, he received a Crown Grant on Mountain Creek near the present day Catawba-Lincoln County line. During most of the American Revolution, his property lay within Burke County (Rowan County at beginning, Lincoln County at conclusion). He was married to Sarah Work, daughter of Alexander Work of Rowan County. In 1774 Francis McCorkle became a member of the Rowan County Committee of Safety.

Summary of Partisan Activity:

After serving on the Committee of Safety, McCorkle received a commission as Captain of militia. He served first under Colonel Christopher Beekman of the 2nd Rowan Regiment. On the creation of Burke County in 1777, he became an officer in Charles McDowell's Burke Regiment.

The still extant North Carolina Revolutionary Army Accounts verify McCorkle's rank and command.

As a militia officer, he took part in the Cross Creek Expedition of early 1776 (sequel to Moore's Creek Bridge action), and the Cherokee Expedition in July 1776.

His participation in the Ramsuer's Mill Battle of June 20, 1780 is well documented (see Sherrill History of Lincoln County). There are also statements saying that he was at Kings Mountain (October 7, 1780) and Cowpens (January 17, 1781). After Cornwallis' crossing of the Catawba in early February 1781, McCorkle participated in the skirmish at Torrence's Tavern. His militia forces were scattered by Tarleton (still smarting after his recent defeat at Cowpens). By the end of the war, Francis McCorkle was a field officer with rank of Major. He was known as Major McCorkle for the remainder of his life.

Summary of Later Life:

Francis McCorkle was married first to Sarah Work (b. before 1750 – d. 2/17/1779) daughter of Alexander Work in 1768. Children of the marriage were:

Matthew (1769-1844) not married
Isabella (1771-1842) m. William Beatty
Jane (1773-1815) m. Abram Alexander
Alexander Work (1775-1854) not married
Rebecca (1777-1863) m. Gilbert Milligan

Francis McCorkle married second Elizabeth (Betsy) Brandon (1761-1801) daughter of Richard and Margaret Locke Brandon (Betsy Brandon McCorkle served as hostess to General George Washington at the Brandon residence near Salisbury on his southern tour in 1791). Children of Frances McCorkle and Betsy Brandon McCorkle were:

Sarah b. 1784 m. John Wilkinson
Elizabeth b. 1786 m. Jeptha Sherrill
Francis b. 1787 d. 1853 m. Elizabeth Abernethy
Richard b. 1790 d. 1823 m. Agnew Sherrill
Rhomas b. 1793 d. Texas m. Casey Sherrill
William b. 1794 d. 1868 m. Mary Marshall
John b. 1796 d. TN m. ____Turbyfill
Other children listed included Margaret, Molly, and Nancy.

Major Francis McCorkle was active in Lincoln County affairs until his death in 1802. At his death, he was a large plantation owner with many slaves (he had ten slaves listed on 1790 census).

Francis McCorkle and his wife Elizabeth Brandon McCorkle are buried in the old McCorkle graveyard two miles north of Denver in Lincoln County. In 1932 a large commemorative boulder was dedicated to their memory.

Land Holdings and Transactions:

1. Burke County NC Land Grant 300 acres on South Fork of
   Mountain Creek. The land lay adjacent to Thomas Little
   and to his own land. Ent. 8 June 1779 #1144 Grant # 351
   Iss. 28 Oct 1782 Bk. 44 p, 132 cc John Reed; Andrew
   Parkes.
2. Burke County NC NC Land Grant 400 acres on South Fork
   of Mountain Creek. The land lay adjacent to that of
   Thomas Little. Ent. 11 Dec 1778 # 1143 Grant # 427 Iss.
   28 Oct 1782 Bk 44 p. 178. cc John Reed; Andrew Parkes.
3. Burke County NC NC Land Grant 150 acres on Hall's
   Creek adjacent to land of Robert McCussick and adjacent
   to land "I now live on". Ent. 11 Dec 1778 # 1143 Grant #
   529 Iss. 28 Oct 1782 Bk. 44 p. 247. cc John Reed; Andrew
   Parkes.
4. NC Crown Grant Tryon County 250 acres on South Fork of
   McCorkle's Creek, a tributary of Mountain Creek.
   Included were Hall's improvements. The land lay adjacent
   to his own land. Grant # 2144 p. 521 Dec 16 1769.
5. NC Crown Grant Tryon County 200 acres on Mountain
   Creek, including Peter Lineberger's improvements. April
   18 1771. Grant # 3000 p. 666.
6. In a 1792 Lincoln County transaction, Robert McCashland
   deeded land originally granted in 1763 to Francis
   McCorkle. Bk 16 p. 276 #746.

Census Locations:

1790 Lincoln County, North Carolina 10th Company
1800 Lincoln County, North Carolina

References:
McCorkle, Louis W. Viking Glory 1982. pp. 213-216.
Sherrill, William L. Annals of Lincoln County NC. (reprint of 1937 ed.) pp.
62-62; 404
Wheeler, John H. Historical Sketches of NC. (reprint of 1851 ed.) pp. 360-377
AIS Census Data. NC 1790, 1800.
Land Grant Data. Burke County Library, Morganton, NC.
Preslar, Charles S. A History of Catawba County. (1954 ed.) pp., 77; 81-82.

Pruitt, Dr. R. B. "Abstracts of Deeds Lincoln County NC 1786-1793" (1988) p. 101.

Hofmann, Margaret M. <u>Colony of North Carolina 1765-1775</u>. Vol. II, Nos. 2144, 3000.

McCracken, David

Summary of Early Life:

David McCracken was born in Maryland ca 1750. During the American Revolution, he and his family were living on Tom's Creek, a tributary of the Catawba River, northwest of present day Marion in McDowell County, North Carolina. During the Revolution, it was a part of Burke County.

Summary of Partisan Activity:

David McCracken served as a private in the North Carolina Continental Line. He later received a military land warrant for his service. David McCracken seems to have been of Loyalist leaning, since his name appears on the 1782 Burke County subpoena docket of suspected Tories. The cases never resolved, as the War was to end four months later along with a general amnesty.

Summary of Later Life:

David McCracken was active in Burke County civic affairs until about 1797. He served as a juror on several court cases and served on road juries. In 1797, he began to sell off his land, possibly indicating the time of his move to East Tennessee. David McCracken appears later in Lincoln County, TN and remained there until his death in 1812. He sold his military land warrant to John McGimpsey in 1806. (Probably related to McCracken's neighbor, John Wilson). David McCracken was married to Elizabeth Wilson (d. 1821). Children were as follows:

James
Joseph b. 1776
Mary m. Birch, Vonell ?
Elizabeth b. 1774 m. George Pierce
Sarah m. William Brown
Elie m. Thomas Jones
Cynthia m. Birch
Margaret b. 1783 m. William Spradley

Malinda b. 1794 m. Daniel Haskins

Both David McCracken and his wife are buried in a family cemetery at Bradshaw near the Lincoln County, Giles County line in south central Tennessee.

Land Holdings and Transactions:

1. 250 acres Burke County NC on both sides of Tom's Creek including the improvements he now "lives on". Ent. 2 Dec 1778 Grant no. 650 Iss. 11 Oct 1783 Book 50 p. 240. c. c. Andrew McClure, John Wilson.

Census Locations:

1790 Burke County, North Carolina 10th Company

References:
Roster of Soldiers and Patriots of the American Revolution Buried in Tennessee. Comp. By Lucy Bates, revised by Helen Marsh. 1979 TN DAR, p. 117.
Huggins, Edith W. Miscellaneous Burke County NC Records in 4soft back volumes, (SHP), Vol. I, p. 102, Vol. II, p. 154, Vol. III, Vol. IV.
NC Land Grant Data in Burke County Public Library, Morganton, NC.
Sullivan, Kathy C. Burke County NC Deeds (Burke County Gen. Soc.), rep. 1804-1813, 1997, p. 48.
Swink, Daniel D. Minutes of the Court of Pleas and Quarter Sessions. Burke County NC in 3 soft back volumes, 1791-1803.
Haun, Wynette P. NC Revolutionary Army Accounts. Military Land Warrant Book, Part XV, (1999 ed.), p. 2113.

McGimsey, John

Summary of Early Life:

Data relating to the McGimsey families of Burke County, North Carolina is extremely mixed. There were two John McGimseys who lived in Burke County during the late 1700's. They were possibly related, but the exact relationship is unknown. The John McGimsey of this sketch came to Burke County during the Revolutionary period. Land entry records show that he settled on Young's Branch, adjacent to the Quaker Meadows tract of Colonel Charles McDowell. He settled on land previously occupied by one James Nicholson. McGimsey may have known the McDowells while in Virginia. The other John McGimsey appears to have arrived in Burke County after the time of the 1790 census, probably in 1793 or 1794. Therefore, events occurring in the 1770's and 1780's refer to John McGimsey of Young's Creek. The John McGimsey who came to Burke County in the 1790's was known as "Colonel John McGimsey" (see seperate biography), who eventually was to move to Tennessee and who died in Maury County, Tennessee in 1821.

Summary of Partisan Activity:

John McGimsey espoused the Liberty movement on his moving to Burke County. His Revolutionary War service is well documented. In the testimony of Revolutionary War soldier Samuel Alexander, speaking about the Battle of Ramsour's Mill, is the following statement:

> "Our force was about 300 and the Tories about
> 1000. We lost about 23 that I counted. Amongst
> our neighbors, John Duckworth wounded, John McGimsey
> wounded, Captain John Bowman wounded, and died
> in a few days, and Captain Falls was killed."
> *From Revolutionary War Pension Application of Samuel Alexander*
> *W1530.*

The battle was a decisive American Victory. How much

disability resulted from his wounds is not known.

Alexander was from Burke County, living near present Lake James. His Revolutionary War pension was approved. McGimsey died before the pension legislation was enacted.

Summary of Later Life:

John McGimsey, after the Revolutionary War, became a prominent citizen of Burke County, serving in several civil capacities. In 1785 he was a deputy sheriff. He also served on various juries and commissions. It is logical to assume that he is the same John McGimsey that was High Sheriff of Burke County in 1796-1798; however, Colonel John McGimsey had arrived in Burke County ca 1794. Colonel McGimsey was also an active public servant and possibly may have been the one who served as High Sheriff. John McGimsey became less active after the turn of the century. He sold off most of his property and may have moved in with his son Joseph. Joseph had acquired acres of property on Linville River from Colonel John McGimsey.

John McGimsey of Young's Branch died ca 1814, as his administrative affairs were handled in the January 1815 session Burke County Court. His son Joseph L. McGimsey acted as administrator.

Family tradition says that he was brought down from Linville to Quaker Meadows on a sled and buried at Quaker Meadows Church Cemetery.

Land Holdings and Transactions:

1. Burke County NC Land Grant 640 acres on Miller's Creek, at tributary of the Catawba River, and including improvements "that James Nichols now lives on". The land lay adjacent to that of Charles McDowell, William Miller, and widow McDowell ent. 5 Sep 1778 #793 Grant #645 Iss, 11 Oct 1783 Bk. 50, p. 238. c.c. William Stewart, Adkins.

2. Burke County NC Land Grant 200 acres on Forney's Mill Branch (also called "Mill Seat Branch"), just above the shoals adjacent to McGimsey's own land. cc William Stewart; Adkins. Ent. 22 Jan 1779 #1738 Grant #698 Iss 11 Oct, 1783 Bk. 50 p. 259.

3. Burke County NC Land Grant 300 acres on Young's Creek, a tributary of Upper Creek, which flows into the Catawba River. The land included "The improvements that said McGimsey lives on..." The land lay adjacent to that of Jacob Forney. Ent 17 Aug 1778 #671 Grant #700 Iss. 11 Oct 1783 Bk 50 p. 260 cc William Stuart; Adkins.

Census Locations:

1790 Burke County, North Carolina 7th Co

References:
McGimsey, Margaret Elizabeth. Article in Burke County NC Heritage Vol. I (1981), p. 300.
McGimsey, James F., Jr. MD, Heritage Vol. I (1981), p. 301.
McGimsey, W. Erwin. Heritage Vol. I (1981), p. 301-302.
Turner, Grace and Philbeck, Miles. "Burke County NC Surviving Will and Probate Abstracts (1777-1910)'. 1983 ed. #338.
Huggins, Edith W. Miscellaneous Burke County Records in 4 Softback volumes.
AIS Census Data NC 1790, 1800, 1810, 1820.
NC Land Grant Data Burke County Library, Morganton, NC.
Swink, Dan. "Minutes of the Burke County Court of Pleas and Quarter Sessions in 3 softback volumes 1791-1803.
Sullivan, Kathy G. "Burke County NC Deeds Registered 1804-1813". (1995), p. 51.
US National Archives. Revolutionary War Pension Data of Samuel Alexander #S6493 W1530.

McMurray, Samuel

Summary of Early Life:

Samuel McMurray was born ca 1755.

Summary of Partisan Activity:

Samuel McMurray was a militiaman of Burke County North Carolina. The regimental commander was Colonel Charles McDowell. His service was government recognized and his grave was marked in 1960.

Note: The Moravian Records, in a contemporary account, tells of some boisterous activity on the part of a militiaman named Samuel McMurray (many western North Carolina militiamen were antagonistic against the Moravians, thinking they were pro-British). There were at least three Samuel McMurray's in the area, one from Burke County, one from Rutherford County, and another from Caswell County.

Summary of Later Life:

Samuel McMurray and his family continued to live in Burke County after the Revolutionary War. His name appears in several court procedures until about the turn of the century. About 1797-1800, he moved to Blount County, Tennessee and remained there the rest of his life. Samuel McMurray was married ca. 1777 to Nancy Bogle (1760-1831). They had the following children:

> Joseph 7/24/1780 – 7/21/1856 m. Rebecca Carswell (1786-1850)
> Betsy 4/11/1781 m. 1827
> Hannah b. 1784 m. 1799 James Boyd
> Polly b. 1787 m. 1821 Andrew McCall
> William b. 1790 m. 1817 Peggy McHenry 1825 (2)
> Margaret
> Malcolm
> Archibald b. 1791 m. Mary Cowan
> Sarah b. 1796 m. 1816 John Sims
> John b. 1797 m. Margaret Carsvan

Fanny b. m. 1819 Thomas McKinney
Henderson
Nancy m. 1825 James Malcolm
Newton b. 1804 m. 1824 Elaine Bogle
Samuel, Jr. Soldier, War of 1812

Samuel McMurray died in Blount County, Tennessee in 1821. Both he and his wife are buried in Eusebia Cemetery in Blount County.

Land Holdings and Transaction:

Burke County NC Land Grant 200 acres on both sides of the south fork of Kennedy's Fork of Silver Creek. The land lay adjacent to that of John Bricey, Jacob Hipps, and Michael Derryberry. cc Jacob Hipps; Andrew Derryberry. Ent. 25 Jan 1779 # 1474 (ent. Orig. by Joseph Farmer) Grant # 826 Iss. Nov 9, 1784. Bk. 57, p. 27.

Census Locations:

1790 Burke County, North Carolina 13th Company
1800 Blount County, Tennessee (tax list)
1805 Blount County, Tennessee (tax list)

References:
Roster of Soldiers and Patriots of the American Revolution Buried In Tennessee. Compiled by Lucy Bates and revised by Helen Marsh (1779 ed.), p. 121.
NC Land Grant Data in Burke County Library, Morganton, NC.
Fries, Adelaide L. Records of the Moravians in North Carolina.
AIS Census Data NC 1790.
Sistler, Byron and Barbara. Early Tennessee Tax Lists (1977 ed.), p. 137.

Mackie, Thomas (Macky, McKey, etc.)

Summary of Early Life:

Thomas Mackie and his family were residents of County Tyrone in Ireland before coming to America ca 1770. According to DAR records, Thomas Mackie was born ca 1740. Thomas Mackie, during the American Revolution, lived on Hunting Creek, Burke County, near present day Morganton.

Summary of Partisan Activity:

Thomas Mackie served as a militiaman with North Carolina troops during the American Revolution. North Carolina Revolutionary Army Accounts show reimbursement for patriotic services during the war. He is listed as a patriot by the DAR.
Note: Draper, in his book on Kings Mountain, says that soldiers were billeted at a "Mr. Mackie" on their march through Burke County following the battle, probably Thomas Mackie.

Summary of Later Life:

After the Revolutionary War, Thomas Mackie obtained grant land by lottery and moved to Wilkes County, Georgia. Later he lived in Madison County, Georgia and died in Danielsville, Georgia ca 1797, the date of his will probate (DAR records say he died 1796). Thomas and Rosannah Mackie had the following children:

John	William
Samuel	Rachel m. Strickland
Rosannah m. Templeton	Mary m. Hemphill
Martha m. Fleming	

Land Holdings and Transactions:

1. Burke County NC Land Grant 100 acres both sides of a branch of Henry's River. Ent. 4 Nov 1778 # 584 Grant # 189 Iss March 14, 1780. cc Thomas Bradley; Jesse

Walker.

2. Burke County NC Land Grant 467 acres on both sides of a fork of Hunting Creek adjacent to land of Mordecai Morgan, Ezekial Springfield, William Bailey, Jesse Walker. Ent 4 Nov 1778 # 585 Grant # 243 Iss. 14 Mar 1780 Bk. 28 no. 242.

3. Burke County NC Land Grant 610 acres on Cherokee Fork of Hunting Creek adjacent to land of Mordecai Morgan, Ezekial Springfield and Jesse Walker. Includes Mackie's improvements. cc Ezekial Springfield, Thomas Bradley. Ent. 31 Dec 1778 # 1321 Grant # 403 Iss.28 Oct 1782 Bk. 44 p. 162.

4. Burke County NC Land Grant 454 acres on Silver Creek. The land lay adjacent to that of Thomas Wilson and Thomas Hemphill. cc Thomas Hemphill, Thomas Mackie. Ent. 30 Nov 1778 # 1101 Grant # 297 Iss. 15 March 1780. Bk 28 p. 296.

Census Locations:

1791 Burke County, North Carolina

References:
Doughtie, Beatrice Mackey. The Mackeys. Decatur, GA, 1957, supplement 1973, p. 587.
Militia Service. Bk ETO G-4-6.
AIS Census Data NC 1790.
Land Grant Data. Burke County Library, Morganton, NC.
NC Revolutionary Army Accounts as given in Haun, Wynette P. Durham, NC in multiple Vols., or parts. Part II, p. 210, part IV, p. 506.
DAR Patriot Index. (Washington, DC 1966 ed.), p. 342.
Draper, L. C. Kings Mountain and Its Heroes.

Martin, Isaac

Summary of Early Life:

Isaac Martin, during the Revolutionary period, was living on Gunpowder Creek in Burke County, North Carolina, now Caldwell County. His rather large plantation lay just east of the present day community of Granite Falls.

Summary of Partisan Activity:

In late 1782, Isaac Martin was cited to appear in Burke County court as a suspected Tory. He was to show cause as to why his property should not be confiscated, for being unfriendly to the American Cause.

Witnesses called in the case included John Wilson, John Martin, William Armstrong, Colonel Daniel McKissick, and Bryant Corpening. Most of the litigation of these cases extended into 1783. There was no definite resolution, as the American Revolution was to end only three months later, along with a general amnesty.

Summary of Later Life:

Isaac Martin was very active in Burke County civil affairs from the late 1790's into the early 1800's.

Land Holdings and Transactions:

1. Burke County NC 400 acres on Gunpowder Creek including the mouth of Silver Branch that flows into Gunpowder Creek. The land lay adjacent to that of Frederick Markel. The land included "improvements that he now lives on". cc William Clark, John Martin. Ent. 24 Oct 1778 # 424 Grant # 513 Iss. 28 Oct 1782 Bk 44 p. 236.
2. Burke County NC 300 acres on both sides Gunpowder Creek, adjacent to his own land. Ent. 1778 # 928 Grant # 545 Iss. 28 Oct 1782. Bk. 44 p. 255.

3. Burke County NC 100 acres on Silver Creek, a tributary of Gunpowder Creek. Ent. 10 Mar 1780 # 1612 Grant # 1435 Iss. 4 Jan 1792 Bk. 75 p. 426.
4. Burke County NC 564 acres on Gunpowder Creek. The land lay adjacent to his own land and to that of William Spencer, Thomas Martin, John Bradburn. The land crossed a portion of Silver Creek and the Horseford Road. c.c. Thomas Martin, James Martin. Ent. 26 Dec 1786 # 32 Grant 3 1458 Iss 4 Jan 1792 Bk. 75 p. 434.
5. Burke County NC 100 acres Gunpowder Creek, adjacent to his own land. Ent. 11 Sep 1790 # 93 Grant # 1746 Iss. 7 Jul 1794 Bk. 85 p. 77.
6. Burke County NC 300 acres on Silver Creek, a tributary of Gunpowder Creek. Ent. 13 Mar 1792 # 153 Grant # 1796 Iss. 7 July 1794 Bk 85 p. 95. cc Jacob Martin, John Griffin.
7. Burke County NC on north side Catawba River and including a small island. The land lay adjacent to his own land. Ent. 20 Jan 1779 # 1118 Grant # 1808 Iss 7 Jul 1794 Bk. 85 p. 101.

Census Locations:

1790 Burke County, North Carolina 2nd Company
1810 Burke County, North Carolina
1820 Burke County, North Carolina
1830 Burke County, North Carolina

References:
Huggins, Edith W. Miscellaneous Burke County NC records in 4 softback volumes. (SHP), multiple references.
AIS Census Data.
Land Grant Data in Burke County Library, Morganton, NC.
Swink, Daniel. Minutes of the Burke County Court of Pleas and Quarter Sessions in 3 soft back vols. 1791-1803 multiple references.

Massy, Jacob

Summary of Early Life:

Jacob Massy was born ca 1760. Jacob Massy appears to have been in Burke County, North Carolina during the latter part of the Revolutionary War. He apparently lived in that part of Burke County in close proximity to Rowan (later Iredell) and Wilkes County, now Alexander County.

Summary of Partisan Activity:

Jacob Massy served as a militiman in Colonel Charles McDowell's Burke Regiment. He served for a year in Captain John Morrison's company. Other offices noted in his tour included Major Daniel McKissick and Captain John Hardin. A pass in extant, issued by Captain Hardin to Massy. Massy hired a substitute on two occasions.

Summary of Later Life:

Jacob Massy was married to Catherine Barrier (b. 1761 d. age 83, 1844) on April 9, 1785. They had the following children:

    Nicholas (1788-1847_ m. Mary McDowell
    Hennrietta m. Daniel Stagdale
    Elizabeth m. Benjamin Reynard
    Sophia m. ____Bullock
    Abraham (1792-1867) m. Rachel Mordrell

Jacob Massy died May 14, 1796. His widow, Catherine Massy, applied for federal pension February 29, 1844 in Johnson County, Indiana.

Census Locations:

1790 Iredell County, North Carolina

References:
US National Archives Federal Pension Data #R7006.
Pyatt, R. L. Valdese, NC. Data submitted to author.

Milstead, John B.

Summary of Early Life:

John Milstead was living in Maryland at the time of his service in the American Revolution. He is listed on a Charles County, Maryland census tabulation of 1775.

Summary of Partisan Activity:

John Milstead enlisted in the Maryland Continental Line for the duration of the war. He served a total of six years and was discharged in 1783. He served as a private soldier in Captain Bruce's Company of Colonel William Smallwood's Regiment (later General Smallwood). The Maryland Line soldiers under Smallwood saw extensive service in both the Northern and Southern Departments.

Summary of Later Life:

Census records show that John Milstead was living first in Charles County, Maryland and later in Prince William County, Virginia (just across the Potomac River from Charles Co.). In 1798, John Milstead was married to Elizabeth Purnell (or Pernell) b. ca 1780. (There may have been an earlier wife as seen in the 1790 census schedules). Later records state "there was a large family". It appears that John Milstead came to North Carolina ca 1810-1820. A William Milstead had settled earlier in Surry County, North Carolina, relationship to John Milstead not definitely known. John Milstead appears on the Wilkes County, North Carolina census in 1820 and on the Burke County, North Carolina census of 1830 (possibly only one location, since this was in the present day Alexander County area, created earlier from Wilkes, Burke and Iredell Counties). In 1828 John Milstead applied for Revolutionary War pension benefits. He was awarded an annual pension of $ 80.00. The Revolutrionary War soldier, John Milstead, died on December 6, 1836. His widow continued to receive his pension. Later she received a bounty land warrant for 150 acres through the Federal Act of 1855. Records indicate she was still living in 1866.

Census Locations:

1775-1778	Charles County, Maryland
1790	Charles County, Maryland
1800	Prince William County, Virginia
1810	Prince William County, Virginia
1820	Wilkes County, North Carolina
1830	Burke County, North Carolina

References:
U.S. Nat. Archives Pension Data   # W 5371
AIS Census Indices NC, MD.,VA. (1775-1830).
Yandle, Suzette Greth Georgetown TX   Data submitted to author 1998.

Morrison, Peter

Summary of Early Life:

Peter Morrison was born in 1748, possibly in Rowan County, North Carolina. He was living in Burke County, North Carolina during the Revolutionary War. This is verified by statements made to the historian Lyman C. Draper by George Morrison, son of Peter Morrison.

Summary of Partisan Activity:

Peter Morrison, during the Revolutionary War, took part in the battle of Kings Mountain, South Carolina. The battle was fought ca October 7, 1780. In later years, Morrison made comments to his son concerning the behavior of Colonel William Campbell of Virginia (there was post war controversy as to whether or not Colonel Campbell was actively engaged during the conflict). Draper interviewed his son relating to Morrison's earlier statements.

Sumamry of Later Life:

Peter Morrison was married to Mary Kirkpatrick. Some of the Morrisons of Rowan County had moved to the Muddy Creek area of Burke County before the war. The Kirkpatricks were near neighbors (Captain Robert Kirkpatrick). Peter Morrison is frequently listed with William Morrison (brother?) who was a Revolutionary War veteran of Burke County, who later moved to Dickson County, Tennessee.

Just at the conclusion of the Revolutionary War, Peter Morrison moved to Sullivan County, Tennessee, Carter Valley section. There was a son George, who married the daughter of Jonathan Wood, a Revolutionary War veteran. A Lawerence Morrison is also present in the same area (son?). A Peter Morrison on 1812 tax lists of Sullivan County, Tennessee (son?).

Peter Morrison died in 1809 and is buried at the Morrison

Chapel Cemetery on West Carter Valley Road, Sullivan County, Tennessee.

Land Holdings and Transactions:

1. Sullivan County TN undated entry, but most likely in the 1780's "100 acres on Oissem Creek joining my former entry no. 299."
2. A land indenture of Samuel Williams of Hawkins County TN mentions 400 acres bounded by "George Crowbarger and Peter Morrison". The land was in Carter Valley of the north fork of Holston River.

Census Locations:

1810 (1809 Hawkins County TN tax lists)

References:
Roster of Soldiers and Patriots of the American Revolution Buried In Tennessee. comp. by Lucy Bates, rev. by Helen Marsh (1979 ed.), p. 127.
Draper, Lymon C. Kings Mountain and It's Heroes. (1997 reprint of orig. 1881 ed.), GPC, p. 579.
White, Katherine Keogh. The Kings Mountain Men. GPC, 1970ed., p. 211.
Moss, Bobby Gilmer. The Patriots at Kings Mountain. 1990 ed., p. 190.
Whitley, Edythe R. Tennessee Genealogical Records. GPC, 1980 ed., (transcribed by Robert Barnes), p. 271, land entry Sullivan Co. TN.

Mullins, John

Summary of Early Life:

The exact location of John Mullins in the pre Revolutionary period is not definitely known. Later family members said that the family had lived earlier in Virginia. There were persons with that name in central North Carolina (Randolph and Montgomery counties) and on Dan River (Stokes and Rockingham counties).

Summary of Parisan Activity:

John Mullins was a member of the North Carolina Continental Line. His nine-month tour of duty started on November 10, 1778 and extended to August 1779. Many of the short-term continentals who were enlisted during this time frame served in South Carolina during the Brier Creek Campaign.

Mullin's Revolutionary War service is verified by the North Carolina Revolutionary Army Accounts.

Summary of Later Life:

Shortly following the American Revolution, John Mullins and his family moved to the westernmost part of Burke County, near the Tennessee line (near Avery County, NC). He lived on the road that led from Grassy Creek to the Limestone Cove (between Spruce Pine and northeast Tennessee). Another account said he lived near the Cranberry Iron mines in Avery County. A John Mullins is listed on Burke County censuses through 1830.

Virginia historical records show that John Mullins, toward the end of his life, moved to Dickinson County, Virginia to be near his son, John Mullins, Jr. A Virginia historical marker notes that he was the only Revolutionary War Soldier buried in Dickinson County. John Mullins name is not on the Revolutionary War pension list. This suggests that he may have died 1830-1833.

Land Holdings and Transactions:

1. Burke County NC Land Grant 100acres on Toe River below the mouth of Snow Creek Ent. 4 Nov 1801 # 3984 Grant # 3119 Iss 27 Nov 1802 . cc Mark Foster, John Mullins (entry states John Mullins, Sr.) Bk. 110 p. 46

2. Burke County NC Land Grant 50 acres north side Toe River. cc Solomon Mullins; John Mullins, Jr. Ent. # 3826 ent 30 Jan 1800 (entry says "John Mullins, Sr.) Grant # 3049 Iss 4Dec 1801. Bk. 114 p 351.

3. Burke County NC Land Grant 100 acres north side of Toe River and on Beaver Creek including improvements made by John Taylor. Entry states "John Mullin's Sr.). cc John Mullins, Jr., Soloman Mullins ent. 30 Jan 1800 # 3823 Grant # 3014 Iss 4 Dec 1801 Bk. 114 p. 337

4. Burke County NC Deeds Registered
   a) John Mullins to Samuel Blalock 100 acres Oct 1810
   b) John Mullins to Isaiah Rose 100 acres July 1808
   c) John Mullins to John Mullins 140 acres 8 Aug 1807
   d) John Mullins to Henry Brown ? acres 21 Aug 1812
   e) John Mullins to Richard Blalock 100 acres 4 July 1809

Census Locations:

1790 Burke County, North Carolina
1800 Burke County, North Carolina
1810 Burke County, North Carolina
1820 Burke County, North Carolina
1830 Burke County, North Carolina

References:
NC Revolutionary Army Accounts as quoted in Haun, Wynette P. (1990), part II, p. 286, part VIII (1996), pp. 1075, 1088.
Roster of Soldiers from North Carolina in the American Revolution. NC DAR reprint of 1932 ed. (1967) GPC. pp. 200, 229, 358.
Land Grant Data in Burke County Library, Morganton, NC.
Huggins, Edith W. Miscellaneous Burke County Records in 4 soft back volumes (SHP).
Sullivan, Kathy G. "Burke County NC Deeds Registered 1804- (Burke Co.

Gen. Soc. 1997), p. 55.

Burke County Court Minutes on microfilm (author's copies) multiple listings. Burke County Library, Morganton, NC vertical file data on Mullins family.

AIS Census Data NC 1790 through 1830.

"A Guidebook to Virginia's Historical Markers". 1994 ed., p. 200.

Nichols, John

Summary of Early Life:

John Nichols was born in Maryland in the year 1752. At the beginning of the Revolutionary War, Nichols was living in Burke County, North Carolina.

Summary of Partisan Activity:

John Nichols first entered military service in 1776 in a company commanded by Captain Reuben White of Charles McDowell's 2nd Rowan Regiment (later Burke County). Captain White was killed by Indians on the North Fork of the Catawba. Nichols served out a six-month tour, stationed at White's Fort and acting as an Indian scout, or "spy". Nichols erroneously gave the date of this service as occurring in 1777.

In 1779, Nichols volunteered for another tour of duty in Captain Joseph White's Company of Charles McDowell's Burke Regiment. They marched into South Carolina where he was place in Colonel Malmedy's Regiment of infantrymen. They were in a skirmish at a place known as Pond Ponds (Colleton County, SC). They drove in their pickets and later they took part in the hard fought battle of Stono Ferry, South Carolina on June 20, 1779. Nichols, in his pension statements, mentioned their attack on the British breastworks, and being subsequently repulsed.

In 1781, under Captain White, Nichols assisted in guarding prisoners taken at the Battle of Cowpens (Jan 17, 1781).

Summary of Later Life:

After the close of the American Revolution, Nichols moved from Burke County, North Carolina to Madison County, Kentucky. Still later he moved to Hardin County, Tennessee. John Nichols applied for Revolutionary War pension in Hardin County, Tennessee on January 20, 1838, age 86 years. Initially his claim was rejected, but there is a short letter, which indicated that his claims were eventually accepted. In 1830 census records Nichols is given as being 70 – 80 years of age, a female in same household, age 70 – 80 year of age, presumably his wife. Also given is a younger female. Other Nichols' in Hardin County in 1830 census included David, John, and Mary Nichols (exact relationship to John Nichols unknown). A Mary Nichols' estate is settled in Hardin County, Tennessee in 1842. The exact relationship, if any, to John Nichols is unknown.

Census Locations:

1830 Hardin County, Tennessee

References:
US National Archives Pension Data. #R7648.
Kentucky Census Records by Volkel, L. M.   (1974) – 1820 census.
Byron Sistler and Associates. Evanston, Ill. 1830 TN census (1971).
AIS 1810 KY census, "Second Census" of 1800 by   GG Clyt (1976).
Boatner, Mark III. Landmarks of the American Revolution. (Harrisburg, PA
         1973), p. 499 (Pon Pon location).
Hays, Thomas A. Hardin County Tennessee Records 1820-1860. SHP 1985, pp.
         17-6.

Nicholson, James

Summary of Early Life:

James Nicholson, during the American Revolution, was living on a tract of land in the Quaker Meadows area of Burke County, North Carolina.

Summary of Partisan Activity:

James Nicholson was an officer in Charles McDowell's Burke Co. Regiment. He served as a lieutenant in Captain Mordecai Clarke's company, Burke County militia. Troops under Clarke fought at the Battle of Cowpens South Carolina on January 17, 1781. Later, they were engaged in the actions relating to Cornwallis' second invasion of North Carolina. The overall American commander was General William Lee Davidson (who was killed at Cowan's Ford on the Catawba River 2 Feb 1781). In late 1781, Nicholson participated in the Wilmington expedition under recently exchanged Brigadier General Griffith Rutherford. In this action, Wilmington was reoccupied by the Americans, following evacuation by the British. Cleanup operations followed, with arrest of Tory partisans, and confiscation of equipment.

Summary of Later Life:

James Nicholson and his wife Sarah were involved in a court case in 1783 relating to charges brought against them by Captain James Murphy, a fellow officer in McDowell's Regiment. It concerned plundered property. Verdict not given, but case appealed in 1784. Disposition unknown. Afterwards, James and Sarah Nicholson appear to have left Burke County. Later whereabouts not definitely known.

Land Holding and Transactions:

Burke Co. NC Land entry data. 100 acres on Miller's Branch (Quaker Meadows area) entered for Nicholson by Samuel Miller. Discontiued. Grant not issued. (Entry # 1120 Ent. Dec 5, 1778).

References:
Huggins, Edith W. Misc. Burke Co. NC records in 4 softback issues (SHP).
     Vol II p. 35 vol III pp. 77, 82,92 Vol IV p.153.

Nicholson, Sarah

Summary of Early Life:

Sarah Nicholson was the wife of James Nicholson. Early in the Revolutionary period, they had entered land in the Quaker Meadows area and were apparently living there during the Revolutionary War.

Summary of Partisan Activity:

The North Carolina Revolutionary Army Accounts verify the patriotic activities of Sarah Nicholson. She received reimbursement for "nursing wounded soldiers". Numerous wounded soldiers were billeted in the Morganton area following the battles of Kings Mountain and Cowpens. (1780 - 1781).

Summary of Later Life:

Just at the end of the Revolutionary War, James and Sarah Nicholson were involved in a court case relating to a "plundered" wedding gown obtained during the Wilmington Expedition of Dec. 1781. Charges were brought against them by James Murphy, a well known patriot and neighbor. The exact nature of the charges and its disposition is not known.

James Nicholson had entered three tracts of land near William Miller at Quaker Meadows. He and his wife departed the area before any grants were issued. Their later whereabouts not known.

Land Holdings and Transactions:

1. Burke Co. NC land entries   Nos. 0242, 0241, 0243.
2. Burke Co. NC   John McGimsey in 1783 received a 640 acre land grant at Millers' Creek "including the improvements James Nichols now lives on". (See John McGimsey, this vol. for details).

References:

NC Rev. Army Accounts Book " 1 - 6 " pp. 9,10. ; Book " A " p. 214.

Huggins, Edith W. Misc. Burke Co. records in 4 softback vols. (SHP), multiple
      listings.

Land Grant Data   Morganton-Burke Co. Library, Morganton, NC.

Osborn, William

Summary of Early Life:

William Osborn was born January 10, 1764. He appears to have been residing perhaps in the Lower Creek area of Burke County, now Caldwell County. In pre-revolutionary Burke (then Rowan) County, there were Osborn families in what are now Catawba and Iredell Counties, exact relationship to William Osborn, the soldier, unknown.

Summary of Partisan Activity:

William Osborn first entered military service as a mounted militiaman in Burke County, North Carolina, in the year 1779. He served for a period of three months in a company commanded by Captain William Adams and Lieutenant William Sumter. He served out his term uneventfully.

He was drafted as a private militiaman in 1780 and served two terms of three months each. He served in a company commanded by Captain William Tabor and Colonel Moffett (Wofford?). Osborn served his tour of duty in Turkey Cove adjacent to North Catawba River. The troops were stationed there as protection against incursions by Indians and Tories. In his pension declaration, Osborn stated that a Bennett Osborn could verify his service.

Summary of Later life:

William Osborn continued to live in Burke County, North Carolina until about 1800, where he moved to Scott County, Kentucky. There he was married (Feb. 20, 1800) to Elizabeth Redden (b. March 20, 1783). By this union were born the following:

Margaret "Peggy" b. Jan. 14, 1810 m. James Sherrill
Abner b. Dec. 11, 1802 m. Eliza Glases
Ipaly b. Dec. 1, 1804 m. Granville Adkins

Kaetherine b. Augu 30, 1806
William b. Nov. 6, 1807
Susan b. Jan. 8, 1810 m. Jacob Dehaven
John T. B. Sept. 21, 1811 m. Permillia Dehaven
Ruben b. March 17, 1813
Martha b. Dec. 8, 1815
Eliza b. Dec. 19, 1819 m. George Glascock

Osborn lived in Scott County, Kentucky until 1827, moving then to Fountain County, Indiana. There he applied for Revolutionary War pension, which was approved. He received a pension of $32.50 per anum. William Osborn died in Fountain County, Indiana on April 5, 1835. His widow continued to receive his pension and later received a bounty land warrant of 160 acres of land. In her later years she moved to Daviess County, Mossuri (1854), but later moved back to Fountain County, Indiana by 1858.

Land Holdings and Transactions:

1. Burke County NC 300 acres on Litten's Creek on west side Catawba River and adjacent to land of Davis, Abraham Robinson and to his own land. Ent. 28 Nov 1778 #679 Grant No. 262 Iss. 15 March 1780 Bk 28 p. 261. cc William Barts, Jeremiah Davis.
2. Burke County, NC 100 acres on both sides Bottle River, a tributary of Mountain Creek and adjacent to land of Henry Taler and William Hambee. Ent. 15 Dec. 1778 #106 Grant No. 343 Iss. 28 Oct. 1782 Bk. 44 p. 128. cc William Hambee; Bennett Ozborn.

Census Locations:

1810 Scott County, Kentucky ("Ozborn")
1820 Scott County, Kentucky
1830 Fountain County, IN

References:
US National Archives.   Pension Data #W4303.
Bounty Land Warrant #80035-160-55.

Huggins, Edith W. Miscellaneous Burke Records (Vols. I-IV).
Land Grant Data. Burke County Library, Morganton, NC.
Byron Sistler and Associates. Nashville, TN. 1830 TN Census.
Kentucky Census Records by AIS (1810) and L. M.Volkel (1810).

Owens, Thomas

Summary of Early Life:

Thomas Owens was living in Burke County, North Carolina during the American Revolution (that part that later was a part of Lincoln County, now Catawba County).

Summary of Partisan Activity:

During the American Revolution, Thomas Owens volunteered in the 10th Regiment, North Carolina Continental Line. He entered in 1779 for a tour of 18 months. He served in a company commanded by Captain (Gee) Bradley. Some of his service was in the Charleston, South Carolina area. Later, according to family sources, he served as a major of militia.

Summary of Later Life:

Thomas Owens lived in Burke County during the entitre Revolutionary War. In Burke County, he was married to Elizabeth McCarry, or McCurry, in 1793. Thomas Owens and Elizabeth McCarry Owens had the following children:

Thomas	John	William
Elizabeth	Pleasant	

Shortly before the turn of the century, Thomas Owens moved to Rutherford County, North Carolina. Thomas Owens died in Rutherford County in 1836. At the time of his death, Thomas Owens was making preparations for federal pension application. His widow later filed for federal pension benefits as a surviving widow. She encountered much diificulty in the process, which was extended over a period of many years, sparked with controversy, and with back and forth harsh exchanges. She was still trying in 1853. Her application was ultimately rejected (there are 81 handwritten pages of data relating to this application).

Census Locations:

1790 Lincoln County, North Carolina 5th Co.
1800 Rutherford County, North Carolina
1810 Rutherford County, North Carolina
1820 Rutherford County, North Carolina
1830 Rutherford County, North Carolina

References:
U.S. Nat. Archives , pension data   # R 16882
AIS Census Indices NC 1790 - 1830
Roster of Soldiers from NC in the American Revolution   NCDAR GPC reprint
        of orig. 1932 ed. p.51.

Ozgathorpe, Richard (Oglethorpe)

Summary of Early Life:

Richard Ozgathorpe was an early settler of Burke County. At the time of the American Revolution, he was living on Hunting Creek, a tributary of the Catawba River, near present-day Morganton, North Carolina.

Summary of Partisan Activity:

The North Carolina Revolutionary Army Accounts verify the military service of Richard Ozgathorpe. He is listed as being a lieutenant of militia. He would have served in Charles McDowell's Burke regiment.

Summary of Later Life:

Burke County records show that Richatrd Ozgathorpe was active in Burke County civic affairs until about the turn of the century. He is listed on the 1790 and 1800 censuses, but not on the 1810 census. A Sarah Ozgathorpe (Oglethorpe) is listed, most likely his wife, or widow. The name Ozgathorpe does occur later, but sporadically, in Tennessee records.

Land Holdings and Transactions:

1. Burke Co. NC 300 acres on East Fork of Hunting Creek, adjacent to Erasmus Mays Mordecai Sutherland, including Ozgathorpes's improvements. Ent. 19 Feb 1778.
2. Burke Co. NC 300 acres on East Fork of Hunting Creek and on a branch of South Fork of Catawba River, including Thompson's Gap Ent. 21 Oct 1778.
3. 200 acres obtained by deed from Edward Poteat. 1794. Walker's Gap. See Vol I., this work.

Census Locations:

1790 Burke County, North Carolina

1800 Burke County, North Carolina
1810 Burke County, North Carolina (Sarah Oglethorpe)

References:
AIS Census Indices NC 1790 - 1810.
Land Grant Records   Morganton-Burke Co. Library Morganton NC.
NC Rev Army Accts. as given in Haun, Wynette P. Durham NC op cit   Vol.
       IX p. 981 Vol. XII p. 1438.
Huggins, Edith W. Misc. Burke Co. NC records in 4 softback iss. GPC Vol. I
       pp. 24, 87.

Patillo, Littleton (Petillo, Pitillo, etc.)

Summary of Early Life:

Littleton Patillo was the son of John and Rachel Patillo and a brother of Middleton (Millington), Susannah, Elizabeth and John Patillo. He was born in Virginia, ca 1757. Relations lived in Brunswick and Mecklenburg counties, Virginia, and Caswell County, North Carolina.

Summary of Partisan Activity:

The North Carolina Revolutionary Army Accounts verify the service of Littleton Patillo, another source says he may have served as long as three years (Crosse).

Summary of Later Life:

Littleton Patillo married Elizabeth Perkins, the daughter of Robert Biggin Perkins. Their children were as follows:

James
John
Millington
Elizabeth m. Roubin Perkins
Susannah m. John Lollar
Polly
Martha

Land Holdings and Transactions:

1. Burke County NC 50 acres on Still House Branch, a tributary of Crooked Creek (now McDowell County NC) ent 12 Aug 1815 #6458 Grant #3755 iss 7 Dec 1816 Bk 130 p. 394.
2. Burke County NC 1815 tax list show Littleton Patillo with 160 acres on Crooked Creek.

References:

Crosse, Malba C. Patillo, Pattillo, Patullo, Pittillo Families. Ft. Worth, TX
    1972, pp. 29-43.

Land Grant Data. Burke County Library, Morganton, NC.

NC Revolutionary Army Accounts. Abstracts by Haun, Wynette P. Durham,
    NC.

Roster of Soldiers from NC in the American Revolution. NC DAR reprint of
    1932 ed., GPC 1967,p. 221.

Pittman, Betsy D. "Burke County NC 1815 Tax Lists", (1990 ed.), p. 7.

Pendergrass, Job

Summary of Early Life:

Job Pendergrass was living in Orange County, North Carolina at the time of the American Revolution. He was born ca 1754 or 1755 (he was age 65 in 1820).

Summary of Partisan Activity:

Job Pendergrass enlisted in the North Carolina Continental Line at Hillsborough in Orange County on May 1776. He enlisted for a term of three years. He was placed in Captain Roger Moore's Company in a regiment commanded by Lieutenant Colonel James Thackston. Continental Line records confirm this service.

Pendergrass, after his initial tour, served again as a nine month Continental. On this tour, he served in South Carolina and was in the battle of Stono Ferry, South Carolina (June 20, 1779). He had enlisted in November 1778.

In 1792, while in the process of applying for settlement, there was testimony in his behalf by Captain John Griffin who stated that Job Pendergrass "was a nine month man to the southard".

Summary of Later Life:

Census records indicate that Job Pendergrass was living in Orange County, North Carolina until the turn of the century. At this time his name began to show up on Burke County records, including the 1810 census.

Job Pendergrass applied for federal pension on March 20, 1820. His affidavits were given before Superior Court Judge Willie Mangum (later US Senator). Pendergrass was awarded a pension of $8.00 per month. In his pension declaration, he mentions a wife (not named) age 56 and two offspring; Henry age twenty and Mary age fifteen years ("subject to fits"). His property consisted of "about fifteen chickens, big and little". His residence was listed as being in Burke County, North Carolina. A later record states that the pensioner Job Pendergrass died in December 1831.

Land Holdings and Transactions:

1. Job Pendergrass received, in 1783, a warrant for 274 acres of land, as payment for his Continental Line services.
2. Tax records for Burke County, NC show a "Charnal" Pendergrass living in Muddy Creek area, relation to soldier not known. There is also a Moses Pendergrass, who later moved to Macon County, NC.

Census Locations:

1790 Orange County, North Carolina St. Thomas District
1800 Orange County, North Carolina
1810 Burke County, North Carolina "Joseph" Pendergrass
1820 Burke County, North Carolina

References:
US National Archives. Pension Data, S41504.
Pittman, Betsy D. "Burke County NC 1815 Tories Lists", op cit, pp. 15, 17.
Huggins, Edith W. Miscellaneous Burke Records Vol. IV, pp. 114, 131, 145.
NC DAR. Roster of NC Soldiers in the American Revolution. op cit, pp. 156, 234.
AIS Census Data NC.
Revolutionary Army Accounts as given in multiple soft back volumes, 1988-1996. (Durham NC) by Haun, Wynette Parks as follows: Vol. I, Bk. 1 and Bk. 2; Vol. II, Bk. 1and Bk. 2, Vol. III, Journal of Commissioners "B"; Vol. X, part 8.
McBride, Ransom. "Revolutionary War Service Records and Settlements", NC Genealogical Journal, Nov. 1988, p. 231.

Pitman, Joseph (Pittman)

Summary of Early Life:

Joseph Pitman was born September 10, 1757. He was living in Granville County, North Carolina at the beginning of the American Revolution. One source states that he may have been the son of Joseph and Elizabeth Pitman of Edgecombe County, North Carolina, members of the Quaker religion. He was a brother of Thomas Pitman, also a Revolutionary War soldier.

Summary of Partisan Activity:

Joseph Pitman first entered Revolutionary War military services as a draftee in 1779 or 1780 probably 1779). He was placed in a company commanded by Captain John Wallis of Colonel William Pill's regiment. They marched from Greenville County to Wilmington on the Cape Fear River, where they remained for three of four weeks, under the overall command of General (John) Butler. From there they marched to Cross Creek (Fayettville), where Pitman was sent home on furlough. After remaining home about two weeks, he again was recalled to service, and was marched to High Rock Shoals of the Haw River. There they took several prisoners. Later Pitman was drafted for another three months tour under Colonel William Moore of Caswell County. His company commander was Captain Abram Potter. They were marching to join General Gate's Army in South Carolina where they heard of his defeat at Camden (August 16, 1780). They then headed toward Wilmington, and then to Pasquotank County to suppress a party of Tories. Later, in lower North Carolina, he was discharged home by Colonel Moore.

About eight or nine months later, Pitman was again drafted for a three month tour, and served in the New Bern area under Colonel Joseph Taylor and Captain Fuller. He was furloughed home after about two months, but recalled to duty shortly afterwards. On this occasion they marched to the home of Colonel (Alexander) Mebane in Orange County, with the intention of joining up with General Nathaniel Greene's Army. Here they heard about the Battle of Guilford Court House (March 15, 1781). He again was discharged and served no further in military service. He does mention the hiring of a substitute by his "class" or militia call group, each man paying the substitute soldier one hundred dollars each to serve a tour in the North Carolina Continental Line.

Summary of Later Life:

Joseph Pitman was married to Sarah Harris, daughter of John and Ann Harris of Greenville County. This occurred before 1784, the birth date of their oldest child. They lived on Aaron's Creek, which later was included in Person County. Pitman is listed on 1784 tax lists of Caswell County ??? on the 1790 census (derived from tax lists).

After some land transactions in Person County, the entire Pitman clan moved to western North Carolina. Thomas Pitman settled in Buncombe County, Joseph in Burke, later Yancey County. He was pensioned in Burke County in 1833 at age ??. He was awarded a pension in the amount of $ per anum.

Summary of Later Life:

Joseph and Sarah Harris Pitman had the following offspring:

Robert m. Mary Gosnell
Stephen m. Abarilla Grindstaff
Harris
Joseph
Sarah m. Samuel Haney

Land Holdings and Transactions:

1. Caswell Bounty NC 1784 tax lists 100 acres Aaron's Creek
2. Burke County NC 1807 tax lists 600 acres Burke County
3. NC 1815 tax lists 500 acres on Mine Creek

Census Locations:

1790 Caswell County, North Carolina
1810 Burke County, North Carolina
1820 Burke County, North Carolina

References:
US National Archives Pension Records #57314.
Pittman, Carroll. Article in <u>Heritage of Toe River Valley Vol. II.</u> pp. 41-42.
        (ed. by Dr. Lloyd Bailey, Durham NC) 1997.
AIS Census Indices
Pittman, Betsy D. 1815 Tax List Burke County, NC.

Pitman, Thomas (Pittman)

Summary of Early Life:

Thomas Pitman was a resident of Edgecombe County, North Carolina during the American Revolution. He was a brother of Joseph Pitman, or Pittman, also a Revolutioary War soldier. The records show that he was born and raised in Edgecombe County.

Summary of Partisan Activity:

Thomas Pitman spent a year in the North Carolina militia in Colonel Jackson's Regiment. He served an additional year as a substitute soldier for his brother, Joseph Pitman (two tours of duty). The North Carolina Revolutionary Army Accounts list Thomas Pitman as a militiaman.

Summary of Later Life:

After the Revolutionary War, Thomas Pitman moved to Buncombe County, North Carolina. He was married to Dicy Newton on August 25, 1793. Four children are listed:

Elizabeth	Thomas
Polly	Lot

Thomas Pitman, the Revolutionary War soldier, died on March 15, 1814.

Census Locations:

1790 Edgecombe County, North Carolina
1800 Edgecombe County, North Carolina
1810 Buncombe County, North Carolina

References:
US National Archives RW Pension Data   # R 8275.
Pittman, Betsy Dodd ; Valdese NC ; data submitted to author. ca 2000.
NC Rev. Army Accts.

<u>Roster of Soldiers from North Carolina in the American Revolution</u>   NC DAR
   GPC Reprint of orig. 1932 ed. p. 186.
AIS Census Indices NC 1790 - 1810.

Pope, George

Summary of Early Life:

George Pope was born January 23, 1731 (another source says 1733), the son of John Henry and Gertrude Kieffer Pope. He came to North Carolina ca 1765 and was living on Clark's Creek. George Pope was a tanner and a tavern owner.

Summary of Partisan Activity:

George Pope was an officer in McDowell's Burke Regiment (earlier, 2nd Rowan Regiment). He served on the Cross Creek Expedition of March 1776 as a Lieutenant of militia (later phase of Moore's Creek Bridge Campaign). Later, he was at Torrence's Tavern, shortly after the death of General William L. Davidson at Cowan's Ford (Feb 1781). By then he was a field officer, with rank of Major.

Summary of Later Life:

George Pope was married to Maria Christina Pope. Their children were as follows:

    Catherine b. 1763 m. George Harlan
    Elizabeth b. 1763 m. Henry Bright
    Henry b. 1775 m. Eve Switzer
    Christina b. 1770 m. (1) Joseph Oatman (2) ____Pittman
    Margaret m. Jacob Swope
    George
    Casper b. 1775 m. Rebecca Harling

George Pope signed his name as "George Bobst". George Pope and family later moved to Lincoln County, Kentucky. Pope probably left Burke County in 1778-1779, the date of his land sale to Joseph Steel. His will is recorded in 1812, Lincoln County, Kentucky.

Land Holdings and Transactions:

1. Burke County NC Land Entry, "George Pope, 640 acres on Clark's Creek joining lines of Simon Hows (Haas), Henry Balinger, Mattias Barringer and Nicholas Frye including Pope's improvements where he now lives." Ent 12 Dec 17 Warrant issued. Transferred to Joseph Steel.

A George Pope, Sr. acquired over a thousand acres of land between 1794 and 1799 in Bourbon, Jefferson, Clarke and Lincoln counties in Kentucky.

Census Locations:

1790 Lincoln County, Kentucky

References:
Pope, C. David, Jr. Article in The Heritage of Catawba County NC Vol. I. 1986 ed. p. 389
US National Archives, Revolutionary War Pension Statements of Richard Matlock W 25701
NC Revolutionary Army Accounts. Abstract by Haun, Wynette P. Durham, NC, Book " A".
Sutherland, James, F. Early Kentucky Landholders 1787-1811. GPC 1986 ed.,p. 276.
Huggins, Edith W. Miscellaneous Burke Records Vols. I-IV, SHP.
Heinemann, Charles B. First Census of Kentucky. 1790, GPC, reprint of 1940 ed. , p. 76.
Pope, Jennings Blaund. Pope Family in the South. (1978 ed.), Austin, TX, pp. 21-46.

Price, Thomas

Summary of Early Life:

Thomas Price and his family were living in Tryon County, North Carolina prior to the American Revolution. During the Revolution, they moved first to the Watauga Settlements (now NE Tennessee), and later in the war, to Burke County, North Carolina. Thomas Price's name is listed on several Tryon County court proceedings 1769 - 1772.

Summary of Partisan Activity:

Thomas Price first served in Watauga as a Captain of militia. He served mainly at Fort Waddell, guarding against the hostile incursions of the Cherokee Indians. Ca. 1779 - 1780, Price moved to Burke County, North Carolina, there serving as a Captain of mounted militia under Major Joseph McDowell of Quaker Meadows. The overall regimental commander was Colonel Charles McDowell. Other officers serving at the same time included Captains Thomas Kennedy and Richard Singleton. Captain Price and his company seved successively at Ned Hampton's Place, Kings Mountain (Oct 1780) and Blackstocks (Nov 1780). All of these were hard fought battles. In South Carolina, Captain Prices' company joined in with the forces under the command of Colonel Elijah Clarke. Under Clarke, Captain Price and his men took part in ther siege and capture of Augusta Georgia (May - June 1781). During this action Captain Price was killed in action. His son, William Price, who fought near his father, said Captain Price received a groin wound and died in about ten minutes. He was buried on the breastworks. Brigadier General Pinketham Eaton of North Carolina also was killed during the same encounter.

Summary of Later Events:

DAR records list a Thomas Price of North Carolina b. 1735 d. 1781. They also give his wife's name as Sally (Llewellyn) Price. The dates fit well with the subject of this sketch. Price's son,

William, was born 1762. There was a younger brother.

References:

US National Archives: Rev War pension data of William Price # W 1072.
DAR Patriot Index Nat. Soc. DAR 1966 ed Washington DC p. 548.
Draper, L.C. Kings Mountain and Its Heroes GPC reprint of orig. 1881 ed. p.
    424.
Holcomb, Brent Tryon Co. NC Court Minutes 1769 - 1779. 1994 ed; multiple
    listings.

Price, William

Summary of Early Life:

    William Price, a son of Captain Thomas Price, was born in York District, South Carolina, December 19, 1762. He was raised in Tryon County (Rutherford County), North Carolina. At the beginning of the Revolution, his father had moved to the Watauga Valley of East Tennessee, then a part of North Carolina. William Price was a brother of Thomas and George Price.

Summary of Partisan Activity:

    William Price ca 1778, as a sixteen year old, entered military service as a musician, a fifer, in Colonel John Sevier's North Carolina Regiment. He served in a company commanded by his father, Captain Thomas Price. He was stationed at a frontier outpost, Fort Waddell, guarding against the incursions of the hostile Cherokee Indians. He served for about twelve months.

    Ca 1779-1780, his father, along with William, moved to Burke County, North Carolina. He lived in Burke County for the remainder of the Revolutionary War.

    In the summer of 1780, Captain Price and his company participated in Charles McDowell's actions directed against the British in western South Carolina. Other officers included Major Joseph McDowell, Major Richard Singleton, and Captain Thomas Kennedy. Price was in the action at Ned Hampton's Place. In the King's Mountain Campaign, Captain Price, with William still serving under him, took part in the hard fought battle of October 7, 1780. Captain Price's company was attached to Colonel Shelby's Company after the battle of King's Mountain.

    Under the leadership of Colonel Thomas Sumter, they fought in another hard fought battle at Blackstocks. Colonel Sumter was wounded in the action. Retreating to Lawson's Fork of the Pacolet, they fought another skirmish with the pursuing British, losing in the action – Captain John Potts.

On the arrival of Colonel Clarke of Georgia in the area, many joined in with him in his aim of freeing Augusta, Georgia from British control. Captain Price and his company then advanced with Clarke to Augusta. At Augusta, William Price left his father's company, and joined up with the mounted troops of Captain Moses Shelby. They captured a garrison commanded by Colonel (Grierson) Grayson. The principle fort (Fort Cornwallis), commanded by Colonel Brown, was assaulted by the main force. During this action, his father Captain Thomas Price received a fatal groin wound, and died a few minutes later. He was buried at the breastworks. After this event, William Price was mustered out of service, though he did spend some time on the frontier in the late phases of the War, guarding against the Cherokee. William Price had spent at least three years on active duty during the Revolution.

Summary of Later Life:

After the Revolution, William Price moved from Burke County to Rutherford County. Shortly after the turn of the century, he moved to White County, Tennessee. On October 9, 1832 William Price applied for Revolutionary War pension. He was awarded a pension of $84.00 per anum.

William Price was married to Elizabeth Hampton on December 19, 1784 in Rutherford County, North Carolina. William Price died October 30, 1844 in White County, Tennessee. His widow continued to receive his pension (she was age 79 in 1846). She died June 11, 1855.

Land Holdings and Transactions:

Rutherford County NC Land entry Jan 9, 1798 150 acres on Cob Creek of First Broad River. #1274.

Census Locations:

1790 (on various jury duties Rutherford County, North Carolina 1783-1785)
1820 (1825 tax list, White County, Tennessee)

1830 White County, Tennessee
1840 White County, Tennessee

References:
US National Archives. Revolutionary War Pension Data   #W1072
The North Carolina Continentals.   Rankin , Hugh F.   Chapel Hill 1971, pp. 332-333.
Newton, Hedy H. Rutherford County, NC Abstracts of Minutes of Pleas and
        Quarter Sessions 1779-1786, 1974.
AIS Census Indices.
Byron Sistler and Associates. 1830 Census TN.

Pugh, John

Summary of Early Life:

John Pugh was born ca 1762 or 1763 in Amelia County, Virginia. At the time of the American Revolution, John Pugh was living in Amherst County, Virginia. Pugh was the son of John Pugh, Sr. His sister was Polly Chewning.

Summary of Partisan Activity:

John Pugh first entered military service in January 1781 as a substitute for his father. He served a three months tour of duty under Captain James Barnett of Amherst County. Their unit was marched to Richmond and then to the York peninsula. They spent most of the time marching and counter marching between Hampton and Williamsburg. No significant encounter took place.

He later re-entered service as a draftee in Captain James Pampalin's company of Virginia militia. They marched to the vicinity of Richmond. He was in no engagement, but could hear the battle sounds near Jamestown (General Anthony Wayne). This service was in June 1781 (three months tour).

Some time later (in 1781), Pugh moved to Burke County, North Carolina. *A cousin was living there in the vicinity. There was a requisition to go against the Indians on the western frontier and Pugh volunteered. He spent his tour of duty at a blockhouse under the command of Captain James McDaniel and Lieutenant James Morris. They were engaged mainly in scouting duties. He mentioned a circumstance in which Captain McDaniel was relieved of duty on suspicion that he may have killed one of his own men. This tour took place in the fall of 1781 (October, November).

Summary of Later Life:

After his last tour of duty, in the spring of 1782, Pugh moved to Amherst County, and remained there about two years.

He then moved back to North Carolina for a year and then to South Carolina for about two years. He then returned to Amherst County until about 1800, went to Monroe County for a year and finally settled in Nelson County, Virginia.

On October 22, 1832 John Pugh applied for Revolutionary War pension benefits in Nelson County, Virginia. He was awarded an annual pension of $30.00. According to DAR records, John Pugh died May 20, 1848.

The kinsman mentioned by John Pugh in western North Carolina, Burke County might have been one David Pugh.

Census Locations:

1810 Nelson County, Virginia
1820 Nelson County, Vrginia

References:
US National Archives. Revolutionary War Pension Data. #S7334. Gwathney, John H. Historical Register of Virginians in the Revolution. GPC 1996 reprint of 1938 ed., p. 641.
Sanchez- Saavedra, Em. A Guide to Virginia.
Military Organizations. in the American Revolution. 1978 ed., p. 37.
1810 VA Census Index (M. W. Critchard) 1971., p. 191.
1820 VA Census Index (J. R. Felldin) GPC 1976., p. 221.
1830 VA Census Index AIS (R. V. Jackson etal) 1976, p. 22.
Burke County NC Land Grant Data. Burke County Library, Morganton, NC.
DAR Patriot Index 1966 ed. Washington, DC, NS DAR, p. 550.

Rader, Conrad

Summary of Early Life:

Conrad Rader was born ca 1765, the son of Henry and Elizabeth Rader, pioneer settlers of the Catawba Valley. He was a brother to Adam Rader, William Rader, and Catherine Rader Smith.

Summary of Partisan Activity:

The North Carolina Revolutionary Army Accounts verify the service of Conrad Rader, or Rather, as a militiman in Burke County, North Carolina. His service was in Morgan Military District.

Summary of Later Life:

Conrad Rader was married to Susannah Winkler (c. 1767-1860) c. 1787. The children by their union included:

Conrad, Jr. b. 1790 m. Christine Keller
David b. 1788 m. (1) Catherine Shell (2) Ebby Givens
Joseph b. 1792 m. Mary Ann Fox
Henry Levi b. 1795 m. (1) Sally Givens (2) Priscilla Barber
Ruthey b. 1801 m. Mattias Rowe
Ann Marie b. 1803 m. Michael Cook

Conrad Rader died 1837 and is buried in Littlejohn Methodist Church Cemetery. His wife is also buried there.

Land Holdings and Transactions:

1. Burke County Tax List shows Conrad Rader with 100 acres on Husband's Creek, now Caldwell County, North Carolina.

Census Locations:

1790 Lincoln County, North Carolina 2nd Co.
1800 Burke County, North Carolina
1810 Burke County, North Carolina
1820 Burke County, North Carolina
1830 Burke County, North Carolina

References:
AIS Census Indices NC 1790-1830.
Pittman, Betsy D. "Burke County NC 1815 Tax Lists". 1990 ed., p. 90.
NC Revolutionary Army Account (Haun op. cit.) Vol. XII, Part XI, p. 1469.
NC DAR Roster of Soldiers from NC in the American Revolution. 1976 reprint
        of 1932 ed., GPC, p. 357.
Burke County Library, Morganton, NC Vertical File Data.

Rector, Lewis

Summary of Early Life:

Lewis Rector was the son of John Rector of Surry County,
North Carolina. He was a brother of Revolutionary War soldier,
Benjamin Rector of Iredell County and of Ephraim Rector of
Burke County, North Carolina. Ephriam was the progenitor of
many of the Burke County Rector's. John Rector lived near the
junction of Surry, Burke and Wilkes County during the Revolution
– probably now in southwest Yadkin County. He lived on a
tributary of Hunting Creek, which flows into the south Yadkin
River. Lewis Rector was in his seventies when applying for
federal pension in 1834.

Summary of Partisan Activity:

Lewis Rector was enlisted in the North Carolina
Continental Line in 1778 for a tour of eighteen months. He served
in Captain Anthony Sharp's Company of Lieutenant Colonel
Archibald Lytle's regiment. Lieutenant Colonel Lytle's regiment
participated in the Battle of Stono Ferry, South Carolina in June
1779. Lieutenant Colonel Lytle was wounded in this battle.
Rector was discharged after serving fifteen months.

Summary of Later Life:

Lewis Rector was married to Frances Lunsford in
December 1788. On the 1790 census, they were living in Burke
County, 8th Company (near present day Alexander County). Ca
1806, the Rector's had moved to Sandy Mush Creek in Buncombe
County, North Carolina, in the Buncombe-Madison County line
near the French Broad River. Lewis Rector applied for federal
pension in 1834 and was issued a pension amount of $50.00 per
anum. Lewis Rector died in Buncombe County, North Carolina on
January 30, 1844.

Lewis Rector's widow applied for and received a
continuation of his pension amount*. The children are not listed,

but other Rector's receiving property in Buncombe County include James, Miajiah, Joel, Elihu, and Andrew Rector, exact relationship to Lewis Rector not established.

Note: Anderson County, Tennessee lists a will by a Lewis Rector ca 1841. Frances Rector pension paid by Tennessee Agency, Greenville, Tennessee.

Land Holdings and Transactions:

1. Buncombe County NC deed from Joseph Hugley Apr 7, 1806 100 acres Sandy Much Creek
2. Buncombe County NC, NC Land Grant #1628 Nov 27, 1807 50 acres Sandy Mush Creek
3. Buncombe County NC NC Land Grant #2147 Dec 7, 1814 150 acres French Broad River

Census Locations:

1790 Burke County, North Carolina 8th Co.
1810 Buncombe County, North Carolina

References:
US National Archives. Revolutionary War Pension llll #W45.
Wooley, James E. Buncombe County NC Index to Deeds 1783-SHP 1983. pp. 412-413.
AIS Census Data. NC 1790, 1810.
Roster of Soldiers from North Carolina in the AmericanRevolution. NC DAR, GPC reprint of 1932 ed., 1967, p. 159.
Duncan, Mary Alice. Article on Rector Family. Burke County Heritage Vol. I, 1981 ed., pp. 366-367.
Garrou, Benjamin W Sr., MD. Valdese NC personal communications, 1990-2000.

Rhinehart, Conrad

Summary of Early Life:

Conrad Rhinehart was the son of Jacob Rhinehart Sr. and a brother of Jacob Rhinehart Jr. and John Rhinehart.

Summary of Partisan Activity:

Conrad Rhinehart's name appears on the 1782 Tory Docket of Burke County, North Carolina, relating to the Confiscation Acts passed by the North Carolina legislature. He however, served on the American side during the Revolutionary War. Conrad Rhinehart served as a sergeant in Captain William McKinzie's company of Colonel William Hill's regiment of South Carolina militia. The overall comander was General Thomas Sumter.

Summary of Later Life:

Conrad Rhinehart married (1) Mary _____ (2) Elizabeth Warlick. There were the following offspring:

Jacob
George m. Barbara Gross
Mary m. Daniel Anthony
Charles m. Elizabeth Loretz
Barbara m. Jeremiah Bennick

Conrad Rhinehart died ca 1808, the date of his will probate.

Land Holdings and Transactions:

In 1794, Conrad Rhinehart acquired 238 acres from John Dietz. Camp Creek, now Catawba Co. NC.

Census Locations:

1790 Lincoln County, North Carolina 6th Co.
1800 Lincoln County, North Carolina

254

References:

AIS Census Indices NC 1790, 1800.

Moss, Bobby G. Roster of South Carolina Patriots in the American Revolution
GPC 1983 ed. p. 810.

Internet source : http://www. mindspring.com(Laura's Reinhardt ancestors).
2004.

Huggins, Edith   Misc Burke Co. Records in 4 soft back issues. SHP Vol II
p. 150.

Pruitt, Dr. R.B. " Abstracts of Land Entrys Lincoln Co. NC 1798-1825". 1987
ed. pp. 90,648.

McAllister, Anne W. and Sullivan, Kathy G. " Lincoln Co. NC Court of Pleas
and Quarter Sessions Apr
1789-Apr 1796". 1987 ed.   p. 85.

Rhinehart, John Article in Burke Co. NC Genealogical Journal May 1995   pp.
3-20.

Rhinehart, Jacob Sr.

Summary of Early Life:

Details are sketchy about the early life of Jacob Rhinehart Sr. He may have been born in Germany ca 1730's. He appears to have been a brother of Christian Rhinehart. Both were early settlers of the Catawba Valley of North Carolina. Jacob Rhinehart was the father of Jacob Rhinehart Jr. Conrad Rhinehart and John Rhinehart.

Summary of Partisan Activity:

Jacob Rhinehart was an active Tory during the American Revolution. He along with his son, Jacob Rhinehart Jr. were members of Nicholas Welch's Loyalist Regiment of North Carolina. They fought conspicously at the battle of Ramsour's Mill North Carolina on June 20, 1780. Jabob Rhinehart Sr., Jacob Rhinehart Jr. and Conrad Rhinehart were all on the 1782 Tory Docket of Burke County, North Carolina relating to the North Carolina Confiscation Acts. Witnesses included Major Daniel McKissock and Captain John Bourlon of Lincoln County.

Summary of Later Life:

Jacob Rhinehart appears to have lived initially on Howard's Creek in Lincoln County, and then later moved to Burke County (now Catawba County). He was under Burke County court jurisdiction in 1782.

Jacob Rhinehart Sr. married Anna _____. There were the following offspring:

Catherine m. William Barks
Margaret m. (1) George Fullbright (2) John Cauvey.
Conrad   m. (1) Mary ___ (2) Elizabeth Warlick
Jacob Jr. m. Nellie Cauvey
John

Jacob Rhinehart Sr. died ca 1800 in Lincoln County, North Carolina (will probate Mar 18, 1800).

Census Locations:

1790 Lincoln County, North Carolina 4th Co.

References:
AIS Census Indices   NC   1790
Internet Source : http://www.mindspring.com (Laura's Reinhardt ancestors.)
    2004.
Clark, Murtie J. Loyalists of the Southern Campaigns of the Revolutionary War
    GPC 1981 ed. pp. 377,403.
Huggins, Edith   Misc. Burke Co. NC records in 4 soft back issues   SHP   Vol.
    II   p. 150.
McAllister, Anne and Sullivan Kathy G. " Lincoln Co. NC Court of Pleas and
    Quarter Sessions Jul 1796-Jan 1805." 1988   ed. p. 119.
Rhinehart, John Article in Burke Co. NC Genealogical Journal May 1995 pp.
    3-20.

Rhinehart, Jacob Jr.

Summary of Early Life:

Jacob Rinehart Jr. along with his Father Jacob Rhinehart Sr. were active Tories during the American Revolution. Both served in Nicholas Welch's North Carolina Loyalist Regiment. They fought conspicously at the battle of Ramsour's Mill on June 20, 1780. Later, Jabob Rhinehart Jr., like his brother Conrad, would serve on the American side, being recruited into the North Carolina Continental Line. (Conrad served in SC militia). Jacob Rhinehart Jr. served 12 months in the 10th North Carolina Regiment, Continental Line, in Captain (Benjamin) Bailey's Company.

Jacob Rhinehart's name (as well as Conrad and Jacob Sr.) appears on the 1782 Burke County North Carolina Tory Docket, relating to the North Carolina Confiscation Acts.

Summary of Later Life:

Jacob Rhinehart Jr. was married to Eleanor "Nellie" Cauvey. They had the following offspring:

Molly m. Christian Knipe	Suzannah m. Daniel Holly
Jacob m. Mary Ann Michel	Christina m. Anthony Shitle
David m. Mary Mason	Mary m. Eli Baker
Isaac m. Elizabeth Wyatt	Margaret m. George Wacaster
Sally m. Levi Hull	Catherine m. John Rudisill
Rachel m. Joshua Lore	

Jacob Rhinehart Jr. died 28 Jan.1834, Lincoln County, North Carolina.

Land Holdings and Transactions:

Lincoln Co. NC Jacob Rhinehart acquired 3 tracts of land totaling 83 acres N. of South Fork of Catawba River, adjacent to his own land.

Census Locations:

1790 Lincoln County, North Carolina 4th Co.
1800 Lincoln County, North Carolina
1810 Lincoln County, North Carolina
1820 Lincoln County, North Carolina
1830 Lincoln County, North Carolina

References:
Internet source : http://www. mindspring.com " Laura's Reinhardt Ancestors "
        2004.
AIS Census Indices NC 1790-1830.
Huggins, Edith W. Misc Burke Co. NC Records in 4 soft back issues   SHP
        Vol II   pp. 150,157.
Clark Murtie J. Loyalists of the Southern Campaigns of the Revol;utionary War
        GPC 1983 ed. pp. 377, 403.
Pruitt, Dr. R.B. "Abstracts of Land Entrys Lincoln Co. NC 1798-1825". 2nd
        index Nos. 974,1073,1075.
Rhinehart, John   Article in Burke Co. Genealogical Society Journal May 1995
        pp. 3-20.

Richardson, James (Richeson, Richason)

Summary of Early Life:

James Richardson was born ca 1763 (he was age 69 in 1832 when applying for Revolutionary War pension). At the beginning of the Revolutionary War he was residing in Rowan County, North Carolina.

Summary of Partisan Activities:

James Richardson first entered military service in Rowan County, North Carolina in a company of militia commanded by Colonel Joseph Dickson (probably 1781). He was marched to the vicinity of Camden, South Carolina and remained on duty there for three months. After returning home, he along with his father and family, moved to Pacolet River section of South Carolina. There he served a tour of duty as a spy, or ranger, in Captain (Thomas?) Price's company of militia. They scoured the countryside, keeping the Tories "in check". After this tour, Richardson along with his father and family moved to Burke County, North Carolina. He served a tour of duty on the Catawba River at Davidson's Fort. He served in Captain (Daniel?) Smith's Company.

Summary of Later Life:

James Richardson continued to live in Burke County, North Carolina until the turn of the century. He moved to Grainger County, Tennessee, and lived there about twenty years and then moved to Monroe County, Tennessee. James Richardson applied for Revolutionary War pension benefits in Monroe County, Tennessee on September 17, 1832 age 69 years. He was awarded an annual pension of $20.00.

James Richardson died in January 1838. His widow later applied for continuation of pension benefits in 1842.

Census Locations:

1800 (1804 and 1805 Grainger County, Tennessee tax lists)
1810 Grainger County, Tennessee (tax lists)
1830 Monroe County, Tennessee

References:
US National Archives. Revolutionary War Pension Data   # S 4112.

Rippetoe, William

Summary of Early Life:

William Rippetoe was born in Albemarle County, Virginia on March 15, 1748. At or near the beginning of the Revolutionary War, he had moved to Burke County, North Carolina, now Caldwell County.

Summary of Partisan Activity:

Family sources say that William Rippetoe served in the American Revolution and was at Yorktown at the time of the surrender of Cornwallis (many from the Albemarle area were at the surrender). There is little documentation of his military service. The relationship of this William Rippetoe to another Virginia soldier by the same name and from the same area is not known. The other William Rippetoe was a pensioned soldier and lived in Orange County, Virginia and Jefferson County, Tennessee. Another source says that he was a bodyguard for General Washington. Probably the best documentation is his tombstone stating that "he was in the War of 1776". This represents a contemporary verification.

Summary of Later Life:

William Rippetoe was married to Ruth Antley (1751-1842 of the Winchester, Virginia area ca 1770. They had the following offspring:

Elizabeth b. 1771
Nancy b. 1774
Anon b. 1775 scalped by Indians, Kentucky, 1810
Mary b. 1779 m. John Bush
David b. 1780 m. (1) Elizabeth Harshaw (2) Priscilla Hall
William b. 1781 m. Elizabeth Vinson
John B. 1784 m. Polly Allen
Sarah b. 1786 m. Jacob Oldacre
James b. 1789 m. Patricia Knight

Peter b. 1790 m. Nancy Robertson

William Rippetoe, along with family members, left Burke County ca 1804 and moved to Russell County, Kentucky. He lived there for the remainder of his life. William Rippetoe died in Russell County, Kentucky on April 16, 1839. His widow, Ruth Antley Rippetoe, died January 5, 1842. They are buried in the Rippetoe Springs Cemetery, Russell County, Kentucky.

Land Holdings and Transactions:

1. 200 acres Burke County on the head branches of Smokey and Gunpowder Creeks adjacent to Chestnut Hill. The land was adjacent to land belonging to John Tabour. Ent. Jan 1, 1779 Grant no. 808 Iss. Nov 9 1784 Book 57 p. 18. c.c. William Tabour, James Ussery.
2. 400 acres Burke County on south side of Gunpowder Creek, including his improvements. The land was adjacent to property belonging to Ezekiel Wilson. Ent Dec 26 1778 Grant no. 849 Iss Nov 9 1784 Book 57 p. 37. c.c. William Murray, Joh Grider.
3. 200 acres Burke County at the head of Smokey Creek and adjacent to land of John Tabour. The land was near Chestnut Mountains. Ent Mar 27, 1779 #1626 Grant no. 1394 Iss. Nov 16, 1790 Bk 77 p. 158.
4. 20 acres Burke County NC The land lay adjacent to his own land and to that of John Clark. Ent Oct 25 1797 #3299 Grant no. 2315 Iss Dec 21, 1798 Bk 100 p 187.
5. In Kentucky he lived on a 125 acre tract in Russell County.

Census Locations:

1790 Burke County, North Carolina 9th Co.
1800 Burke County, North Carolina
1820 Adair County, Kentucky
1830 Russell County, Kentucky

References:
Caldwell County NC Library, Lenoir, NC, vertical files.
Burke County NC Land Grant Data. Burke County Library, Morganton, NC.
AIS Census Indices.

Robinson, James

Summary of Early Life:

James Robinson was one of the early settlers of the Catawba Valley of North Carolina. In the early 1750's he received Crown and Granville grants on South Fork of the Catawba River, near Clark's Creek. By the time of the American Revolution, he was a substantial landowner and slave owner.

Summary of Partisan Activity:

James Robinson was an officer in the 2nd Rowan Regiment of Militia, later to become the Burke Regiment. He served under both Colonel Christopher Beekman of the 2nd Rowan Regiment and under Colonel Charles McDowell of the Burke County, North Carolina Militia. He and his company participated in the Cross Creek Expedition under Brigadeir General Griffith Rutherford, Commandant of the Salisbury District Militia. This was a followup action following the Moore's Creek Bridge battle of February 1776. They assisted in cleanup operations, confiscating equipment and supplies and arresting suspected Tories.

Later Robinson and his men served on the Catawba frontier, guarding against the hostile actions of the Cherokee Indians, then operating in concert with the British agents.

Summary of Later Life:

James Robinson and his wife Catherine had the following offspring:

Sarah	Jesse	David
James, Jr.	John	

In 1785 James Robinson deeded possesssion of his slaves to three of his sons, David, Jesse, and James. James Robinson is not listed on the 1790 North Carlina Census.

James Robinson is buried in the Wilson - Robinson cemetery at Startown, Catawba County, North Carolina.

Land Holdings and Transactions:

1. Anson Co. NC 400 ac on N. side of South Fork of Catawba River. 27 Sep 1751 Crown grant " Robertson "
2. Tryon Co. NC 180 ac. on N. side of South Fork of Catawba River. 11 Dec 1770 Crown grant.
3. Granville grant to James Robinson 144 ac. 8 Dec 1753.

References:
Hofmann, Margaret <u>Colony of NC</u> 1765 - 1775 Vol. II 1984 ed. p. 193.
Hofmann, Margaret <u>Colony of NC</u> 1735 - 1764 Vol. I 1982 ed. p. 9.
U.S. National Archives: Rev. War pension data of Michael Houck # S 32329 and Joseph Painter # S 3240
NC Rev. Army Accounts as given in Haun, Wynette P. <u>op cit</u> Part I p. 5.
McAllister, Anne and Sullivan, Kathy " Lincoln Co. NC Court of Pleas and Quarter Sessions 1796 - 1805" 1988 ed. p. 11.
Plyler, Mattie Adams Article: " The Robinson Family " in Catawba County <u>Heritage</u> Vol I 1986 ed. p. 416.

Robinson, Samuel (Robertson)

Summary of Early Life:

Samuel Robinson was born in Baltimore County, Maryland on September 7, 1760. His family was living in Burke County, North Carolina at the time of his first enlistment.

Summary of Partisan Activity:

Samuel Robinson first entered military service in late 1778 as a volunteer militiaman in Burke County, North Carolina under the command of Luetinant Colonel Hugh Breverd and Captain Bennett Osborne. He enlisted for a tour of five months. Robinson was marched from Burke County to Salisbury and then to lower South Carolina, joining in with the troops of General Rutherford's brigade. Later they marched to the well known "Two Sisters" and then to Matthew's Bluff, overlooking the Savannah River. On March 3, 1779, Robinson was at the disastrous Brier Creek Battle. Just across the river on the Georgia side, American forces under General John Ashe were soundly defeated by the British in a battle that lasted only five minutes. The Americans were thrown in disorder, many died attempting to swim across the Savannah River to safety. Robinson was recalled back across the river shortly before the battle, and thus missed the action. In his pension declaration, he gives an interesting commentary concerning the post-battle events that occurred.

Robinson stated that before embarking for the American side at Matthew's Bluff, General Ashe "came running up, having lost his way and requested me to carry him across the river in the canoe in which I had went across". "When General Ashe got across to our encampment, General Rutherford demanded to know where his men were." Robinson said that he thought General Ashe stated, "they were gone to hell for aught he knew." Robinson also said that, at this time, Rutherford took Ashe's sword from him.
This is an interesting historical tidbit – The author has never, to his knowledge, read anything about this encounter. Rankin, in his book on the North Carolina Continentals, does relate "Ashe made it to Matthew's Bluff some four miles

away where General Rutherford's brigade of North Carolina militia was stationed". (The North Carolina Continentals. Rankin, Hugh F. UNC Press Chapel Hill 1971., p. 196.)

Robinson returned to the encampment at Two Sisters where he remained until his enlistment had expired (about April 1779).

After returning to Burke County and about eighteen months later, he was drafted for a three-month militia term under Captain Smith and Lieutenant Isaac Stockley. He was marched south, joining some detached troops of General Nathaniel Greene, who were stationed at Rugley's Mill, South Carolina above Camden. They conducted a siege maneuver designed to flush out a group of Tories that were sequestered in a large barn owned by Henry Rugley. Several hundred Tories were inside, including Major Rugley, armed and ready. Here, Colonel William Washington utilized the old "Quaker Gun" trick in order to impress the Tories, and it worked. The Tories surrendered without a shot being fired. Robinson interestingly described (in his pension statements) how the Quaker gun was built. It was built by sawing a large log in two and mounting a portion of it between the two wheels of a caisson. Robinson accompanied the prisoners to Salisbury, North Carolina. Here, he assisted in building a stockade jail to house the prisoners.

Robinson's final military duty was as a drafted militiaman serving on the frontier at the head of the Catawba River (now Old Fort, North Carolina). His commanding officer was Captain Samuel Davidson.

Summary of Later Life:

After the Revolution, Robinson moved from Burke County, North Carolina to Pendleton District, South Carolina. He was living there at the turn of the century. Between then and 1823, Robinson lived at various times in Limestone County and Madison County, Alabama and in Hickman County, Tennessee. In 1823 he moved to Hardin County, Tennessee, remaining there the remainder of his life. He is listed on the 1830 census along with one female over seventy years of age, presumably his wife.

Robinson applied for Revolutionary War pension in Hardin
County, Tennessee on March 18, 1834 at the age of seventy-three.
He received a pension in the amount of $33.33 per anum.
*See Tennessee Will Books, Hardin County 1836, b.21. A Samuel Robinson
estate was inventoried and sold in 1836, Hardin County, Tennessee – see
reference.*

Census Locations:

1790 Ninety-Six District, Pendleton County, South Carolina
    (2 Samuel Robinsons)
1800 Pendleton District, South Carolina
1820 Limestone County, Alabama (Robertson)
1830 Hardin County, Tennessee (Robertson)

References:
US National Archives Pension Data #S4155
Boatner, Mark IV. Encyclopedia of the American Revolution. New York, 1966,
    p. 951.
Huggins, Edith W. Burke County Data Vol. II. (court martial minutes, C.
    McDowell)
Rankin, Hugh. The North Carolina Continentals. Chapel Hill Press, 1971, p.
    193. (Brier Creek Battle).
AIS Census Indices.
Byron Sistler, and Associates. 1830 TN Census (Nashville, TN).
Hays, Thomas A. Hardin County Tennessee Records 1820-1860. SHP 1985, p.
    158.

Roderick, Frederick

Summary of Early Life:

Frederick Roderick was born in Germany in 1758 (another source says 1760). He lived in the vicinity of Hesse. He came to America in 1776.

Summary of Partisan Activity:

Frederick Roderick came to America as a hired professional soldier, or mercenary. The British had recruited them to help bolster their forces in America. They were generally called "Hessians", since most, but not all, came from the province of Hesse. After landing at Staten Island, Roderick deserted and was pursued by Tories and escaped, later joining the American Army of General George Washington. He served for the duration and then moved to Virginia, Albemarle County.

Summary of Later Life:

Frederick Roderick moved to Albemarle County and lived there about twenty-five years. He and his wife Mary had four children as follows:

William
Charles
Nicholas m. Julia Gavins
Anna m. Kesley

Frederick Roderick's first wife died and he then married Elizabeth Phillips Burgy, a widow, while still living in Albermarle County. There was one child, a son Daniel Roderick (m. Elizabeth Spainhour). Daniel was born 1804. Ca 1813, Frederick Roderick left Virginia and came to Burke County, North Carolina, where he lived the remainder of his long life.

Frederick Roderick was by occupation a stone mason. He built many structures in and around Burke County. One of his last projects was the building of the Burke County Court House, which still stands. Frederick Roderick died March 15, 1842.

See separate articles by Richard Lane and Dixon Lackey in Burke Heritage I, pp. 373-4.

Land Holdings and Transactions:

Frederick Roderick purchased 200 acres of land in Linville Township from Waighstill Avery (present day Jamestown Road and Kerley Creek).

Census Locations:

1810 Albemarle County, Virginia Frederickville Parish
1820 Burke County, North Carolina (William Roderick)
1830 Burke County, North Carolina
1840 Burke County, North Carolina

References:
Lackey, Dixon A. Article in Burke Heritage I. p. 373, Winston Salem 1981).
Lane, Richard N. Article in Burke Heritage I. p. 374.
AIS Census Indices. (NC 1830, 1840).
Crickard, M. W. Index to the 1810 Virginia Census. (1971).
Potter, D. W. Index to the 1820 North Carolina Census. (1974).
Hallyburton, Rick and Wood, Alice (Hallyburton), (Rutherford College, NC).
        Personal conversation with author 1980-1999, descendants of Frederick
        Roderick.

Russell, John

Summary of Early Life:

John Russell was born April 13, 1758. During the American Revolution, John Russell was living on a lower branch of Little River, a tributary of the Catawba River, then Burke County, North Carolina.

Summary of Partisan Activity:

Captain John Russell began his Revolutionary War activities on the Catawba frontier guarding against the hostile Cherokee Indians (summer 1777). Captain John Russell was a commissioned officer in Captain Charles McDowell's Burke Regiment. At Ramseurs' Mill (June 20, 1780), his company arrived just after the battle, but did not participate in it. Shortly afterwards his company joined up with McDowell's troops and played an active role in the South Carolina actions of McDowell, which culminated in the American victory at Musgrove Mill (Aug. 1780).

Later on October 7, 1780 Captain John Russell and his company served in the Battle of Kings Mountain. There, Russell witnessed the capture of Ben Whitson, one of the Burke County Tory leaders.

In the summer of 1782, Russell and his company were on the Catawba frontier at Wofford's Fort. In September, his company took part in one of the last, if not the last acts of the American Revolution which was directed against the Cherokee Indians.

In early 1782, Russell served on the court martial board in the trial of Captain Charles McDowell of Burke County.

Summary of Later Life:

John Russell was married to Rachel Hobbs. The

Revolutionary War soldier, Captain John Russell died August 3, 1838. Russell seems to have moved west, first into Rutherford County, and then into Buncombe County.

Land Holdings and Transactions:

1. Land Grant Burke County NC 100 acres on the south side of the Naked Mountain on water of Mountain Branch of the Lower Little River, a tributary of the Catawba River. The land included a part of the road leading "from Mineral Springs to Morrison's Mill". Ent. #309 16 Oct 1778 Bk 28/208.

Census Locations:

1790 Rutherford County, North Carolina 10th Co.

References:
DAR Patriot Index. Washington, DC, 1966 ed., p. 587.
US National Archives Pension Statements of Philip Anthony (S6800), Charles Baker (S31536), Enoch Berry (W8128), John Penly (S7302), and Henry Wakefield (W35).
Huggins, Edith W. Miscellaneous Burke Records in 4 volumes. Vol. II, (SHP).

Sailors, John

Summary of Early Life:

John Sailors was born in Maryland ca 1756. During the Revolutionary War, he was living in eastern Burke County, North Carolina, later Lincoln and then Catawba County. John Sailors was the son of Abram and Catherine Sailors. What, if any relation the Revolutionary War soldier Michael Sailors is unknown.

Summary of Partisan Activity:

According to family records, John Sailors was present at an early Revolutionary War skirmish between the Tories and Liberty men, known as the "Battle of Old Store". Later he was to participate, as a patriot, in the battle of Ramsuer's Mill (June 20, 1780) and Kings Mountain (October 7, 1780).

Summary of Later Life:

John Sailors married Fanny Osborne (1759-1784). *Details of later marriages not known.* There were supposedly three children born in South Carolina. Two sons are mentioned in later records, Jacob and Conrad. John Sailors moved from NC to the Abbeville area in South Carolina ca 1784. Later in 1810, he moved to Scott County, Kentucky and then to Franklin County, Indiana. His last move was to Rush County, Indiana, where he died in 1822. He is buried six miles southeast of Rushville, Indiana.

Census Locations:

1800 Pendleton District, South Carolina
1810 Indiana Territory 1807, Dearborn County

References:
Leavell, Jane, A. Internet data: little calamity @ yahoo.com.
Holcomb, Brent. Index to 1800 Census of South Carolina. GPC 1980.
Census of Indiana Territory for 1807. Indianapolis 1980.

Sailors, Michael

Summary of Early Life:

Michael Sailors was born ca 1756 in Pennsylvania. As a small child, his family moved to North Carolina. During the Revolutionary War, he resided in Burke County, North Carolina on the south side of the Catawba River.

Summary of Partisan Activity:

Michael Sailors first entered military service in Burke County, North Carolina as a draftee for a tour of one month. He served his time on the Catawba frontier guarding against Indian incursions. His company commander was Captain William Davidson. This was probably in late 1780, early 1781.

He served next as a draftee for a three-month tour of duty. He was detached from the Army headed toward Cheraw, South Carolina and sent to Salisbury. Here he assisted in building a stockade and subsequently guarded some prisoners. He dates this tour at about the time General William L. Davidson was killed (February 1781).

His third tour of duty was with South Carolina troops (many North Carolina soldiers were being recruited for service in South Carolina units). He served in Colonel Charles S. Myddleton's Regiment under Captain Godfrey Adams and Ensign Daniel Killian (General Sumter's Corps). They marched to the vicinity of Columbia, South Carolina, in the process taking possession of many slaves, formerly owned by Tories. They were detached from the main army and proceeded to Camden, South Carolina. In the meantime, the main Army under General Nathaniel Greene attempted to take the British held fortress of Ninety-Six, which was unsuccessful because of the arrival of British reinforcements. His unit then marched to Congaree River and crossed at McCord's Ferry. There, Sailors became sick and was hospitalized for several weeks. After recovering, he joined the main Army at Orangeburg, South Carolina, but became sick again.

On recovery, he was engaged in hauling grain to Colonel Sumter's mill. He continued these duties until the end of his tour of duty until May 1782.

Summary of Later Life:

After the Revolution, Michael Sailors moved from Burke County, North Carolina to Georgia. From there he moved to Blount County, Tennessee and finally to Jackson County, Tennessee. He spent a short time in Missouri, but moved back to Jackson County.

Michael Sailors applied for Revolutionary War pension benefits in White County, Tennessee (it was closer and easier to access than the County Seat of Jackson County, where he resided). He was awarded an annual pension of $30.00.

References:
US National Archives Revolutionary War Pension Data #S21463.
Land Grant Data. Burke County Library, Morganton, NC.

Scott, Levi

Summary of Early Life:

Levi Scott was born near Hagerstown, Maryland in 1762. At the time of the American Revolution, he was residing in Burke County, North Carolina. Many of the Scotts were living on Upper Creek section of Burke County. He was the son of Baptist and Betsy Farquhar Scott.

Summary of Partisan Activities:

Levi Scott first entered military service in May 1780 (1781?). He was placed in a militia horse company commanded by Major Joseph McDowell. There was a Lieutenant Williams and Ensign Talbott. The overall commander was Colonel Charles McDowell of Burke County. Their company was marched to South Carolina. There was no general action during this tour, only a few small skirmishes. In November the same year, he moved to Kentucky and settled at McGary's station. There he volunteered as a private soldier and was placed in Captain Michael Kirkham's Company.

They marched to Louisville, joining up with troops under the command of Colonel George Rogers Clark. They embarked upon a mission against the Indians near Chillicothe, destroying their towns and burning their crops. The tour lasted three months, the later part of which he served as an Indian scout, or "spy". As a draftee in 1783, he assisted in building a fort in the Louisville area.

Summary of Later Life:

Levi Scott m. Nancy Carter (b. 1772) in 1793. Children are as follows:

Mary Polly b. 1794 m. Willima Mead
Elizabeth b. 17997 m. Hamilton Wilson
Lydia b. 1799
George m. Mary Hawtthorn

Jean (Jane) b. 1803 m. James Hisle
Levi b. 1805
Nancy b. 1807
Rowland b. 1809
Madison b. 1812

Levi Scott had moved to McGary Station in Mercer County, Kentucky during the War. He continued to live for a while in Mercer County after the War. About 1800 he moved to Henry County, Kentucky.

Levi Scott applied for Revolutionary War benefits in Henry County, Kentucky on October 11, 1843. He was awarded an annual pension of $30.00. Levi Scott died in Henry County, Kentucky on January 16, 1844. His wife had died earlier in 1822.

Census Locations:

1820 Henry County, Kentucky

References:
US National Archives Revolutionary War Pension Data #S30690.
Hill, H. Edgar at www.hile-ky.org/reports/scott. LC PDF.
Feldin, Jeanne R. and Inman, Gloria K. V. Index to the 1820 Census of
        Kentucky. GPC, 1981 ed.

Sellers, James

Summary of Early Life:

James Sellers was living in Chatham County, North Carolina at the time of his first enlistment in 1778. He was age seventy-four in February 1833, when applying for federal pension.

Summary of Partisan Activity:

James Sellers first entered military service in the fall of 1778 as a nine-month Continental Soldier, then being actively recruited by North Carolina authorities. His company commander was Captain Matthew Ramsey of the 4th Continental North Carolina Line Regiment. They marched from Chatham County, North Carolina to Guilford and Rowan Counties in North Carolina, then southward through Mecklenburg County, North Carolina. Entering South Carolina, they passed through Camden and then to Purysburg. Their regimental commanders were Colonel James Thackston and Lieutenant Colonel Archibald Lytle. Crossing the Savannah River, they advanced to Augusta and then down across to the mouth of Brier Creek. Crossing the Savannah again, they advanced toward Charleston so as to intercept the British. The British were then beginning their first attempt to take Charleston. This was in June of 1779. On June 20, 1779, the hard fought battle of Stono Ferry took place. Sellers was in this battle. The British were forced to retire toward Savannah and try again at another time (they were successful in 1780). As the armies were still in proximity to each other after the battle, Sellers was discharged by Colonel Thackston on August 2, 1779. He returned home to Chatham County.

In his declaration he mentions, besides Colonels Thackston and Lytle, Colonel Martin Armstrong (John ?) and General (Benjamin) Lincoln.

In Sellers statements relating to pension application, he was a little confused as to dates – the dates given are a year later. Eg. Battle of Stono Ferry was June 10, 1779, not 1780.

Summary of Later Life:

Probably at the end of the war, it appears that James Sellers moved to Burke County, North Carolina. The Burke records mention James Sellers on numerous occasions. They also indicated there were two James Sellers, one the son of James, the other the son of John. His name appears on the 1810 census and on 1815 tax lists, but not on 1820 census. In his pension file, a document of 1842 stated that he had lived in Tennessee for about twenty-six years and in Burke County, North Carolina before then. This would suggest that he left Burke County somewhere between 1815 and 1820. In Tennessee, he lived first in Bradley County and then Grainger County. The soldier James Sellers applied for Revolutionary War pension in Grainger County, Tennessee on February 19, 1833 and was awarded an amount of $30.00 per anum. Later documents indicate that his wife predeceased him, though she appears to have been living at the time of the 1830 census. The documents also list a son James Sellers and two other sons.

James Sellers died in Grainger County, Tennessee on December 20, 1842. Of interest is that "the other James Sellers" of Burke County, North Carolina died sometime prior to 1820, as indicated by probate records.
Check Tennessee Wills and Probate, Grainger County. W5-247, 1843.

Land Holdings and Transactions:

1. Burke County, NC. 71 acres South Muddy Creek including the top of a mountain between Muddy Creek and Silver Creek. Ent. 14 Jan 1795, #1045 Grant no. 2548 Iss. 7 June 1799. Bk. 101, p. 75. cc John Cauden orBensen, James Sellers.
2. Burke County, NC. 50 acres South Muddy Creek adjacent to Thomas Morrison and William Morrison. Ent. 19 Nov 1792 #210 Grant no. 2587, Iss. 7 June 1799. Bk. 101, p. 92.
3. Burke County, NC. 50 acres South Muddy Creek adjacent to land of Charles McDowell (previously William

McDowell). Ent. 20 July 1802 #4450 Grant no. 3252 Iss. 19 Dec 1803.

4. Burke County, NC. South Muddy Creek adjacent to land of Colonel Charles McDowell. Ent. 25 Feb 1812 #5944 Grant no. 3617 Iss. 24 Nov 1813 Bk. 128, p. 17. cc John Sellers; Michael Sellers.

5. Grainger County, TN. 1815 tax lists show James Sellers as being in Captain John Arwine's militia district and owning 100 acres of land.

Census Locations:

1790 Burke County, North Carolina 6th Company
1800 Burke County, North Carolina (2 by this name)
1810 Burke County, NC 1815 Burke County NC tax lists (250 ac)
1820 (1815 Tax lists Grainger County, Tennessee)
1830 Grainger County, Tennessee

References:
US National Archives Pension Data #S3872
AIS Census Indices. NC 1790, 1800, 1810.
Huggins, Edith W. Burke County Data Vols. I-IV. 1977 et. Seq.
Pittman, Betsy D. Burke County, NC 1815 Tax lists (1990), p. 33.
Philbeck, M. S. and Turner, G. "Burke County NC Surviving and
        Will Probate Records, 1983. Chapel Hill. p. 486.
Byron Sistler and Associates. Nashville, TN, 1830 TN Census.
"Grainger County Tennessee Tax Lists", 1815, WPA Records
        1936, p. 30.

Settlemeyer, Jacob (Suttlemeyer)

Summary of Early Life:

Jacob Settlemeyer was living on "Cold Arse" Creek in Burke County, North Carolina (now Mountain Creek, Connelly Springs, NC) during the American Revolution.

Summary of Partisan Activity:

A Jacob Settlemeyer (or Suttlemeyer) served with South Carolina troops under Colonel Charles S. Myddleton and Captain Francis Moore (Sumter's Brigade) in 1781. These units took part in the Battle of Eutaw Springs, South Carolina in September 1781.

In 1782, Settlemeyers name was included on the Tory list of Burke County Court, to show cause as to why his property should not be confiscated (for being inimical to the American cause). Witnesses included Colonel Joseph McDowell, Captain Robert Patton, James Morris, Joseph Dobson, and James and Rebecca Cooper.

Summary of Later Life:

Jacob Settlemeyer married Mary _____. Children were, Jacob, John, David, Catherine, and Mary. Jacob Settlemeyer died in 1813. He left a will; Burke County North Carolina dated August 2, 1813.

Land Holdings and Transactions:

Jacob Settlemeyer was a large landowner. North Carolina land grant records are as follows:

1. Burke County NC 150 acres on both sides of Cold Arse Creek and on both sides of the wagon road extending from the Line Kilns to Sherrill's Ford (now present day Rutherford College – Connelly Springs). The property included "the improvements whereon he now lives". Grant

#359, Iss. 28 Oct. 1782. Ent. 1778. Bk. 44.137.
2. Burke County NC 100 acres Ceney Fork of Rocky Fork (tributary Drowning Creek). Grant #375. Iss. 28 Oct. 1782. Ent. 1778. Bk. 44/146.
3. Burke County NC 100 acres Drowning Creek. Grant #1444, 1792. Bk. 44/146.
4. Burke County NC 250 acres Cold Arse Creek. Grant #874. Iss. 1784. Bk. 57/47.
5. Burke County NC 200 acres Husbands Creek. Grant 1144, 1789. Bk. 71/38.
6. Burke County NC 100 acres Zadack Smith's Creek. Grant 1419. 1792. Bk. 75/420.
7. Burke County NC 12 acres south side Catawba River, containing his fishery. Purchased from John Gibbs. Grant #1448. 1792. Bk. 75/430.
8. Burke County NC 111 ½ acres south side Catawba River. Grant #1556. 1792. Bk. 80/51.
9. Burke County NC 100 acres south side Catawba River. Grant #1748. 1794. Bk. 85/78.
10. Burke County NC 100 acres Caney Fork of Drowning Creek. Grant 1725. 1794. Bk. 85/70.

Census Locations:

1790 Burke County, North Carolina 2nd Company (4 females, 4 males)
1800 Burke County, North Carolina

References:
Moss, Bobby G. Roster of South Carolina Patriots in the American Revolution. GPC Baltimore (1983). P. 909.
NC Land Grant Records. Burke County Public Library, Morganton, NC.
AIS Censuses
Huggins, Edith W. Burke County Records Vol. II.
Philbeck, Miles and Turner, Grace. "Burke County North Carolina Surviving Will and Probate Records 1777-1910". (1983) #487.

Sharpe, Thomas

Summary of Early Life:

Thomas Sharpe was born in Lancaster County, Pennsylvania in 1755. Before the American Revolution, he had moved to Mecklenburg County, North Carolina.

Summary of Partisan Activity:

At age twenty years, Thomas Sharpe volunteered to serve a three month tour of duty. He served in a cavalry company commanded by Captain Robert Maybon (or Mebane) and Colonel William Polk. The overall commander was Colonel High Montgomery of Salisbury. His first tour was the Cross Creek Expedition of March 1776. This was under Brigadier General Rutherford. Arriving in Cross Creek after the Moore's Creek Battle of late February, they assisted in mop-up activities and conveyed prisoners to Hillsborough. He was discharged after ending his tour of duty.

He next volunteered as a militiaman in Captain Joseph Hardin's Company of General Rutherford's Brigade. He then took part in Rutherford's Cherokee Expedition of August and September 1776. The Cherokee's were effectively subdued by this action.

Summary of Later Life:

At the end of the war, he lived in Lincoln County for about nine years and then moved to Burke County. He remained in Burke County for over twenty years. From Burke County, he moved to Buncombe County, where he spent the remainder of his life.

Thomas Sharpe and his wife, Rhoda or Rhody, were married in 1775. They had twelve children. Thomas Sharpe applied for Revolutionary War pension in Buncombe County, North Carolina in October 1832, age seventy-eight years. His pension was approved in the amount of $22.50 per annum.

The Revolutionary War soldier, Thomas Sharpe, died in Buncombe County on January 25, 1834.

Summary of Later Life:

The widow of Thomas Sharpe lived until 1844-1845. Her will was probated in 1845, April court. She had continued to receive his pension after his death.

Land Holdings and Transactions:

1. Buncombe County NC 50 acres Grant from James Gudger, on Newfound Creek BIC 28 p. 110. Jan 17, 1829. (other Sharpe's receiving grants on Newfound Creek include James Sharpe, Jason Sharpe, William Sharpe).
2. In Burke County, Sharpe lived on a branch of South Muddy Creek adjacent to Andrew Woods and Charity Patton.
3. In Lincoln County, NC Thomas Sharpe received a deed from Frances Guthry 150 acres 20 June 1789. This was conveyed to George Brock Aug 19, 1793. (Howard's Creek).

Census Locations:

1790 Lincoln County, North Carolina 4th Co.
1800 Burke County, North Carolina
1810 Burke County, North Carolina
1820 Burke County, North Carolina
1830 Buncombe County, North Carolina

References:
US National Archives Pension Data W17803.
AIS Census Indices NC 1790-1830.
Wooley, James E. Buncombe County NC Index to Deeds 1783-SHP (1983 ed.), p.445.
Huggins, Edith W. Burke County Records Vol. I, p. 22.
McAllister, Anne and Sullivan, Kathy. "Lincoln County NC Court of Pleas and Quarter Sessions." Jul 1796- Jan 1805 pp. 80-81, (1988 ed)

Shenalt, Nimrod (Shinalt, Chennault, etc.)

Summary of Early Life:

The records are sparse concerning Nimrod Shenalt. Persons by this name were living in central Virginia in the Pre-Revolutionary period. Later some moved into Surry County, North Carolina. There are descendents by that name still living there today. Land records indicate that Nimrod Shenalt was living in Burke County, North Carolina during the Revolution, probably on Laurel Creek, southeast of Morganton.

Summary of Partisan Activity:

South Carolina records show that Nimrod Shenalt was serving in the South Carolina militia following the Charleston siege and surrender (May 1780). In 1782, his name appears in the Tory List as a suspected Tory; relative to the North Carolina Confiscation Acts. His name also appears on the trial docket with Captain George Walker and John Bourlin as witnesses.

Summary of Later Life:

Nothing is known definitely. Persons by the name of Shinalt appear in the middle Tennessee census enumerations.

Land Holdings and Transactions:

A Burke County, North Carolina land entry of Elias Alexander on Laurel Creek states, "including an improvement by John Shenalt". This probably was a relative of Nimrod. George Walker, a witness in the Tory trial of Nimrod Shenalt, also lived on Laurel Creek.

References:
Huggins, Edith W. Miscellaneous Burke County North Carolina Records Vol.
    II. Pp. 40, 150, 154.
Moss, Bobby G. <u>SC Patriots in the Am, Revolution</u>.GPC Balt. 1983ed. pg 859.
Miscellaneous census records Virginia, North Carolina, and Tennessee.

Sherrill, Moses

Summary of Early Life:

Moses Sherrill was born Aug. 8, 1742 in Augusta County, Virginia. He was the son of Adam Sherrill, a pioneer settler of the Catawba Valley of North Carolina. The Sherrills settled on the west bank of the Catawba. This region lay in Burke County during most of the Revolutionary War, later in Lincoln and then in Catawba County.

Summary of Partisan Activity:

Moses Sherrill received a commission as a Lieutenant of Militia in 1775, issued by the Rowan County Committee of Safety. In early 1776, Lieutenant Sherrill marched with General Rutherford to the Cross Creek area of North Carolina (now Fayetteville). His company was part of the Second Rowan Regiment of Militia. There they assisted in suppressing Tory activity following the battle of Moore's Creek Bridge.

Summary of Later Life:

Moses Sherrill was married to Sarah Simpson. By this union were born the following offspring:

Michael	William	Absalom
Acquilla	Cassandra	Sarah
Aaron	Moses	Japtha

Moses Sherrill continued to be active in Lincoln County affairs. He died ca 1813. (another source says 1830).

Land Holdings and Transactions:

1. Moses Sherrill received from his father 341 acres Apr. 10, 1769. This was part of a Granville Grant of 623 acres.
2. Burke Co. NC. 220 acres both sides of a branch of Clarks Creek and on waters of Litten's Mill Creek.he land lay

adjacent to that of James Clark, John Jones, John Robeson and James McLean. Grant # 282 Mar 14, 1780.

Census Locations:

1790 Lincoln County, North Carolina 1st Co.
1800 Lincoln County, North Carolina
1810 Lincoln County, North Carolina

References:
Internet acquisition (2003) members@ aol.com/ mysherrills/
Hofmann, Margaret NC Land Grants   Abstracts of State Grants Vol I # 282
        (1998 ed).
Wheeler, John Hill History of North Carolina (Rowan Co. NC Committee of
        Safety minutes.) op cit
Land Grand Records   Burke Co. NC Library Morganton NC.
AIS Census Indices NC 1790, 1800, 1810.
NC Rev Army Accts. as abstracted by Haun, Wynette P. Durham NC.
DAR Patriot Index   Nat. Soc. DAR Washington DC (1966 ed) . p. 612.

Shuford, Daniel

Summary of Early Life:

　　Daniel Shuford was born 1759, the son of John Shuford, Sr. and Maria Clara Shuford.

Summary of Partisan Activity:

　　Like his father and all of his brothers, Daniel Shuford was a Loyalist during the Revolutionary War. His name is on the subpoena docket for suspected Tories of Burke County, North Carolina, late 1782. Sworn witnesses relating to his Tory activity, included Captain Henry Whitener and Major Daniel McKissick. The cases were never resolved, as peace was to be declared several months later, along with a general amnesty.

Summary of Later Life:

　　Daniel Shuford was married to Mary Elizabeth Ramseur. By this union were the following children:

>David b. 1787 m. Rhoda Coulter
>Elizabeth b. 1789 m. Michael Shireman
>Daniel b. 1793 m. Hannah Robinson
>John b. 1794 m. Elizabeth Roberston
>Henry b. 1798 m. Mary Ann Warlick
>Barbara b. 1800 m. John Slagle
>Ephraim b. 1802 m. Susan Hoyle
>Solomon b. 1804

　　Daniel Shuford died ca 1833/1834. His will probated in 1834.

Land Holdings and Transactions:

1. Lincoln County NC 527 acres on South Fork of Catawba River received from his father, John Shuford, June 3, 1778.

Census Locations:

1790 Lincoln County, North Carolina 4th Co
1810 Lincoln County, North Carolina
1820 Lincoln County, North Carolina

References:
Shuford, David Wilson. <u>Origins of the Shuford Family in America</u>. Gateway
    Press, Baltimore MD.
Shuford, Reverand Julian H. <u>A Historical Sketch of the Shuford Family</u>. 1901,
    copy in Catawba County Library, Newton, NC.
AIS Census Indices NC 1790-1820.
Huggins, Edith W. Miscellaneous Burke Records Vol. II. Jury Docket.
Meyerling, Joan. Catawba County <u>Heritage</u>.

Shuford, David

Summary of Early Life:

David Shuford was born 1761, the son of John Shuford, Sr. and Maria Clara Shuford. Before the Revolutionary War, he was living on his father's estate, on the South Fork of the Catawba River.

Summary of Partisan Activity:

David Shuford was an active Loyalist during the American Revolution. The still extant minutes of the court martial of Colonel Charles McDowell expressly pinpoints David Shuford's Tory activities. Captain Henry Whitener stated that he fought against the Americans at the Battle of Ramseur's Mill on June 20, 1780 and that "he did not surrender for sometime". Captain Joseph Steel stated that Shuford later was with Cornwallis' Army at the Battle of Camden, South Carolina on August 16, 1780. The British military rolls further verify his Loyalist activity (as a member of Nicholas Welch's Regiment of Loyalist militia, listed as being "on furlough").

Summary of Later Life:

David Shuford was married to Elizabeth Ramseur. Their children were as follows:

John
George
Maxwell
Sally m. John Rhine
Anna m. David Robinson
Clarissa m. John Jarrett
Elizabeth

After the conclusion of the Revolutionary War, David Shuford became an active public servant. He served on many committees and juries. He served as sheriff of Lincoln County

291

1801-1803. David Shuford served several terms in the North Carolina Senate (1806, 1812, 1813, 1815, 1816, 1820).

Land Holdings and Transactions:

1. Lincoln County NC from John Shuford to David Shuford, 2 tracts of land on south side of South Fork of Catawba River. 527 acres and 443 acres July 1790 Book 4 pp. 28039. Book 15, pp. 379-381.

Census Locations:

1790 Lincoln County, North Carolina 4th Co
1800 Lincoln County, North Carolina
1810 Lincoln County, North Carolina
1820 Lincoln County, North Carolina

References:
Minutes of the Court Martial of Colonel Charles McDowell, facsimile of original minutes, copy presented to author by the late Mrs. Eunice Ervin, Morganton, NC. Printed version in Huggins, Edith. Burke County Miscellaneous Records (SHP), Vol. II.
Pruitt, Dr. R. B. "Abstracts of Deeds Lincoln County NC 1786-1793". 1988 ed., #514, 515.
AIS Census Indices, NC.
Philbeck, Miler and Turner, Grace. "Lincoln County NC Will Abstracts 1779-1910". 1986 ed., #514, 515.
Clark, Murtie June. Loyalists in the Southern Campaign Vol. I. Genealogical Publ. Co., Baltimore, MD, 1981 ed., p. 403, 377.

Shuford, Jacob

Summary of Early Life:

Jacob Shuford was born in 1756, the son of John Shuford, Sr. and Maria Clara Shuford. At a young age, he came with his family from Pennsylvania to the Catawba Valley of North Carolina.

Summary of Partisan Activity:

Like his father and his brothers, Jacob Shuford was an active Loyalist during the American Revolution. British war records confirm his presence in an organized Loyalist regiment. The regiment participated in the Battle of Ramsour's Mill (June 20, 1780) and Camden (August 16, 1780). His name appears on the Tory docket of Burke County, North Carolina in late 1782.

Summary of Later Life:

Jacob Shuford remained in Lincoln County (later Catawba County) after the Revolutionary War. He settled in the Potts Creek section of Lincoln County (south central Catawba County). Jacob Shuford was married to (1) Mary Blair, no children, and (2) to Barbara Hoover. By this union were born the following children:

Jacob
Ephraim b. 1797 m. Elizabeth Bradford
Israel b. 1797 m. Mary Davis
Clarissa m. Jacob Martin
Polly m. John Clay
Sarah m. Jacob Link

List of children - Joan M. Meyering in Lincoln County Heritage, 1997 ed., p. 208.

Jacob Shuford was active in Lincoln County civic affairs, appearing on various juries and committees. Jacob Shuford died in 1828.

Land Holdings and Transactions:

1. #937 50 acres Potts Creek adjacent to David and Daniel Shuford, Aug 11, 1798.
2. #983 55 acres Henrys Creek, Nov 16, 1798.
3. #1108 25 acres Henry River May 27, 1799
4. #1627 50 acres Potts Creek Jan 7, 1802
5. #1828 80 acres Potts Creek Jul 6, 1803
6. #2021 30 acres Jacobs River Sep 9, 1805
7. #2102 55 acres South Fork Catawba River Oct 7, 1806
8. #2103 100 acres South Fork Catawba River Oct 7, 1806

Census Locations:

1790 Lincoln County, North Carolina 4th Co
1800 Lincoln County, North Carolina
1810 Lincoln County, North Carolina
1820 Lincoln County, North Carolina

References:
Shuford, David Wilson. Origins of the Shuford Family in America. Gateway Press, Baltimore MD.
Shuford, Rev. Julius H. A Historical Sketch of the Shuford Family. 1901, copy in Catawba County, NC Library.
AIS Census Indices NC 1790-1820
Clark, Murtie June. Loyalists in the Southern Campaign. Genealogical Publ. Co., Baltimore, MD, 1981 ed., Vol. I pp. 336, 377, 403.
Huggins, Edith W. Tory Docket Burke County, NC 1782.

Shuford, John, Sr.

Summary of Early Life:

John Shuford was born in Germany in 1723, the son of George and Gertaud Hubener Shuford. The family came initially to Pennsylvania and then to the Catawba Valley of North Carolina, arriving near the conclusion of the French and Indian War. John Shuford was married to Maria Clara (or Clare), last name not definite, either Conrad or Wagner*. The Shuford's settled on the south fork of the Catawba River. George Shuford died shortly later, ca 1762.

*DAR records show an earlier marriage to Sarah _____

Summary of Partisan Activities:

John Shuford was a Loyalist during the time of the American Revolution. His name is on the Suspected Tory Docket, Burke County, North Carolina, late 1782, relating to the Confiscation Acts.

He, like his neighbor in Burke County, Conrad Hildebran, may have played on both side of the fence. Shuford did furnish supplies to the American Army. For this, he was designated a patriot by the DAR.

Summary of Later Life:

John Shuford lived through the Revolutionary War, dying ca 1790. He was buried near the home place on South Fork of Catawba River. His widow Mary Clare (Maria Clara) Shuford died after 1790

Land Holdings and Transactions:

1. Mecklenburg County NC Grant #5960 230 acres on west side of South Fork of Catawba River, on both sides of a Jumping Branch adjacent to land of Isaac Johnson and Legamir. Oct 26, 1767. Book 23, p. 100.

2. Mecklenburg County, NC #5961, 250 acres joining his own land west side of South Fork of Catawba adjacent to Michael Whitener. Oct 26, 1767 Book 23, p. 100.
3. John Shuford 443 acres, part of the estate inherited from his father, George Shuford.   June 3, 1788.

References:

Shuford, David Wilson. Origins of the Shuford Family in America. Gateway Press, Baltimore, 1998 ed.

Shuford, Rev. Julius H. A Historical Sketch of the Shuford Family. Hickory, NC, 1901, copy in Catawba County Library, Newton, NC.

Philbeck, Miles and Turner, Grace. "Lincoln County NC Will Abstracts 1779-1910". 1986 ed., #1143.

Huggins, Edith. Miscellaneous Burke County Records Vol II. Tory docket of 1782.

Hofmann, Margaret M. Colony of North Carolina 1765-1775 Abstracts of land patents, Weldon, NC 1984, p. 448.

Patriot Index. National Society DAR, Washington, DC, 1966 Ed., p. 615.

Shuford, Martin (John Martin Shuford)

Summary of Early Life:

Martin Shuford was born in 1744, the son of John Shuford, Sr. and Mary Clare Shuford. The family came to North Carolina from the York, Pennsylvania area ca 1760.

Summary of Partisan Activity:

Like his father and brothers, Martin Shuford was a Loyalist during the American Revolution. Martin Shuford was an active participant in the Battle of Ramsour's Mill fought on June 20, 1780. During this battle, Martin Shuford was mortally wounded. He died two days after the battle and is buried on the battlefield site.

Summary of Later Events:

Martin Shuford was married to Eva Catherine Warlick, daughter of Johann Daniel Warlick and Marie Schindler Warlick. There were six children.

Jacob	Daniel
John	Elizabeth
Martin	Philip

After the death of her husband, she later was married to Jacob Summey and had three additional children. Eva Warlick Shuford died January 24, 1822 and is buried at the old White Church in Lincoln County, North Carolina.

Land Holdings and Transactions:

1. Anson County NC 100 acres west side of the south fork of the Catawba River adjacent to land of Michael Whitener Grant #107 Oct 26, 1767.

References:

Shuford, David Wilson. <u>Origins of the Shuford Family In America</u>. Gateway Press, Baltimore, MD, 1998 ed.

Shuford, Rev. Julius H. <u>A Historical Sketch of the Shuford Family</u>. Hickory, NC, 1901, copy in Catawba County Library, Newton, NC.

Sigmon, Balser (Palser)

Sumamry of Early Life:

Balser Sigmon was born in Pennsylvania in 1753 or 1754. At the time of the American Revolution, he was living near Lyle's Creek in Burke County, North Carolina, near Catawba County.

Summary of Partisan Activity:

The North Carolina Revolutionary Army Accounts verify the revolutionary service of Balser Sigmon. Balser Sigmon was commissioned as an ensign of militia by the Rowan County, North Carolina Committee of Safety in November 1775.

Summary of Later Life:

Balser Sigmon was married to Margaret Cline (1757-1842). They had the following children:

Catherine m. Tobias Moser
Regina m. William Fullbright
Polly m. Philip Baker
Agaline m. Frederick Smith
Henry
Eli
Martin m. Susannah Lineberger
Harriet m. John Gabriel
Bennett m. Martha Ann Lineberger
George

Balser Sigmon died in 1820.

Land Holdings and Transactions:

1. Burke County NC 640 acres on third branch of Lyle's Creek and Jonas' Little Creek adjacent to Bernard Stoway and John Isenhower ent#182, 22 Jan 1778. Grant #203, Iss. 14 March 1780. Bk. 28, p. 202. cc Bernard Stoway,

Valentine Isenhower (with Abraham Barrier). The land included Barrier's and Sigman's improvements.

Census Locations:

1790 Lincoln County, North Carolina 5th Co
1800 Lincoln County, North Carolina
1810 Lincoln County, North Carolina

References:
NC Revolutionary Army Accounts. Abstracts by Haun, Wynette P. Durham NC, Vol. VII, Bk. 26, p. 1.
NC Land Grant Data in Burke County Library, Morganton, NC.
Catawba County Library, Newton, NC, William Sigmon file.
AIS Census Indices. NC 1790-1810.
Rowan County NC Committee of Safety Minutes as given in Wheeler, John H. History of North Carolina, p. 374.
Family Data via internet: Rootsweb.com/Sigmon.txt.

Sigmon, Barnet (Sigman)

Summary of Early Life:

Barnet Sigmon was born in Bucks County, Pennsylvania in 1754, the son of Barnet Sigmon, Sr. and Clara Sigmon. Barnet, or "Barney", Sigmon was living on Lyle Creek in what was then Burke County, North Carolina, later Lincoln County, now Catawba. He, along with his parents and siblings, had settled near Lyle Creek ca 1769.

Summary of Partisan Activity:

Barnet Sigmon was an officer in Charles McDowell's Burke Regiment; being commissioned a Lieutenant. His immediate superior was Captain John Hasselbarger. His company took part in the Wilmington Expedition of late 1781. The Americans, under Brigadier General Griffith Rutherford, occupied Wilmington after the British departure.

The North Carolina Revolutionary Army Accounts verify the service of Barnet Sigmon during the Revolutionary War.

Summary of Later Life:

Barnet Sigmon was active in Burke County civic activities, serving on various juries. He continued these activities in Lincoln County (after the expansion of 1782) until after the turn of the century. Barnet Sigmon and Elizabeth Sigmon had the following children:

David	John
Barnet	George
Elizabeth	Susanna

Barnet Sigmon died ca 1821, the date of his will probate.

Land Holdings and Transactions:

1. Rowan County deed of 320 acres on Lyle's Creek in 1753 was probably Barnet Sigmon the elder.
2. There were grants issued in Burke County, late Lincoln County, In 1778-1779 from land on Mull's Creek and Lyle's Creek. 450 acres Mull's Creek, 1779. 300 acres Lyle's Creek, 1778, 296 acres Lyle's Creek, 1779, and 374 acres Lyle's Creek, 1779. It must be remembered that there were three Barnet Sigmons in Lincoln County at the time of the 1790 census.

Census Locations:

1790 Lincoln County, North Carolina (3 Barnet Sigmons)
1800 Lincoln County, North Carolina
1810 Lincoln County, North Carolina
1820 Lincoln County, North Carolina

References:
Burke County Land Records. Burke County Library, Morganton, NC.
Linn, Jo White. Abstracts of the Deeds of Rowan County NC 1983 ed., Salisbury, p. 99.
AIS Census Indices. NC 1790-1820.
NC Revolutionary Army Accounts Vol. XII, Book 7, Folio X.

Sigmon, John (Sigman)

Summary of Early Life:

John Sigmon was born in Pennsylvania ca 1750. In 1771, he received a Crown Grant for 44 acres of land on the west side of Clark's Creek, where he lived.

Summary of Partisan Activity:

Early in the Revolutionary War, in November 1775, John Sigmon was commissioned a Lieutenant of militia and served under Captain Rudolph Conrad. The commission was issued by the Rowan County Committee of Safety. His unit served in the Cross Creek expedition of February and March 1776, which was the latter part of the Moore's Creek Bridge action against the Tories of southeast North Carolina.

In the summer of 1776, Conrad's company took part in Rutherford's Campaign against the Cherokee Indians. By 1780, John Sigmon had been commissioned a Captain of militia. Under Colonel Charles McDowell, he served in the small skirmishes preceding the Kings Mountain Campaign. Under McDowell (after retreating to Watauga), they advanced southwesterly into North Carolina into South Carolina on the trail of Major Patrick Ferguson and his command (containing loyalist militia along with provincial (regular) troops). On October 7, 1780, Sigmon led his company in the epic Battle of Kings Mountain, a great American victory.

Summary of Later Life:

John Sigmon married Mary _____. Children by this marriage included John, Sally (m. William Short), Nancy, George, and William. John Sigmon was a blacksmith by trade. John Sigmon died ca 1789 or 1790. Administrative papers presented in Lincoln County Court January 1791 session.

The 1790 census of Lincoln County, North Carolina show four John Sigmon's and a Mary Sigmon, wife of John Sigmon, deceased.

Note: The administrative papers and Lincoln County Court Records show that the John Sigmon who died ca 1790 was a relatively young man, since children were involved. The birth date of John Sigmon is given as ca 1750. This would indicate a person of about forty years of age. This would fit right for a person leaving at least five young offspring. It also seems that he was too young to have a son of military age during the Revolutionary War. The author therefore assumes that the John Sigmon who was born in 1750, who served as a Revolutionary War officer, and who died ca 1790 leaving a wife Mary and several young children was one and the same person.

Land Holdings and Transactions:

1. Crown Grant (state of NC Josiah Martin, Governor). #4797, p. 302, <u>John Sigmon</u> 25 November 1771, 44 acres in Tryon County on the west side of Clark's Creek, joining Peter Johnston, Mill's Line, Whitley's line and Shuffle (Christopher) Sigmon.
2. Land Entry Burke County NC. #423, p. 142 <u>John Sigmon</u> 200 acres on Clark's Creek, between the lines of Nicholas Fry's, Simon Horne, Peter Eigate (Icard), Hugh Montgomery including improvements whereon he now lives. Ent. 24 May 1778.

Census Locations:

1790 Lincoln County 3rd Company (Mary Sigmon)

References:
Minutes, Rowan County, North Carolina Committee of Safety as presented in
        Wheeler, John Hill, <u>Historical Sketches of North Carolina</u> Vol. II.
        Orig. 1851, reprint Reg. Pub. Co. Baltimore, 1964. pp. 360-381.
US National Archives. Revolutionary War Pension Statements. Philip Anthony,
        #S6800, John Wilfong, #S7951.
White, Katherine Keogh. <u>The Kings Mountain Men</u>. GPC 1970 Reprint, p. 25.
Revolutionary Army Accounts. Treasurers and Comptrollers Account Books
        "A" p.178. "Cpt. John Sigmons Co. of Horsemen", 5498, Sept. 1781.
Huggins, Edith. Burke County Records Vol. I, p. 40.
Land Grant Data. Burke County Library, Morganton, NC.
Hoffman, Margaret. <u>Colony of North Carolina 1765-1775</u> Vol. II.
AIS Census Records.
McAllister, Anne W. and Sullivan, Kathy G. "Lincoln County NC Court of
Pleas and Quarter Sessions, April 1789 - April 1796. " 1987., p. 32.

Simpson, Reuben

Summary of Early Life:

Reuben Simpson was born October 6, 1743 in Baltimore, Maryland. He was the son of William and Avarilla (Perkins) Simpson. Reuben Simpson, at the beginning of the American Revolution was living on land adjacent to the Catawba River, now Catawba County, North Carolina, but within Burke County during most of the Revolutionary War. His land lay just south of Sherrill's Ford.

Summary of Partisan Activity:

Reuben Simpson was an active Loyalist. In June 1780, he fought in the Battle of Ramseur's Mill, near Lincolnton. His brother, William Simpson was a Whig. Because of his Loyalist activity, family history says that he was forced to leave the area.

Summary of Later Life:

Reuben Simpson was married, in 1761, to Sarah Sherrill (b. 1743), another source says 1746, daughter of William Sherrill and Agnes White Sherill. Reuben and Sarah Simpson had the following offspring:

Avarilla b. 1763	Moses b.177
William	Sarah
Mary b. 1769	Samuel
Joshua White b. 1771	Elizabeth
Agnes Anne (or Agnes) b. 1773	Elisha b. 1787
Reuben b. 1775	Ruth Ann
	Avington Wayne b 1792

Land Holdings and Transactions:

1. Burke County NC. NC Land Grant #579.
2. Burke County NC. 640 acres Beaver Dam Creek on west side Catawba River adjacent to Stephen Fisher, Francis

Cunningham, Frances McCorkel, and James Henry. c.c.
James Henry, James Johns. Ent 16 Dec 1778 #1225, Grant
#581, Iss. 11 Oct. 1783, Bk. 50, p. 206.

Census Locations:

1800 Wayne County, Kentucky (1801 tax list)
1810 Wayne County, Kentucky
1820 Wayne County, Kentucky

References:
Sherrill, William L. Annals of Lincoln County NC. 1967 reprint of orig. 1937
    ed. (Rep. Publ. Co. Balti.), p. 39.
Beatty, M., Drum, P., and Beatty, S. (1990) Newton NC, "Through the years
    with Jane and John Robinson". (both of the above refer to recollections
    of Mr. W. A. Day, Grandnephew of William and Reuben Simpson).
Burke County Land Grant Data. Burke County Public Library
    Morganton, NC.
Internet acquisition (2004), "Ancestors of Hill and Smith",
    http://users.htcomp.net/benny/d143.htm.
Sherrill, Steven L. Internet acquisition source at
    http://members@aol.com/mysherrills/.
Wagstaff, Ann T. 1810, 1820 Census Indexes, Kentucky (1980 1981 reprinted
    by GPC, Balti.).

Sims, John

Summary of Early Life:

John Sims was born in Halifax County, North Carolina on the Roanoke River ca 1761. At the time of the American Revolution, he was living in Burke County, North Carolina.

Summary of Partisan Activity:

While a resident of Burke County, North Carolina, John Sims enlisted, about 1777, in Captain John Starnes' Company of Mounted Militia, under the overall command of Colonel Martin Phifer. Lieutenant Frederick Plyler was a subaltern officer. The division commander was General William L. Davidson. Sims went with his company to the Charleston South Carolina area in the Spring of 1780. He took part in the American defeat at Monck's Corner, South Carolina on April 14, 1780. This action sealed off the American units trapped in the city. The city surrendered on May 12, 1780. After the surrender, Sims and his unit joined in with the forces of General Thomas Sumter of South Carloina. Near Camden, at a place called Fishing Creek, Sumter and his men were surprised by the British under the well known Colonel Banastre Tarlton. During this encounter, Sims was captured and remained a prisoner for about three years. Later he walked away or "deserted". This ended his military career.

Summary of Later Life:

John Sims was married to Milly Bowling. After the Revolution, they moved to Rutherford County, Tennessee, then to Roane County, Tennessee, and to Blount County, Tennessee, where he was pensioned. John Sims' pension was approved in Blount County, Tennessee at a rate of $100 per annum, beginning in 1833. Later John Sims moved to Monroe County, Tennessee, where he died at about a hundred years of age. One source says he was buried in Eusebia Cemetery.

Land Holdings and Transactions:

In Blount Co. TN, Sims lived on Nine Mile Creek.

References :
US National Archives, R.W. Pension Data, # W 10252
Bates, Lucy and Marsh, Helen C. " Roster of Soldiers and Patriots of the
        American Revolution Buried in Tennessee." 1974 ed. (rev 1979) TN
        DAR p. 158.

Smalley, Abner

Summary of Early Life:

Abner Smalley was living in the area of Wilkes County and Caldwell County, North Carolina during the American Revolution.

Summary of Partisan Activity:

Abner Smalley appears to have been a member of the so called New River Tories. They conducted partisan activities in Wilkes and Ashe counties, the New River Valley of Virginia, and were constantly in strife with Colonel Benjamin Cleveland and his militiaman of Wilkes County. Other Tory members included Thomas Elledge and Micajah Pennington.

Later in the War Smally joined in with Colonel David Fanning, North Carolina's most famous and gifted Loyalist leader. Smalley became a Captain of mounted troops under Fanning. Under Fanning, Smalley led his men in the many raids into central North Carolina. At the war's conclusion, both he and Fanning took refuge in Charleston. Fanning eventually left North Carolina and immigrated to Nova Scotia. Smalley returned to Burke County.

Summary of Later Life:

Smalley returned to Burke County where he continued to live until the 1820's. Smalley was married in 1774 to Nancy Murray, daughter of Jeremiah Murray. The Murray's were prominent members of the Tory establishment in Burke County. Smalley seems to have moved to Cumberland County, Kentucky ca 1819, 1820. He purchased land from William Ballew, one of his former loyalist neighbors in Burke County. Children of Abner and Nancy Smalley were:

Joseph	Rachel m. George Fleming
Abner	Nancy m. William Fleming
Abrahan	

309

Land Holdings and Transactions:

1. Wilkes County NC Land Entry #541, 8 Dec. 1778. 200 acres on Howard's Creek, marked out Ebenezer Fairchild written in.
2. Wilkes County NC Land Entry# 542, 8 Dec. 1778, 200 acres end of Plat Mountain. Abner Smalley crossed out – Benjamin Herndon written in.
3. Wilkes County NC Land Entry #553, 9 Dec. 1778, 300 acres on Howard's Creek near a gap. Abner Smalley crossed out – Benjamin Herndon written in.

References:
Absher, Mrs W. O. "Land Entry Book Wilkes County NC 1778-1781", SHP 1955.
Absher, Mrs, W. O. and Hayes, Mrs. R. K. :"County Court MinutesWilkes County NC 1778-1784". Wilkes Gen Soc., Wilkesboro, NC.
Fanning, David. "The Narrative of Colonel David Fanning". Reprint Co. Publ, Spartanburg, SC, 1973 ed., pp. 21. 49.

Smith, George

Summary of Early Life:

George Smith and his family first came to the Catawba Valley in early 1764, settling on a tract on Elk Creek, now Catawba County, North Carolina. During the Revolutionary War, it was a part of Burke County, later Lincoln County.

Summary of Partisan Activity:

George Smith was a Captain of militia in Charles McDowell's Burke Regiment. Many of his men were of German extraction.

In early 1782, Smith was a member of the Court Martial board in the trial of his commanding officer, Colonel McDowell. Smith testified that he lived near one of the men associated with McDowell's actions, Captain John Eslinger. McDowell was convicted and removed from command, but restored a few months later.

Summary of Later Life:

Smith continued to be active in local affairs after the conclusion of the war. His son, George Smith, Jr., lived nearby. Both George Smith, Sr. and George Smith, Jr. are listed on the 1790 census.

Lincoln County court records show probate of a nuncupative will of a George Smith in April 1790. Presumably this was George Smith, the Revolutionary War soldier; however there were other persons of the same name in the area.

Land Holdings and Transactions:

1. Rowan County NC Bastan (Bastian) Cline to George Smith 320 acres of Elk Creek adjacent to Philip Jacocbs. March 29, 1764.

2. Rowan County NC Bastian Cline to George Smith 282 acres of Elk Creek adjacent Bernard Sigman, "Where Smith now lives on since March 29, 1764". Nov. 6, 1771.

3. NC Crown Grant Patent Book 18 #503, "Mecklenburgh County" on branch of Elk Creek, near Smith's own lines. 350 acres Oct. 30, 1765.*

Author's note: Even though grant states "Mecklenburgh County", numerous crown grants were issued in Granville's District, because of the then indeterminate western boundary of the district. The land described was clearly in Rowan County and well within Granville's jurisdiction.

Census Locations:

1790 Lincoln County, North Carolina 5th Company

References:
AIS Census 1790, NC 1978 Reprint.
Linn, Jo White. "Abstracts of the Deeds of Rowan County North Carolina 1753-1785". (1983) Salisbury, NC,pp. 78. 112.
US National Archive Revolutionary War Pension Statements. Philip Burns S30909. (See Vol. I, this work).
McAllister, Anne W. and Sullivan, Kathy G. "Lincoln County Court of Pleas and Quarter Sessions April 1789 - April 1796". (1987), p. 39.
Court Martial Records of Trial of Colonel Charles McDowell. Copy of original transcript, presented to author by late Ms. Eunice Erwin of Morganton, NC.
Huggins, Edith W. Miscellaneous Burke Records Vol. II. NC Revolutionary Army Accounts: Vol. XII, Part XI, Bk. 7 Folio 11, #214.
Roster of Soldiers from North Carolina in the Revolutionary War. (NC DAR), reprint of original 1932 ed., p. 397. GPC.
"Militia – Captain George Smith, #5046 Morgan District".
Hofmann, Margaret M. Colony of North Carolina 1765-1775.
Abstracts of Land Patents Vol. II. (1984 ed.), p. 39.

Sorrells, Walter

Summary of Early Life:

Walter Sorrells, according to family data, was born ca 1732 in Virginia, the son of Richard and Mary Sorrells of Augusta County, Virginia. Later Walter Sorrells appears in Burke County, North Carolina. He lived on Silver Creek, near present day Morganton, North Carolina.

Summary of Partisan Activity:

There are numerous references in the North Carolina Revolutionary War Accounts relating to the patriotic and military service of Walter Sorrells. Family records say that he fought in the battle of Kings Mountain South Carolina on October 7, 1780. There were other Sorrells who served in the Burke militia. These include John Sorrells and Lieutenant Samuel Sorrells. Another John Sorrells was in Rutherford County, North Carolina. DAR records show Walter Sorrells as a militiaman, Morgan Military District.

Summary of Later Life:

According to family historian, Marion Pettegrew, Walter Sorrells was married to Alfira Newberry. It is assumed that this marriage took place in Virginia ca 1765-1769. (There are numerous Newberrys in Wythe Co. VA.). Walter and Alfira Sorrells had the following offspring:

David	George Washington
Green	Samuel
Richard	Nancy
Ethan Allen	

Walter Sorrells was active in Burke County affairs until the end of the century, serving on various juries and exercising court duties.

Walter Sorrells died sometime before 1811, the date of his will probate.

Land Holdings and Transactions:

1. Burke Co. NC 200 acres on both sides of Silver Creek. His land lay adjacent to that of John Nail, John Mackey. It also bordered a wagon road. Ent. 5 Feb 1778. Grant # 59 20 Sep 1779.

Census Locations:

1790 Burke County, North Carolina 13th Co.
1800 Burke County, North Carolina

References:
Roster of Soldiers from North Carolina in the American Revolution   NC DAR
      Reprint of 1932 ed. p. 399.
AIS Census Indices NC 1790, 1800.
Land Grant Records   Burke Co. Library Morganton NC.
NC Rev Army Accts. as given in Haun, Wynette P. Durham NC Multiple soft
      back vols. Vols I - XII.
Huggins, Edith Misc Burke Co. records in 4 soft back issues SHP Vol. I p. 11.
Swink, Daniel " Burke Co. NC Minutes of Court of Pleas and Quarter Sessions
      1791-1795 " pp. 33- 34.
Philbeck, Miles and Turner, Grace " Burke Co. NC Surviving Will and Probate
      Absracts 1777-1910." 1983 ed. # 504.
Internet acquisition 2003 " Sorrells Families of the South "
http://www.-+oursouthernancestors.com/sorr-001/

Stepp, Moses

Summary of Early Life:

Moses Stepp was born in Orange County, Virginia in 1763. During the American Revolution, he was living in Burke County, North Carolina. He probably was related to the Burke County Loyalist, Joseph Stepp.

Summary of Partisan Activity:

Moses Stepp entered military service as a volunteer militiaman in 1778 (1776?). He served in Captain Thomas Whitson's Company of Colonel Charles McDowell's Regiment. He was stationed at the head of the Catawba River, guarding against the incursions of the hostile Cherokee Indians. He describes the North Cove skirmish in which Captain Whitson was wounded and Captain (Reuben) White killed (most sources date this in the summer of 1776). After returning home, he re-enlisted in a company of militiaman under Lieutenant John Sumter (of Lower Creek, Burke County, now Caldwell County, North Carolina). Under Lieutenant Sumter, they were marched to Congaree River, South Carolina (near Columbia, SC), where they were placed in South Carolina troops. Their Company commander was Captain John McKenzie (Charles S. Myddleton's Regiment); the overall commander was General Thomas Sumter of South Carolina (directly related to the Sumters of Lower Creek).

They were marched to Eutaw Springs, South Carolina, and several of his company were placed in charge of guarding the baggage wagon supporting the Army. They, therefore, did not take part in the battle of Eutaw Springs on September 8, 1781. After the battle, General Thomas Sumter issued a proclamation of amnesty for those who would come in within a certain period of time. After that, his group was instructed to hunt for Tories and "take no prisoners". Between Brown's Old Fields and the Santee swamps, they killed approximately twenty-four Tories. In the following year (1782), he was discharged at General Sumter's mill on the Santee, after which he returned home to Burke County.

315

Summary of Later Life:

     After the Revolution, Moses Stepp left Burke County and moved to the Tugaloo section of South Carolina. From there he moved to Russell County, Virginia (probably that portion, that later became Scott County, Virginia, as he is listed on 1820 Virginia census schedules in Scott County). From Virginia, he moved in the mid 1820's to Pike County, Kentucky.

     Moses Stepp applied for Revolutionary War pension in Pike County, Kentycky on November 26, 1835. He was awarded an annual pension of $63.10. Moses Stepp died in Pike County, Kentucky on December 13, 1856, age ninety-three years. He also received a bounty land warrant of 160 acres by the Act of 1855.

Census Locations:

1820 Scott County, Virginia

References:
US National Archives Revolutionary War Pension Data #S15655.
Bounty Land Warrant #34511-160-55.
Moss, Bobby Gilmer. Roster of Soldiers from SC in the American Revolution
     op cit.

Stringfield, Ezekial

Summary of Early Life:

Ezekial Stringfield was living in the Hunting Creek area of Burke County during the Revolutionary War. He was a brother of Richard Stringfield.

Summary of Partisan Activity:

Ezekial Stringfield's name appears on the subpoena docket of late 1782 relating to the Confiscation Acts. He was a suspected Tory and had to show cause as to why his property should not be confiscated for being disloyal to the American cause.

Disposition of these cases was not finalized in many cases due to the imminent Treaty of Peace in early 1783. Most Loyalists were given amnesty as per agreement with treaty provisions.

Summary of Later Life:

Ezekial Stringfield was married 1785 to Rebecca Sorrells, born April 28, 1768. Children by this marriage are as follows:

Christand Sept 2, 1786
Sara b. Oct 22, 1787
Mary b. July 20, 1789
Richard b. July 19, 1795
Schuesaner b. June 5, 1793
Elizabeth b. Aug 22, 1807
Rebecca b. May 6, 1809
William b. Dec 21, 1820
James b. April 15, 1816
John b. 1811?

Ezekial, along with his brother Richard, moved to East Tennessee at the conclusion of the Revolutionary War.

Land Holdings and Transactions:

1. Burke County NC 320 acres at the head of Hunting Creek and near the heads of Dry Creek and Cattail Branch. His land lay adjacent to that of John Burgess and Thomas Mackey. The property included "improvements that said Stringfield lived on". cc Thomas Mackey, Jesse Walker. Ent. 8 dec 78, #480, Grant No. 285, 14 March 1780, Bk. 28, p. 284.

Census Locations:

1790 Rutherford County, North Carolina 3rd Co
1807 Knox County, Tennessee – tax lists (Rebecca Stringfield)

References:
Huggins, Edith. Miscellaneous Burke Records Vol. I
Land Grant Data. Burke County Library, Morganton, NC
Internet Source: http://www.boonefamily.org., by Boone, Thomas.
AIS Census NC 1790.

Stringfield, James

Summary of Early Life:

James Stringfield was born in Surry County, Virginia on December 19, 1735. He was the son of Richard and Mary Stringfield. By 1774, James Stringfield had moved to Rowan County, North Carolina, that part that would later become Burke County.

Summaryof Partisan Activity:

During the Revolutionary War, James Stringfield served as a captain of militia in Charles McDowell's Burke Regiment. His service was mainly on the Catawba frontier, guarding against the hostile actions of the Cherokee Indians, then allied with the British cause. A pensioned soldier of the Revolution, John Smith stated that he served under Captain Stringfield and was discharged by him on December 17, 1781 at Davidson's Fort. Both James Stringfield and his son, John Stringfield, are listed as American patriots by the National Society DAR.

Summary of Later Life:

James Stringfield was married to Mary Ann Ray of Queen Anne's County, Maryland. They had the following offspring:

John m. Sarah Boylston
James m. Nancy Simmons
William Ray m. Marie Love
Nancy m. Elias McFaddin
Delilah m. James Brittain
Bida m. ____Downs.
Brittain

After settling initially in Burke County near Hunting Creek, the family moved to western Rutherford County, that part which was later included in Buncombe County, then Henderson County (Mills Creek area). Several years later James Stringfield and his family moved farther west to western Kentucky, Warren and Barren Counties (near present day Glasgow KY, east of Bowling Green). James Stringfield apparently died sometime after 1810. His wife, Mary, died July 13, 1813.in Warren County, Kentucky.

Land Holdings and Transactions:

Burke Co. NC 1779 500 acres Hunting Creek adj to Jos. Morgan, Geo. Killian.
Burke Co. NC 1780 100 acres Henry Fork on Walnut Mtn..
Buncombe Co. NC 1792 300 acres Boylston Creek 2 tracts
Barren Co. KY 1799 200 acres Beaver Creek.
Warren Co. KY 1799 147 acres Sinking Creek.
Barren Co. KY 1804 100 acres Beaver Creek.

Census Locations:

1790 Rutherford County, North Carolina 14th Co.
1800 Barren and Warren Counties, Kentucky (land acquisitions, 1799, 1804 , above).

References:
AIS Census NC 1790
Smith, John Rev. War pension data # S 1931.   See also Vol I this work.
Hofmann, Margaret. NC Abstracts of State Grants Vol. I.1998 ed. Nos. 92, 109.
Wooley, James E. Buncombe Co. NC Index to Deeds 1783 - 1950 SHP 1983 ed. p. 479
Jillson, W.R. The Kentucky Land Grants Part I GPC 1971 reprint of 1925 ed. p. 413.
DAR Patriot Index . Nat. Soc. DAR Washington, DC 1966 ed p. 656.
Cawyer, Shirley B. Stephensville TX Internet acquisition Jan 2004.
        http:/www.obcgs.com/stringfield.
        See also Vol II this work   re James Brittain.

Swearingen, Richard C.

Summary of Early Life:

Richard Cheek Swearingen was born in 1760 in Edgecombe County, North Carolina. His family later moved to Montgomery County, North Carolina. He was living in Montgomery County before and during the Revolutionary War.

Summary of Partisan Activity:

Richard Swearingen first entered military service in Montgomery County. He was marched to the Narrows of the Yadkin River where they joined in with the regiment commanded by Thomas Polk of Mecklenburgh County, North Carolina. His regiment marched to Philadelphia, Pennslyvania, then being threatened by the British. He remained here for about three months. This was probably in 1776.

In the summer of 1776, he was marched to the Charleston, South Carolina area, then being threatened by the British. He served in Captain Taylor's Company of Colonel Dewey Ledbetter's Regiment. In Charleston, they were commanded by Governor Rutledge.

Swearingen next was placed in Captain Brevard's Company of Colonel William L. Davidson's Regiment (later General Davidson). Under Colonel Davidson, he took part in the actions at Colson's Place in Anson County.

Serving in Captain Lilly's Company of Colonel Topp's regiment, he participated in the skirmish at Rafyt Swamp, South Carolina. Under Colonel Loftin, he was in the action at Cross Roads in Randolph County. Swearingen took part in the battle of Cowpens, South Carolina on January 17, 1781. In this battle, he served in Captain Pilcher's Company. One of his last actions was at Eutaw Springs, South Carolina on September 8, 1781 under Captain Jarrinck. Swearingen also served in the Wilmington Expedition in late 1781 under Brigadier General Griffith

321

Rutherford.

Summary of Later Life:

After the Revolution, Richard Swearingen moved to Burke County, North Carolina after acquiring property from Samuel Swearingen. Still later he lived in Lincoln County, North Carolina, Jackson County, Tennessee, Ashe County, North Carolina, and finally to Greene and Pulaski counties in Tennessee.

While living in Ashe County, North Carolina, Richard Swearingen applied for Revolutionary War pension benefits on November 13, 1832. He was awarded an annual pension of $80.00. Richard Swearingen was married to Mary Penley. Richard Swearingen died September 4, 1852. Richard and Mary Penley Swearingen had the following offspring:

>Mary (Polly) Swearingen m. James Wiles
>William Cheek Swearingen b. 1785-90 m. Polly Brown
>Austin Swearingen b. 1796
>Elender Swearingen b. 1805 m. Jesse Tubbs
>David Swearingen b. 1807 m. Mahala Vaught
>Richard Cheek Swearingen b. ca 1810
>James Swearingen

Land Holdings and Transactions:

1. Burke County NC Samuel Seaaringen to Richard Cheek Swearingen Land on Acck's Fork 100 acres (now Caldwell County, NC) 1 February 1791.
2. Burke County NC Richard Cheek Swearingen to Soloman Smith 100 acres 10 August 1795.

Census Locations:

1790 Burke County, North Carolina 9th Company
(Cheek Swearingen)

References:
US National Archives Revolutionary War Pension Data #S31402
DAR Patriot Index. NSDAR Washington DC, 1966 ed., p. 662.
Roster of Soldiers from North Carolina in the American Revolution. GPC
        reprint of 1932 ed., p. 585.
www.homeneo.com/thorn/swearingen/main-outline.html Internet source,
        material by Whyte, Kenel L., Jan 2004.

Tate, Samuel ("Rock")

Summary of Early Life:

Samuel Tate was born May 24, 1730 in County Derry (Londonderry), North Ireland. He was married to Elizabeth (Betty) Caldwell Tate (b. 1733). The Tates, along with their children, came to America in 1765, settling at Shippensburg, Cumberland County, Pennsylvania. They were living here during the American Revolution.

Summary of Partisan Activity:

Samuel Tate served in the Pennsylvania militia during the Revolutionary War.

Summary of Later Life:

After the American Revolution, Samuel Tate (now in his fifties), along with his family, moved to Augusta County, Virginia and then to Burke County, North Carolina. Sons Robert and Samuel remained in Pennsylvania. It appears that son John had preceded them to Burke County (see sketch of John Tate, Vol. II). In Morganton, John and William opened a store; David became a tavern owner, and Hugh a farmer.

Samuel and Elizabeth Tate were affiliated with the Quaker Meadows Presbyterian Church. Samuel and Elizabeth Tate had the following children:

Margaret b. Derry County, Ireland m. Joseph L. Alexander
Robert b. 1754 (a Revolutionary War soldier) Derry County, Ireland m. Nancy Campbell
John b. 1758 (a Revolutionary War soldier) m. Ann Oliphant moved to Georgia
Samuel b. Pennsylvania m. Elizabeth Alexander
William b. Pennsylvania 1765 m. Mary Bowman, daughter of Captain John Bowman
Catherine b. Pennsylvania 1767 m. Benjamin Newland

David b. Pennsylvania 1770 m. (1) Nancy Ann Elizabeth
    McCall, (2) Christinia Wakefield
Hugh b. Pennsylvania 1772 m. Margaret "Peggy" Ervin
    daughter of Colonel Alexander Ervin
Elizabeth b. Pennsylvania unmarried d. Burke County, NC

Samuel "Rock" Tate died in Burke County, North Carolina
March 23, 1813, age 83 years. Elizabeth Caldwell Tate died Burke
County, North Carolina on January 8, 1818, age 85 years. Both are
buried in the old Quaker Meadows Cemetery, overlooking
Morganton, North Carolina.

Census Locations:

1790 Cumberland County, Pennsylvania "Tait"
    (this may be Samuel Tate, Jr.
1800 Burke County, North Carolina
1810 Burke County, North Carolina

References:
Simpson, Jr. Roberts and Ervin, Samuel J. Jr. Article in Burke County Heritage
        Vol. I., pp.421-422. (Winston-Salem, 1981).
AIS Census indices.
Ervin, Jr. Samuel J. Articles in Burke County Heritage Vol. I On Hugh Tate,
        David Tate, and William Tate. pp. 414-426.
White, Emmett R. Revolutionary War Soldiers of Western North Carolina
        Burke County Vol. II. Sketch of John Tate.

Taylor, Parmenas

Summary of Early Life:

Parmenas Taylor was born in Prince William County, Virginia on April 4, 1753. He was living in Burke County, North Carolina during most of the Revolutionary War.

He was the son of William Taylor and Mary (Bradford) Taylor and a brother of Captain LeRoy Taylor (See Vol. I).

Summary of Partisan Activity:

Parmenas Taylor served as an officer in the militia regiment of Colonel Charles McDowell of Burke County, North Carolina. During most of the war, he carried the rank of Major. After the Revolutionary War he was known as "Colonel Parmenas Taylor".

Summary of Later Life:

Parmenas Taylor was married to Betty White, daughter of William White of John's River. One source gives the marriage date as 1779. Children are as follows:

> William B. 1780 m. Mary Lingfeller
> Alfred b. 1782 m. Jane Inman
> Leanna m. Alex McClannahan
> LeRoy b. 1787 m. Mary McSpadden
> Mary "Polly"
> Matilda b. 1789 m. Ezekial Inman
> Mahala b. 1792 m. John C. Turnley
> Argyll
> Willie b. 1798 m. Ann Harrison
> Elizabeth m. John Langdon
> Albert

Shortly after The Revolutionary War, Parmenas Taylor and his family moved to Jefferson County, Tennessee, on a bend of the

French Broad River, known as "Taylor's Bend." Taylor became a dedicated and well known public citizen. He was a member of the Legislator and helped in framing the Constitution of Tennessee. By profession, he was a surveyor and farmer.

The Revolutionary War soldier, Parmenas Taylor died February 28, 1827 at the age of 74. His wife, Betty White Taylor, died in 1838, age 74 years.

Land Holdings and Transactions:

1. Burke County NC 200 acres on Warrior Fork of John's River received from Samuel Simpson. 20 Dec 1778.
2. Burke County NC 100 acres White's Mill Creek. 1 June 1779.
3. Greene County TN 640 acres with David Stewart. Grant #729, Bk. 2, p. 39.
4. Jefferson County TN. 325 acres from Robert and James Lamme. North side French Broad River. 17 April 1798. *1800 tax list show house with 390 acres, Captain Copeland's Company.*

Census Locations:

1800 (tax lists) Jefferson County, Tennessee
1822 (tax lists) Jefferson County, Tennessee.

References:
Whitley, Edythe. Tennessee DAR records 1961.
Patriot Index. National Society DAR, 1966 ed., Washington, DC, p. 668.
Creekmore, Pollyanna. Early East Tennessee Taxpayers. SHP, 1980, p. 135.
Hollaway, Boyd. "Land Records of Jerrerson County, Tennessee, SHP 1991, p. 80.
Sistler, Byron and Barbara. Early Tennessee Tax Lists. Evanston, IL, 1977, p. 194.
Bates, Lucy.Rev. rev. by Marsh, H. "Roster of Soldiers and Patriots Buried in Tennessee". TN Soc. DAR, 1979, p. 167.

Thompson, James

Summary of Early Life:

James Thompson was born in Pennsylvania December 18, 1763. James Thompson was living in Burke County, North Carolina during the Revolutionary War. He possibly was related to the "well known rebel"* of Burke County, Alexander Thompson. Alexander Thompson had a son James. After the Revolutionary War, both Alexander and James Thompson moved to the same region of Georgia, Alexander to Elbert County, and James to adjoining Madison County.

*As described by the British officer Anthony Allaire in his diary.

Summary of Partisan Activity:

In March 1776, as a young teenager, James Thompson entered revolutionary service as a private volunteer militiaman in Charles McDowell's regiment, Captain Cain's Company. Burke County was then part of Rowan County. He was stationed at Cathey's Fort at the head of the Catawba River, guarding against the intrusions of the hostile Cherokee Indians. He served a tour of six months. The following year, in May 1777, he served a three-month tour of duty under Captain Thomas Kennedy of McDowell's regiment. He was stationed at John Davidson's Fort on the upper Catawba. In the summer of 1778, he served another three months tour of duty at George Davidson's Fort, under the command of Captain (Daniel) Smith. Thompson again served a short tour of duty in the summer of 1779 and 1780 under Captains' John McDaniels and Jonathan Camp, respectively.

In the fall of 1780, Thompson served in Captain Samuel Wood's Company of McDowell's regiment. Under Woods, he fought in the epic battle of Kings Mountain on October 7, 1780.

Thompson's final military service was a tour of duty directed against the Cherokees. Joseph McDowell was the commanding officer. This was in May 1781. (This may have been McDowell's well-known raid in the spring of 1782.)

Summary of Later Life:

James Thompson lived for a while in Burke County, North Carolina and then moved to Wilkes County, Georgia. He moved from Wilkes County to Madison County, Georgia.

He applied for federal pension in Madison County, Georgia on May 1833 and was allowed a pension in the amount of $69.00 per annum. Census records of Madison County list a James Thompson, Sr. and a James Thompson, Jr.

Census Locations:

1790 Wilkes County, Georgia (1793 militia list)
1800 (Burke County, North Carolina?)
1820 Madison County, Georgia
1830 Madison County, Georgia

References:
US National Archives Pension Records #S32014.
AIS Census Index. NC 1800.
Draper, LC. Kings Mountain and It's Heroes. (1885), (Allaire's Diary, appended).
White, Emmett R. Vol. II , this work, relating to Alex Thompson.
De La Mar, Marie and Rothstein, Elizabeth. The Reconstructed 1790 Census of Georgia. GPC 1985, p. 177.

Thornton, Samuel

Summary of Early Life:

Samuel Thornton was born at Matthew's Bluff, South Carolina in July 1755. At the time of the American Revolution, he was living on South Fork of the Catawba River in Burke County, North Carolina. There was a Sammuel and Mary Thornton of nearby Fourth Creek in Rowan, now Iredell County, North Carolina. The relationship to the subject is unknown.

Summary of Partisan Activities:

Samuel Thornton entered military service in Colonel Charles McDowell's Burke Regiment as a volunteer militiaman in Major Joseph McDowell's mounted battalion. Thornton and his fellow troops advanced into South Carolina to assist in the defense of that state against a planned British invasion. This was probably in the spring of 1781, following the battle of Cowpens. The British, on their failure to take Charleston, were retreating back toward Savannah. The Americans engaged the British at Stono Ferry, South Carolina. Thornton took part in this hard fought battle. He describes the American defeat and the carrying away of 343 wounded American soldiers. He mentions the leadership of Captain Casimir Pulaski. Thornton even gave the length of the battle, sixty-seven minutes. After Stono, he served companies commanded by Captain Ryone, Turner, and Butler. He was marched to the vicinity of Orangeburg, where they were involved in several skirmishes, all to the advantage of the Americans.

At the conclusion of his pension statements, Thornton stated that he was in the Battle of "Ferguson's Defeat', (Kings Mountain, October 7, 1780), and "several others', the details he couldn't recall.

Summary of Later Life:

Following the Revolutionary War, Samuel Thornton moved to South Carolina on Savannah River. Still later he moved to the

Savannah River area of Georgia and resided in several contiguous counties (Scriven, Burke, Effingham, Chatham, and finally Appling).

Samuel Thornton applied for Revolutionary War pension benefits in Appling County, Georgia on October 2, 1832. This pension was denied, but there were vigorous efforts to secure it for the heirs. Samuel Thornton had the following children: Isaac, Bedie, Ezekial, and Elbert. Samuel Thornton died March 7, 1847. *October 1859 – Letter from John T. Wilson of Blackshear, Georgia addressed to Commissioner of Pensions: "Please inform me whether a pension has ever been issued for these services; if so, who stained it".*

References:
US National Archives. Revolutionary War Pension Data #R10571.
AIS Census Indices.

Tinney, Samuel

Summary of Early Life:

Samuel Tinney was born ca 1756, possibly in the Orange County section of North Carolina. He was by occupation a farmer and lived in the Lower Creek section of Burke County. There was also a James Tinney in Burke County. Several of the Tinneys in Orange County served under Colonel John Pyle (Loyalist).

Summary of Partisan Activity:

Samuel Tinney entered military service in August 1782. He was placed in Captain Henry Highland's Company of Burke militia, but was delivered to the Continental Line Establishment, 10th Regiment. He was placed in a company commanded by Lieutenant Colonel Archiblad Lytle. Samuel Tinney was described as being 26 years of age, 5'10" in height, with brown hair, blue eyes and dark complexion. His name was omitted in 1783.

Summary of Later Life:

Samuel Tinney died in 1782 or 1783, as indicated by Burke County North Carolina Estate Papers (Oct 22, 1783) administrative bond by Mary Tinney. Inventory of estate December 5, 1783 by Mary Tinney. It is not known whether or not his demise was of a military nature. 1819 tax records of Giles County, Tennessee refer to a "widow Tinney", relationship to family not known.

Land Holdings and Transactions:

Burke County, North Carolina Land Entry records show Samuel Tinney as entering 100 acres of Jumping Branch of Burke County. This small stream enters the north side of Catawba River just downstream from mouth of Lower Creek. His land entry was adjacent to land of John Harper and Edmund Fears.

References:

Huggins, Edith. Miscellaneous Burke County NC Records. Vol. I, pp. 86, 94.
    Vol. II, pp 156, 171.

Sistler, Byron and Barbara. <u>Early Tennessee Tax Lists</u>. Evanston, Il. 1997, p.
    195.

NC DAR <u>Roster of North Carolina Soldiers in the American Revolution</u>. Orig.
    publ. 1932. GPC Reprint Issue 1976, p. 170.

Underdown, Stephen

Summary of Early Life:

Stephen Underdown was born in Caroline County, Virginia June 9, 1755. At about age eighteen or nineteen, he came with his family to Granville County, North Carolina. After staying there only a short while, they moved to Caswell County, North Carolina.

Summary of Partisan Activity:

Stephen Underdown, in September 1775, while a resident of Caswell County, volunteered for a six month tour of duty in the First North Carolina Regiment, commanded by Colonel (James) Moore and Lieutenant Francis (Frank) Nash. Underdown was placed in a company commanded by Captain Alfred Moore and Lieutenant L. Thompson. Their regiment assembled at Hillsborough and then marched to Cross Creek (Fayetteville) and then to the vicinity of Wilmington. At a place called Barnet's Creek they constructed barracks. Under Colonel Moore they served in the Wilmington area and frequently crossed the Cape Fear to Brunswick. Later they captured Fort Johnston and tore down its walls (Southport). Their main duty was to defend the coast and prevent a proposed British invasion. In February, troops under Moore's command (commanded by Caswell and Lillington) defeated the Tories at Moore's Creek Bridge (Feb 27, 1776). Following this action, Underdown's tour ended and he was discharged home by Colonel Moore.

Following his return from his six-month tour of duty, Underdown was married and moved to Rutherford County, North Carolina. There he was drafted for a three-month tour in Captain Vanzant's Company. He stated (in his pension declarations) that his "wife was in a situation which would not justify his leaving her…" He therefore, with the consent of his officer, hired a substitute, Daniel Singleton. He paid him forty pounds. Singleton served out the full three months.

Later Underdown served a short tour of duty at Earle's Fort

334

(on Pacolet River), usually guard duty. His off and on duty continued throughout the remainder of the war. He stated that he served at least twelve short tours. He was commanded usually by Colonel Earle and Lieutenant John Anderson.

Summary of Later Life:

Stephen Underdown, shortly after the Revolution, moved back to Caswell for a short while. He then moved to Burke County, North Carolina ca 1791-1796, and lived there until 1825, moving then to Russell County, Kentucky (later Todd County). Underdown was still living in 1836. According to data given by Bill Crook, Underdown had married a second time to the widow Betty Crook, mother of John Crook. There is also a statement that Underdown at one time may have been a Tory, but this is not documented. Underdown applied for Revolutionary War pension benefits (defined by Act of 1832) on October 1832, Russell County, Kentucky. He was awarded a pension of $33.33 per anum.*

A Jesse and George Underdown listed in Burke County (now Caldwell County) North Carolina, relationship to soldier not known. Many of the Underdowns are buried at Colliers Methodist Church, south of Lenoir North Carolina.

*Apparently there was some difficulty in classifying Underdown's type of service. Initially he was listed as a militiaman. From his statement, many duty locations and officers, it is apparent the he indeed was a member of the 1st Regiment of Continental Line, commanded by the able Colonel James Moore. See reference by Rankin, Hugh F.)

Land Holdings and Transactions:

1. 1777 Caswell County Tax Lists. St. James District, no acreage given.
2. 1796 Tax List Burke County 115 acres. Captain Sumerall's District (now Caldwell County, NC)
3. 1815 Burke County Tax Lists (now Caldwell County)
   a. 100 acres Lower Creek
   b. 150 acres Husband's Creek

c. 200 acres Lower Creek
d. Conveyance from John Tucker to Stephen Underdown 100 acres 1806. pr. 1808

.

Census Locations:

1790 Caswell County, North Carolina St. Lawrence District
1800 Burke County, North Carolina
1810 Burke County, North Carolina
1820 Burke County, North Carolina
1830 Russell County, Kentucky

References:
US National Archives Revolutionary War Pension Statements #S 30760.
AIS Census Data. NC 1790, 1800, 1810.
Potter, Dorothy W. Tullahoma. TN 1974. 1820 NC Census Index.
Smith, Dora Wilson. 1820 KY Census index. 1974 ed.
Rankin, Hugh T. The North Carolina Continentals. UNC Press Chapel Hill, 1971. pp. 38-39.
Pittman, Betsy D. "Burke County NC 1815 Tax Lists" 1990 p. 79.
Sullivan, Kathy C. "Burke County NC Deeds Registered 1804-1813". 1995. Burke County NC Gen. Soc. p. 77.
T.L.C. Genealogy. Miami Beach, FL. 1990, "Caswell County NC Tax Lists". (1777, 1780, 1784), p. 17.
Crook, Wilson (Bill) W., Jr. from internet source. http:/ gen 1 Starnet.com/crook. htm

Van Horn, Isaac

Summary of Early Life:

During the American Revolution, Isaac VanHorn was living in eastern Burke County, North Carolina, that part that would later be a part of Lincoln County, now Catawba County, North Carolina. He was living on Betts Creek, a tributary of the upper portion of Clark's Creek. Van Horn was a neighbor of Captain John Sigmon, under whom he would later serve.

Summary of Partisan Activity:

Isaac VanHorn was a commissioned officer during the Revolutionary War. He served as a lieutenant in Captain John Sigmon's Company of Colonel Charles McDowell's Burke Regiment. Under Sigmon, he took part in Indian skirmishes and later served in the Kings Mountain South Carolina campaign and battle (Oct 7, 1780). A pensioned soldier of the Revolution, John Wilfong, gave sworn testimony telling of his service under Lieutenant VanHorn.

Summary of Later Life:

During and after the Revolutionary War, Isaac Van Horn continued to live in the Betts Creek area (near present day Startown). In the 1790 census he is listed with a relatively large family (4 males, 4 females). 1797 records show VanHorn as re-marrying. He married at that time, Christina Ashenbrunner, a daughter of Urban Ashenbrunner. She was married earlier to (1) John Stamey and (2) John Borland. Isaac VanHorn, after his second marriage, moved to eastern Burke County, on Camp Creek. Census records show an Isaac VanHorn on Burke County rolls until at least 1830. Some of the enumerations may be that of Isaac VanHorn, a son of John VanHorn.

Land Holdings and Transactions:

Burke Co. NC 350 acres on waters of Bett's Creek and Mull's Mill

Creek. The land was adjacent to that of Henry Reader (Rader), Lutz and William Coon. The entry data states "improvements whereon he lives ". cc John Sigmon, Adam Rader.
Ent.#1177 ent 12 Dec 1778 Grant # 726 11 Oct 1783. Bk50/270. Burke Co. NC 24 Apr 1809. 150 acres. Deed from Isaac VanHorn to John VanHorn.

Census Locations:

1790 Lincoln County, North Carolina 3rd Co.
1800 Burke County, North Carolina
1810 Burke County, North Carolina
1820 Burke County, North Carolina
1830 Burke County, North Carolina

References:
AIS Census Indices NC 1790 - 1830
Land Grant data. Morganton-Burke Co. Library. Morganton, NC.
U.S. Nat. Archives. Rev. War federal pension data John Wilfong # S 7159
Sullivan, Kathy G. " Burke. Co. NC Deeds Registered 1804 - 1813 ". 1995 ed.
        p. 78

Waggoner, Christopher ("Stoffel")

Summary of Early Life:

     Christopher Waggoner was born in Bucks County, Pennsylvania five miles from Bethlehem on June 20, 1755. The family moved from Pennsylvania to Rowan County, North Carolina and located about nine miles below Salisbury. Later, during the Revolutionary Period, the family moved to Burke County, that part that later became a part of Lincoln County, the later Catawba County, North Carolina.

Summary of Partisan Activity:

     Christopher Waggoner served three successive three-month tours of duty as a volunteer militiaman in late 1775 and 1776. His company commander was Captain George Barringer of Rowan County; General Griffith Rutherford was Brigade Commander. He first served in the "Snow Campaign" of late 1775, directed against the Scovellite Tories of upper South Carolina. He mentions the capture of the noted Tory, Colonel Thomas Fletchall.

     He served a three-month tour in the Cross Creek Expedition of February and March 1776, again under Captain Barringer. This was the later phase of the Moore's Creek Bridge Campaign. The western militia mainly conducted mop-up operations and conveying of prisoners, etc. In the summer of 1776, Waggoner took part in the Cherokee campaign of General Rutherford, mainly taking place in August and September of 1776. The large force assembled and subdued, at least for a while, the hostile Cherokees. After this tour, Waggoner and his family moved to Burke (later Lincoln) County North Carolina. From then until the end of the war, he was a member of the Burke County militia.

     He describes a short Indian raid, probably in 1779, under Major Joseph McDowell and Captain Daniel Whitener. In 1780, Waggoner took part in the Kings Mountain Campaign of September and October 1780, serving under Captain John Sigmon and Major McDowell. In early 1781, he served in Captain Whitener' Company once again and participated in the Battle of Cowpens on January 17, 1781. He mentions seeing Colonel (William) Washington.

Waggoner's last military service was in 1782, under Captain Whitner. He took part in both the spring and fall action against the Cherokee Indian. The first was headed up by Major (now Colonel) Joseph McDowell. The later raid (against the Chickamauga element) was in August and September 1782, under the overall command of the newly appointed commanding officer of Morgan District, General Charles McDowell.

Summary of Later Life:

After the war, Waggoner moved from Lincoln County into Burke County. He moved later to Pendleton County, South Carolina and then to Davidson County, Tennessee. He lived in Davidson County for about twenty-six years and moved last to Humphreys County, Tennessee. Waggoner applied for Revolutionary War pension in Humphreys County, Tennessee on October 27, 1834, age seventy-nine years. His claims were rejected. There were efforts by family members to obtain approval. There were verified payment records made by the State of North Carolina for military service. One Elisha Waggoner is listed, possibly his son.

Census Locations:

1790 Burke County, North Carolina 7th Co.
1810 (Davidson County, Tennessee Tax List 1811)
1830 Humphreys County, Tennessee
1840 Humphreys County, Tennessee

References:
US National Archives Pension Data #R 10995
AIS Census Indices. 1790 NC and 1840 TN.
Byron Sistler and Associates. Nashville TN, 1830 TN Census.
Byron Sistler and Associates. Early TN Tax Lists (1977).

Wallace, John

Summary of Early Life:

John Wallace was born December 22, 1758. He was living in western North Carolina at the time of the American Revolution.

Summary of Partisan Activities:

John Wallace, along with six of his friends, entered military service in Burke County, North Carolina, January 1779. They wanted to enter for an extended period of time, but were told by the Regimental Commander, Colonel Charles McDowell, that they could enlist in successive three month tours of duty instead. Their first enlistment was in a company commanded by Captain Roger Topp and Lieutenant John Baker. Captain Topp later resigned because of poor health, his command being taken over by Lieutenant Baker (Captain Topp died shortly later). After this tour, Wallace re-enlisted under Captain Micajah Lewis. They spent their tour ranging and scouting in western North Carolina. In June 1780, he volunteered again and served under Captain Lewis until August 1780. Colonel McDowell then placed him in Captain James Alexander's Company of McDowell's Regiment. He served until shortly after the Battle of Cowpens in January 1781. Wallace took part later in the Battle of Kings Mountain (October 7, 1780), and Cowpens (January 17, 1781). Wallace was twice wounded at Kings Mountain.

Summary of Later Life:

John Wallace, after the Revolutionary War, lived for about twenty-five years in Blount County, Tennessee and then moved to Bibb County, Alabama.

John Wallace applied for Revolutionary War pension benefits in Bibb County, Alabama. He was awarded an annual pension of $80.00.

John Wallace was married to Margaret Thompson. There

341

was a son listed, Matthew Wallace. John Wallace died in Bibb County, Alabama on Jun 18, 1847.

Census Locations:

1790 Burke County, North Carolina 4th Co.

References:
US National Archives. Revolutionary War Pension Data #S32572.
DAR Patriot Index. National Society DAR, Washington DC, 1966
        Ed. p. 713.

Warren, Robert

Summary of Early Life:

Robert Warren was living in the Upper Little River area of Burke County, North Carolina during the Revolutionary War, now Alexander County.

Summary of Partisan Activity:

According to the late distinguished historian, Edith Warren Huggins, Robert Warren was a Revolutionary soldier of Burke County. There are several references to a Robert Warren in the North Carolina Revolutionary Army Accounts. (Some of these probably refer to a Continental Line Surgeon, Dr. Robert Warren).

Summary of Later Life:

Alexander County, North Carolina records indicate that Robert Warren and his wife Mary lived on Upper Little River. Land grant records show this clearly also. A son, Hugh Warren is given. According to Ms. Huggins, Robert Warren died in Iredell County, North Carolina in 1795. She also lists court records of Burke County, listing him as a juror in 1790. Most of the fellow jurors were from the western part of the county, later Buncombe County. This may have been his son of the same name. Several Warrens appear in post- Revolutionary War records of Buncombe County including Robert, James, William, Joseph and Uriah Warren. These may well be his progeny.

Robert and Mary are probably buried in the Warren Cemetery near Macedonia Baptist Church and the old Warren school, south of present day Taylorsville.

Land Holdings and Transactions:

Burke Co. NC Robert Warren entered 150 acres on Upper Little River adjacent to land of Hugh Fox. The tract included his "inmprovements". 1778

Census Locations:

1790 Burke County, North Carolina 8th Co.
(Robert Warren is shown in the 1790 census with 4 additional males in household, including an older one). This would go along with those seen later in Buncombe Co.

References:
Huggins, Edith Warren Misc Burke Co. NC records in 4 soft back issues   SHP
        Vol I. p.50 ; Vol. II p. 179. Vol III p. 158. Vol IV pp. 31, 32, 35.
Huggins, Edith Warren. and her husband , Dewey Huggins.   Multiple
        conversations with author while doing research at NC State Archives.
        Raleigh. ca 1978.
Wooley, James E.   Buncombe Co. NC Index to Deeds 1783 - 1850. pp.
        504, 505. SHP 1983 ed.
NC Rev Army Accounts as given in Haun, Wynette P. Durham, NC   Multiple
        soft back issues. Part IV pp. 554,555.Part V p. 610Part VI p. 726 Part
        VIII p. 1027.
AIS NC Census 1790.

.

Whitson, Thomas

Summary of Early Life:

Thomas Whitson was born ca 1734 in Stafford County, Virginia, the son of Williams and Margaret Whitson. Before and during the Revolutionary War, he was living in the Lower Creek area of Burke County, now Caldwell County, North Carolina.

Summary of Partisan Activity:

Thomas Whitson, early in the Revolutionary period appears to have espoused the cause of liberty. In August 1775, he was appointed to the Rowan County, North Carolina Committee of Safety (Burke was then part of Rowan County). Appointed a Captain of militia, he led his company against the hostile Cherokee Indians in the summer of 1776. Captain Whitson was wounded at a skirmish with the Cherokees on the North Fork of the Catawba in July, 1776. Later he led his company again on the Cherokee Expeditions of General Griffith Rutherford (Aug. – Sept. 1776). Following the Cherokee Expedition, Captain Whtson served as a frontier commander in guarding against further incursions. He served at various times at Davidson's Fort and Crider's Fort in 1777 and 1778.

Thomas Whitson was now recognized as one of the ranking officers in McDowell's Burke Regiment of militia. In 1779, he served as Burke Representative in the Wartime General Assembly, meeting that year in Smithfield. Whitson's military activities continued into early 1780, serving in McDowell's mounted troops.

1780 was a turning point in sentiment for Captain Whtson, as it was for many Partisans. After mid 1780, his name no longer appears as an active participant. There are those who say he became a Tory and fought against the Americans at Ramsour's Mill at Kings Mountain. One author thinks that he may have been killed at Ramseur's Mill. One fact is certain; his son Benjamin Whitson was active at Ramseur's Mill and Kings Mountain. In the court martial records of Colonel Charles McDowell in 1782, one

Captain relates how he saw the capture of Ben Whitson, and how he was sentenced to hang, and his subsequent reprieve.

Later that same year, the so called "Tory Docket" was introduced. This related to the Confiscation Acts passed by the legislature. Both Benjamin Whitson and Thomas Whitson are listed as suspected Tories. The case was never resolved, as peace was declared a few months later in April 1783, along with a generalized amnesty for the Loyalists.

Summary of Later Life:

Prior to the Revolution, Thomas Whitson was married to (1) Ann White, (2) Mary M. ca 1759. Their children were John, Mary, Isbell, and Benjamin.

Thomas Whitson, after the conclusion of the war, moved to the mountain area of northeast Tennessee, now Carter County, Tennessee. He lived on a branch of Doe River. The Revolutionary War partisan, Captain Thomas Whitson, died in Johnson County, Tennessee ca 1808.

Land Holdings and Transactions:

1. 441 acres Burke County, NC on Little's Branch, a tributary of Lower Creek, and adjacent to land belonging to Henry Pearson, Alexander Clark and William Ursery. The land included "his own improvements." cc Thomas Littlejohn and Jonas White. Ent. 29 Dec. 1778, #1361, Grant No. 668, Iss. 11 Oct. 1783, Bk. 50, p. 247.
2. 200 acres Burke County, NC on Husband's Creek, a tributary of Lower Creek including the Mill Fork and improvements of Condell on Condell Branch. cc John Baldwin, John Little, Ent. 8 Nov. 1778, #591, Grant No. 178, Iss., 14 March 1780, Bk. 28, p. 177.
3. North Carolina (later Tennessee) Land Patents as follows:
   23 Nov. 1792. 100 acres First fork of Little Doe River.
   23 Nov. 1792. 100 acres First Fork of Little Doe River.
   23 Nov. 1792. 100 acres on Little Doe River, a branch of

of Rowan Creek.
23 Nov. 1792. 50 acres south fork of Little Doe River.

Census Locations:

1800 (1796, 1798 tax lists), Carter County, Tennessee

References:
Wheeler, John Hill. <u>Historical Sketches of North Carolina</u>. Reprint of original
        1851 ed. (1964 Rep. Publ. Co., Balti..), (Committee of Safety Minutes,
        Rowan County, NC), p. 369.
US National Archives Whasington Pension records of:
        Smith, Samuel (R9833), (Davidson, Crider Forts).
        Sumter, Thomas (R10312), (McDowell, 1780).
        Cathey, George (S16699)
        Coffee, Benjamin (S1655), (Cherokee Expedition 1776).
        Grider, John (W358), (Catawba Frontier 1778).
        McFalls, Arthur (W9187), (N. Catawba 1776).
        Jackson, James (S38077), (N. Catawba 1776).
Internet data: jinman.org/inman/dat21.html. Jinman.
<u>Carter County, Tennessee and It's People 1796-1993</u>. (1993 ed. Elizabethton,
        TN.), p. 590.
McDaniel, Seth. "Loyal to the Last". (2005), p. 11.

Wilfong, George

Summary of Early Life:

George Wilfong was born in Pennsylvania, the son of German immigrant Johannes Wilfong. He was a brother of Nicholas and Jacob Wilfong. He was born November 3, 1740. George Wilfong came to the Catawba Valley of North Carolina. Ca 1761 he was married to the widow Mary Mull ree Poffh (b. 1844). (There may have been a short sojourn in South Carolina to escape the violence of the French and Indian warfare in western Carolina.)

Summary of Partisan Activity:

George Wilfong first entered military service at the beginning of the Revolutionary War. Earlier he had served in the Colonial militia as a Lieutenant (probably) between 1770 and 1775. The military structure of the North Carolina Provincial Troops was reorganized at the Halifax Congress in April 1776. Wilfong was appointed 2nd Major of the 2nd Rowan Regiment of militia. His superior officers were Colonel Christopher Beekman, Lieutenant Colonel Charles McDowell. Hugh Brevard was 1st Major. The Brigade Commander was General Griffith Rutherford of Rowan.

Wilfong took part in the Cherokee Expedition of General Rutherford in the summer and fall of 1776. It appears that Wilfong may have become inactive on creation of Burke County in 1777. McDowell became the Colonel commanding the Regiment. Brevard was Lieutenant Colonel Joseph White and Joseph McDowell were 1st and 2nd Majors. (The 2nd Rowan Regiment had become the Burke Regiment.) One source did state that he participated in the Kings Mountain Campaign and the Battle of September – October 1780. There are anecdotal events relating to the Tory plundering of the Wilfong home and the subsequent capture and execution of the accused, using Mrs. Wilfong's clothesline in the hanging. See Catawba County Heritage I and Draper, L.C. for details. Wilfong was a witness in the court martial trial of Colonel Charles McDowell in early 1782.

Summary of Later Life:

George and Mary Wilfong had the following children:

Mary m. Daniel Whitener
Peter m. Susannah Catherine Hayle
Elizabeth m. Jacob Cline
Sarah m. Adam Gross
Catherine m. Andrew Hoyle

In 1777 George Wilfong served on a committee to select a courthouse site for newly organized Burke County. (Wilfong's home was then in Burke until nearly the end of the war, then Lincoln County, and finally Catawba.) After the war, Wilfong became one of the county's most prominent citizens and appeared in many civil actions. He served as a jury member on numerous occasions.

George Wilfong died on November 3, 1818. His wife had died earlier in 1816. Both are buried at the Old St. Paul's Church Cemetery near Newton, North Carolina.

Land Holdings and Transactions:

Lincoln County NC 1790 – 118 from Christopher Ryan to George Wilfong
Lincoln County NC 1791 – 150 from George Wilfong to J Moyer
Lincoln County NC 1786 – Henry Whitener, Sr. to George Wilfong 134 acres South Fork Catawba in Finley's Branch

Census Data:

1790 Lincoln County, North Carolina 4th Co
1800 Lincoln County, North Carolina
1810 Lincoln County, North Carolina

References:

North Carolina Revolutionary Army Accounts as cited in several volumes by Haun, Weynette P. (Durham NC Argonne Dr.) (These auditors' accounts verify Wilfong's wartime service as well as his rank of Major.) Vol. VIII Book F-2 Folio 76 # 2052 "George Wilfong, Major". Vol. VI Book 25, p. 36.

Clark, Murtie June. Colonial Soldiers of the South. 1732-1774. GPC 1983, p. 646.

Wheeler, John Hill. Historical Sketches of North Carolina. (Reprint Reg. Publishing Co. Baltimore) 1964 orig 1851. Vol. I. (early militia Morganton, NC), p. 81.

McAllister, Anne Williams. Through Four Generations. (1992), p. 925

AIS Census Indices, North Carolina.

McAllister, Anne W. and Sullivan, Kathy G. Lincoln County NC Court of Pleas and Quarter Sessions. 1789-1796. (1987).

Pruitt, Dr. R. B. "Abstracts of Deeds: Lincoln County NC 1786-1793.

Draper, Lyman C. Kings Mountain and It's Heroes. (Gen. Publishing Co., Baltimore) Reprint of 1881 ed., pp. 436-437.

350

Williams, James

Summary of Early Life:

James Williams was living in Burke County North Carolina at the time of his first military service enlistment in 1779. He mentions Morgantown (then Burke Court House). He was age sixty-eight when applying for federal pension in 1832.

Summary of Partisan Activity:

James Williams enlisted in the North Carolina Continental Line in 1779 and was placed in the 3rd Regiment. The regiment was commanded by Lieutenant Colonel Robert Mebane and Major Thomas Hogg. His company commander was Captain (Reading) Blount. Williams participated in the military activities in and around Charleston, South Carolina under the overall command of General Benjamin Lincoln. In May 1780, Charleston was captured by the British. The entire regiment was made captive including Colonel Mebane and General Lincoln. After being held prisoner for about three months, Williams managed to escape his captors and returned to Burke County. Back in Burke County, he became a mounted rifleman and served in McDowell's Burke Regiment. Later he took part in several important military actions including Kings Mountain (October 7, 1780).

He was assigned to South Carolina and served as a mounted rifleman under Colonel Malmedy. Williams fought in the Battle of Eutaw Springs on September 8, 1781. After Eutaw Springs, he returned to Rowan County, North Carolina and was discharged by Colonel Matthew Locke.

Summary of Later Life:

Williams applied for federal pension in West Feliciana Parish, Louisiana on August 4, 1836 at the age of sixty-eight. He was awarded a pension of $60.00 per annum.

351

Land Holdings and Transactions:

Burke County NC land entry data shows a James Williams entering land. James Williams was awarded 274 acres of bounty land warrant for his service in the North Carolina Continental Line. Warrant # 1628.

References:
US National Archives Pension Data #S31487.
DAR (NC). <u>Roster of Soldiers from North Carolina in the American Revolution</u>. Pp. 266, 173. (Winston-Salem) 1931 reprint issue.

Wilson, Samuel

Summary of Early Life:

Samuel Wilson was born in Lancaster County, Pennsylvania in the year 1761. During the Revolutionary War he was living in Burke County, North Carolina. At the time of his pension application, he was living in Iredell (possibly that part of Burke that later was included in Iredell County).

Summary of Partisan Activity:

Samuel Wilson first entered military service as a volunteer militiaman in the year 1778. He served on the Catawba Frontier under Major Joseph McDowell. This was a short tour of only one month.

His second tour again was as volunteer militiaman in Major Joseph White's company of Colonel Charles McDowell's Burke Regiment. He was marched to South Carolina, serving in the campaigns of General Brigadier Lincoln. The battle of Stono Ferry is mentioned. This tour lasted four months. Shortly afterwards he served under Lieutenant Colonel Robert Holmes, first in Lincoln County in pursuit of Tories and later in the Guilford Court House campaign and battle (March 1781).

Summary of Later Life:

Samuel Wilson applied for Revolutionary War pension in Iredell County, North Carolina on August 23, 1832, age seventy-one years. He was awarded a pension in the amount of $26.33 per annum.

Land Holdings and Transactions:

Burke County North Carolina Land Entry records show John McGee entering 200 acres "on Muddy Fork of Lower Little River, joining Thomas Willson and Samuel Willson....28 Oct 1779." This may be Samuel Wilson, Sr. (Jr. and Sr. listed on 1790

Iredell County NC census) The locale would be consistent with military service area and officers.

Census Locations:

1790 Iredell County, North Carolina
1800 Iredell County, North Carolina
1810 Iredell County, North Carolina
1820 Iredell County, North Carolina
1830 Iredell County, North Carolina

References:
US National Archives Pension Data #S7944.
AIS Census Records NC. 1790, 1800, 1810, 1830.
Potter, Dorothy W. 1820 NC Census Index.
Burke County NC Land Entry Data as given in Huggins, E. W. Burke County
        Records Vol. II, p. 14.

Withrow, James

Summary of Early Life:

James Withrow was born on June 10, 1764 in Rowan County, North Carolina. His family moved to the South Fork section of Burke County. He was living at this location when he entered Revolutionary War service. What relationship to John and James Withrow of Rutherford County, North Carolina is not definitely known.

Summary of Partisan Activity:

James Withrow first entered military service in mid 1780. He was drafted for a service term of three months and was placed in Captain John Sigman's Company of Charles McDowell's Burke Regiment. He marched with the regiment to the Broad River section of South Carolina, and then withdrew into Burke County on the approach of Ferguson's wing of Cornwallis' Army. He participated in the skirmish at Cane Creek (near Brindletown, Burke County) on September, 12, 1780. In this action Peter Brank was killed and Major Joseph White wounded. Withrow, with McDowell's troop, withdrew further into what is now East Tennessee. Withrow then took part in the great Kings Mountain Campaign. He had lost use of his horse and joined with the foot soldiers (under Major Herndon of Wilkes County). He therefore missed the Battle of October 7, 1780 that was conducted only by the mounted troops. He then assisted in conveying the prisoners to Greenlee's Ford of the Catawba River. He was discharged at this point, but shortly afterwards, joined in with a group of Whigs searching out Tories. They dispersed a group that had gathered at Isaac Martin's place.

In the fall and winter of 1781, Withrow took part in the Wilmington Expedition, headed up by General Griffith Rutherford and Colonel McDowell. He was discharged "after the surrender of Cornwallis". Withrow joined in the spring of 1782, the Cherokee Raid led by Colonel Joseph McDowell of Quaker Meadows. He was in a company commanded by Captain Daniel Whitener.

355

Withrow's final military service was in August 1782, being a member of another Cherokee raid under the overall leadership of General Charles McDowell of Burke County. In this action, Whithrow was a member of Captain James Wilson's Company.

Summary of Later Life:

After the Revolution, Withrow moved from Burke County to Knox County, Tennessee and then to Madison County, Kentucky. His last move was to Warren County, Tennessee, where he remained for the rest of his life. On December 5, 1836 Withrow applied for federal pension in Warren County, Tennessee. At that time he was seventy-two years of age and had lived in Warren County for about twenty-five years. He was granted a pension in the amount of $20.00 per annum. Pension records indicated that Withrow was dead per a final payment form of 1850.

Land Holdings and Transactions:

1. Burke County Land Entry records give a James Withrow adjacent to land of Jacob Gortner (now Catawba County), possibly father of the soldier, James Withrow? (Huggins I/52).

Census Locations:

1790 Lincoln County, North Carolina *(Earlier Burke County NC – Later Catawba Co NC)*
1800 Garrard County, Kentucky (?)
1820 Warren County, Tennessee
1830 Warren County, Tennessee *(listed as "James Wethrow" on printed census)*

References:
US National Archives Pension Data #S6403.
AIS Census Indices.
Huggins, Edith W. Burke County Records Vol. I. (Raleigh 1977).
Byron Sistler and Associates. Nashville, TN. 1830 TN Census.

Yates, John

Summary of Early Life:

John Yates was born ca 1769 in Georgia, seven miles from Augusta. His father died while they were living in Georgia. His mother then took the family to Burke County, North Carolina. Yates was only about thirteen years old when first entering military service.

Summary of Partisan Activity:

At the age of thirteen, John Yates was drafted into the Burke Regiment of militia. His company commander was Captain Joseph McDowell (P.G.?). John McDowell served as lieutenant. The regimental commander was Colonel Charles McDowell. The Burke militia joined other militia units to form a brigade headed by Brigadier General Griffith Rutherford. In late 1781, the brigade began the Wilmington Campaign. The object was to free Wilmington of British control. Yates, in his pension declaration, stated that they marched through Rowan County, North Carolina through "General Butler's battleground". (Guilford C.H.), through, Duplin County, North Carolina to Wilmington. At Wilmington, only one man was killed (by a sentry posted in a sentry box at the bridge). Wilmington was liberated. Yates served out a tour of six months.

Summary of Later Life:

After returning to Burke County, North Carolina where he remained for a "few years", Yates moved to Madison County, Kentucky. Still later he moved to Williamson County, Tennessee, and finally to Pulaski County, Missouri. John Yates applied for Revolutionary War pension in Pulaski County, Missouri on July 26, 1851. Due mainly to passage of time and lack of clear documentation, his claim was rejected. Documents from North Carolina verified that he had received allowances for military services.

Land Holdings and Transactions:

1. Burke County NC land records show a land grant issued to a John Yates, north side of Catawba River. Exact relationship to applicant unknown. (Ent 11 Dec 1778 Grant #400 Issued 28 Oct 1782).

Census Locations:

1800 Madison County, Kentucky
1810 Madison County, Kentucky
1820 Madison County, Kentucky
1830 Madison County, Kentucky
1840 Williamson County, Tennessee

References:
US National Archives Pension Data #R11928.
KY Census Records by G. G. Clift (1800); AIS (1810).
L. M. Volkel (1820), D. W. Shith (1830).
AIS – 1840 TN Census.
Revolutionary Army Accounts Morgan District. Vouchers #1773 #3397.

Yount, Jacob

Summary of Early Life:

Jacob Yount was born in the Catawba Valley of North Carolina in 1752 (another source says Pennsylvania). He was the son of pioneer settler John Yount (Jundt) and Anna Elizabeth Zimmerman Yount. The Younts lived near Newton, now Catawba County, North Carolina. Jacob Yount was one of the older offspring of a large family.

Summary of Partisan Activity:

According to Houts, Jacob Yount served in the South Carolina actions of General Nathaniel Greene. He was at Charleston when that port was evacuated (1781-1782). While on duty, his home was burned by Tories. The DAR has recognized Jacob Yount as an American Patriot.

Summary of Later Life:

Jacob Yount was married to Marellis Killian, the daughter of John and Elizabeth Killian, and the granddaughter of pioneer settler, Andreas Killian. Children of the union follows:

John B. Yount b. 1782
Elizabeth b. 1784 m. Reuben Farmer
Henry Yount b. 1787 m. Sophia Grounds
Jacob Yount. b. 1788 m. (1) Catherine Murray, (2) Charity
    Murray
Sarah b. 1780 m. Peter Welker
George Calvert Yount b. 1794 m. (1) _____ Gashwiler
    (2) Eliza Wilds
Christina b. 1796 m. Wesley Polk
David Yount b. 1798
Catherine Yount b. 1800 m. Jacob Thomas
Susannah Yount b. 1802 m. Azariah Tinnin
Jesse Yount b. 1804 m. Sibella Tinnin
Sophia Yount b. 1806

In 1794, Jacob Yount sold his land near Henry and Jacob's Fork in what is now Catawba County and moved to Burke County, North Carolina on a 350 acre tract on Drowning Creek. He remained active in Burke County civic affairs until the turn of the century, serving on various court functions, juries, and etc. In 1804, Jacob Yount and family migrated to the Mississippi River Valley, settling in Bollinger County, Missouri, just west of Cape Girardeau. Prior to his departure, he sold his land on Drowning Creek to Jacob Rudisill.

Jacob Yount, the Revolutionary War soldier, died in Bollinger County, Missouri in 1818. He was buried near the village of Patton, in the northern part of the county.

It is noteworthy that one of his sons, George Calvert Yount, moved to the Napa Valley of California and became one of the nations leading wine growers. The town of Yountville in the middle of Napa County, California is named for the family.

Land Holdings and Transactions:

1. Lincoln County, NC. Deed from Jacob Yount to Jesse Robinson, 200 acres Nov. 9, 1795.
2. Burke County, NC. Deed William Baldwin to Jacob Yount, 350 acres March 11, 1794, purchased by Phillip Killian.
3. Burke County NC. NC Land Grant, 50 acres north side of Henry River, Ent. 25 Oct. 1779, to Peter Sharpe.
4. Burke County NC. NC Land Grant 50 acres Stoney Creek, ent. 25 Oct. 1779. Not paid.
5. Burke County NC. 359 acres Drowning Creek Deed from Jacob Yount to Jacob Rudisail purchased by Jason Campbell 31 August 1804.

Census Locations:

1790 Lincoln County, North Carolina 4th Company
1799 Burke County, North Carolina (jury list)
1814 Cape Girardeau, Missouri (tax list)

References:

Huggins, Edith W. Miscellaneous Burke Records (SHP), Vol. IV, pp. 21, 159.

McAllister, Anne and Sullivan, Kathy G. Lincoln County North Carolina Court of Pleas and Quarter Sessions 1789-1796. (1897 ed.), p. 127.

Huggins, Edith. Op. cit. Vol. II, p. 13.

AIS Census Index North Carolina 1790.

Sullivan, Kathy G. Burke County North Carolina Deeds Register 1804-1813. Burke County Gen Soc. Publ., 1995 ed., p. 84.

Sherrill, William L. Annals of Lincoln County North Carolina. 1967 reprint of 1937 ed. (GPC), p. 418.

DAR Patriot Index. National Society DAR, Washington, DC, 1966 ed., p. 770.

Houts, Alice. Revolutionary Soldiers Buried in Missouri. (1966 ed.), (copy in Rowan Public Library, Salisbury, NC).

Internet: www.geocites.com/heartland/ranch 8239/yount.html.

Swink, Dan D. "Burke County Minutes of the Court of Pleas and Quarter Sessions". (1791-1795) and (1795-1798).

INDEX